Appalachia in an International Context

Cross-National Comparisons of Developing Regions

Edited by
PHILLIP J. OBERMILLER
and
WILLIAM W. PHILLIBER

Westport, Connecticut
London

Library of Congress Cataloging-in-Publication Data

Appalachia in an international context : cross-national comparisons of
  developing regions / edited by Phillip J. Obermiller and William W.
  Philliber.
        p.   cm.
      Includes bibliographical references and index.
      ISBN 0–275–94835–8 (alk. paper)
        1. Regionalism—Appalachian Region, Southern.   2. Regionalism.
      3. Appalachian Region, Southern—Civilization.   4. Appalachian
      Region, Southern—Economic conditions.   I. Obermiller, Phillip J.
      II. Philliber, William W.
      F217.A65A653   1994
      975—dc20   94–6380

British Library Cataloguing in Publication Data is available

Library of Congress Catalog Card Number: 94–6380
ISBN: 0–275–94835–8

First published in 1994

Praeger Publishers, 88 Post Road West, Westport, CT 06881
An imprint of Greenwood Publishing Group, Inc.

Printed in the United States of America

The paper used in this book complies with the
Permanent Paper Standard issued by the National
Information Standards Organization (Z39.48–1984).

10 9 8 7 6 5 4 3 2 1

Copyright Acknowledgments

*To Ernie Mynatt, Mike Maloney, and Maureen Sullivan
whose vision of Appalachians has always transcended
conventional boundaries.*

Contents

Illustrations

Preface

Appalachia has always existed within an international context. As early as the 16th century, Spanish explorers searched the Southern mountains for gold, while French trappers roamed the Northern mountains taking furs. The Amerind natives of Appalachia, themselves descendants of earlier migrants from Asia, taught the 17th and 18th century newcomers from Scotland, Ireland, France, Germany, and England how to survive in the mountains. In the 19th century, people stolen from Africa found refuge from slavery in the mountains or used Appalachian valleys and passes as corridors to freedom. Later, Poles, Serbs, Croats, and Italians came to help fell timber, mine coal, build railroads, and weave textiles in the townships and villages of the Appalachian region.

The international context of Appalachia has sometimes been obscured by bucolic images and "backwoods" stereotypes, but some notable regional institutions have recognized the international aspects of Appalachian life. The Highlander Research and Education Center in New Market, Tennessee, has strong ties with people and grassroots organizations in India and Africa, as well as Central and South America. The Appalachian Center at the University of Kentucky has ties with scholars from Canada, Great Britain, and Italy. Berea College actively recruits Tibetan students to its campus in Eastern Kentucky.

Although *Appalachia in an International Context* explicitly acknowledges the region's location in the global community using the comparative method, this approach to Appalachia does not guarantee insight. In Volume II of *A Study of History*, Arnold Toynbee made an unflattering association of mountaineers with "the latter-day white barbarians of the Old World—Rifis, Albanians, Kurds, Pathans, and

Hairy Ainus," insulting all those mentioned. The essays in this volume demonstrate, however, that comparative analyses need not be odious; done well, cross-national research can be instructive and insightful.

As the subtitle of this volume suggests, the essays that follow focus on the region as the primary unit of analysis. In his Introduction, William Philliber outlines the social science background of the concept of regionalism. The cross-national themes in individual essays use Appalachia as the standard case study for comparison. In Chapter One, Richard Couto provides a framework by analyzing political and economic conditions in the Appalachian region.

In Chapter Two, John Stephenson examines the interplay of in- and outmigration and the dynamics of social change in the highland communities of Shiloh in North Carolina and Ford in Western Scotland. In Chapter Three, Graham Day finds that in both Wales and Appalachia regional identity is affected by patterns of development and the activities of grassroots organizations. In Chapter Four, Richard Couto identifies the structural elements shared by coalminers' strikes in Great Britain and Appalachia. In Chapter Five, Nelda Pearson compares the roles of "familiar outsiders" in women's community action groups in Atlantic Canada and in Appalachia.

The next three chapters offer anthropological interpretations of regional dynamics. In Chapter Six, Glenn Mitchell compares the local economic survival strategies in the Catalonian region of Spain with those in Appalachia. In Chapter Seven, Benita Howell examines the similarities of the "mountain man" stereotype in the Philippines and in the United States. In Chapter Eight, Susan Abbott presents survey research on the relationship of gender roles to the mental health of youth in Kenya and Appalachia.

In Chapter Nine, John Gaventa shows the economic impact of capital mobility on regions through tracing the moves of one manufacturing firm from Michigan to Tennessee to Alabama and, finally, to northern Mexico. In Chapter Ten, I compare regional planning agencies and strategies for economic development in southern Italy and in Appalachia. In Chapter Eleven, Peter Sinclair provides a theoretical overview that ties together the cross-national comparisons throughout the volume.

Appalachia in an International Context goes beyond comparative methodology to make several substantive points. First, there are "core" and "peripheral" regions in both developed and developing countries. Second, while public attention is focused on the problems associated with rapid urbanization, the truly impoverished locales throughout the world are frequently rural and most often mountainous. Third, regional economic disparities are structural—inherent in the ways that governments, societies, and economies are organized—

not the result of cultural dysfunction or geographic isolation, the typical explanation. Finally, the Appalachian region may be unique, but similar regions around the globe share its problems, and in some cases offer guidelines for solutions.

PJO
Cincinnati

NOTE

In 1987, I received a James Still Fellowship for Advanced Research in the Humanities and Social Sciences from the Andrew W. Mellon Foundation. I began work on this volume the following year during postdoctoral research at the University of Kentucky. I am especially grateful for the assistance of the Appalachian College Program in obtaining the fellowship and for the contribution of the University of Kentucky Appalachian Center in making it so productive.

Introduction:
Appalachia and the Study of Regionalism

William W. Philliber

The focal point of pre-industrial societies was the local community. In many ways these communities were almost closed societies. People were born and died in the same community. In between, they learned the values of those around them. They chose a marital partner from among their neighbors. They earned their living, did their trading, and made friendships from within that context.

Industrialization expanded the frame of reference within which people functioned. Of necessity, the volume of goods produced by factories had to be traded outside of the community. Locals could not consume all that they produced themselves, but at the same time did not produce many of the things available elsewhere. Developments in communication and transportation made large distances less important. It became possible to travel across a continent in a matter of hours and to talk to anyone anyplace almost instantaneously. People began to identify with the nation-state as strongly as they had previously identified with a local community. They sang national anthems, said pledges to their flags, and volunteered to fight in national wars.

While the nation-state grew in importance as a result of industrialization, in many ways it has remained too large. While people do trade outside of their local community, their trade is not random. Trade continues to be more common among people who are close to each other than among people separated by greater distance. People in proximity to one another have more in common than people who live far apart. People in proximity share similar ways of speaking, customs, and prejudices. What emerges is the importance of region.

Although regionalism has been a concept used in the social sciences for most of this century, its definition remains elusive. Everyone usually agrees that a region is a place and can therefore be identified from a geographic perspective. However, there is often a lack of consensus about the exact area of a particular region—especially its borders.

Part of the reason is that a region often lacks clear borders. There are, for example, three major identifications of the region of Appalachia. John Campbell (1921) included 256 counties in nine states. He used the boundaries of the Mason-Dixon Line on the north, the Blue Ridge Mountains on the east, and the Allegheny-Cumberland Plateau on the west to form a triangle. Thomas Ford (1962) limited the area to 190 counties in seven states, eliminating western Maryland and northwestern South Carolina. In 1965, the Appalachian Regional Commission defined Appalachia as including 397 counties located in 13 states. Portions of Ohio, Pennsylvania, New York, and Mississippi were included for the first time.

Part of the reason for these differences in definition is that Ford and the Appalachian Regional Commission considered more than geography. Ford used the boundaries of state economic areas to obtain data from the U.S. Bureau of the Census. Only those areas entirely within Appalachia were included. This produced a smaller region than identified by Campbell. The Appalachian Regional Commission, on the other hand, needed political support. To obtain it they made the widest possible definition of the region. The issue of who is right is irrelevant. What is clear is the fact that the geographic boundaries of a region are moveable.

In part, the boundaries of a region are fluid because they are not tied to anything that is permanent. Physical features like rivers, oceans, and mountain ridges can make for borders because they do not move, and political treaties establish the borders of nations and states. But region is often a matter of consensus—a consensus that is strong about the center but weak around the edges.

Sometimes regions are identified from an economic basis. Often this is because the areas within them have a common economic foundation. Regions may be noted for manufacturing (such as the Northeast) or for farming (such as the Midwest). The Civil War in the United States more than a century ago was fought between regions defined on this basis. The industrial North sought and benefited from high tariffs that restricted imports; the South, with an economy based on farming, wanted low tariffs which produced cheaper imports and foreign markets for tobacco and cotton.

Other times, regions are identified economically because they have a dominant hub around which areas orient. For example, the Boston-to-Washington corridor, Chicago, Atlanta, Houston, Los Angeles, and St. Louis function as hubs, to varying degrees. Their economic dominance expands beyond their borders to impact on a wide area. Within these regions, people orient to the hub and are influenced by its actions. Such hubs may partially account for the fact that one area of the country may experience a severe recession while other areas experience strong growth.

There does not appear to be an especially strong economic basis for claiming that Appalachia is a region. It lacks any hub which serves as a focal point for economic activity. In fact, much of the region orients to hubs outside of the region, such as Atlanta, Baltimore, and Cincinnati. Although the region is not especially industrial, it lacks any dominant economic factor that would serve to bring it together. Part of the region is noted for mining, and other parts for farming. Timber extraction provides employment in other areas. Recreation has increased in importance, but not evenly throughout.

In recent years there has been an emphasis on the importance of culture in identifying regions. This orientation holds that people who are of the same region share a common culture, often in conflict with others outside the region. Bruce Ergood (1976) reviewed 20 studies of Appalachia and found 11 different cultural traits. Most frequently cited were independence, religious fundamentalism, strong family ties, living in harmony with nature, traditionalism, and fatalism.

Many of these traits are believed to conflict with the requirements of an industrial society and therefore account for the failure of Appalachians to achieve in the larger American context. For example, an independent person may have difficulty taking directions from others and therefore not get along in a large organization. A person who is fatalistic may not believe that it is possible to get ahead by working hard. A religious fundamentalist may even believe that rewards are from the grace of God and not the result of personal efforts. These beliefs would appear to be in conflict with what contemporary society requires.

Most recently there has emerged a perspective that argues for a psychological basis of regionalism. From this perspective, people who live in proximity with one another and identify with one another are seen as belonging together. John Shelton Reed (1983) has spent much of his career studying the South from a psychological perspective. He argues that people think of themselves as Southerners and identify with other people who are Southerners. They are even seen as Southerners by outsiders.

Studies have also been made of the extent to which people from Appalachia who identify themselves as Appalachians are seen by others as Appalachians (Miller 1977; Philliber 1983). In general, these studies find only a weak level of identification.

At times the debates about Appalachia as a region have taken on a life of their own. What has been lost is the recognition that the same issues that exist within and about Appalachia are typical of areas within other regions of the United States and other parts of the world. This volume attempts to place those issues in perspective through the presentation of a number of comparative studies of Appalachia and other regions. What may become increasingly clear is the realization that Appalachia is not especially unique. Many of the same issues, many of the same problems are found throughout the world.

■ 1 ■

The Future of the Welfare State: The Case of Appalachia

Richard A. Couto

Appalachia is central to the American welfare state. Conditions there have inspired legislation and regional development efforts unique to American public policy. The Tennessee Valley Authority (TVA) was an early response within the New Deal to problems that a portion of the Appalachian region was suffering—problems the Depression exacerbated. The Appalachian Regional Commission, or ARC, was a later government response to the Appalachian region's problems that President John F. Kennedy rediscovered and that President Lyndon B. Johnson invoked in fashioning his Great Society programs. Like boats, some socio-economic measures rose with the tide of social legislation. But in Appalachia at present, that tide is out; socio-economic measures are therefore down, and they are predicted to fall even lower.

A catalog of inequality and human deprivation is easily assembled in assessing conditions in the Appalachian region—the Central Appalachian region, in particular. It is more difficult to assess why welfare policies have not had greater effect on improving conditions and what needs to be done now and in the future. Those questions will be addressed in this chapter. Central to the assessment here is an effort to understand the economic changes in the Appalachian region as part of a de-industrialized and post-industrialized American economy. These economic changes have fostered a general decline in demand for labor as well as a demand for a different kind of labor force within the region. It is the nature of the labor force and of work in Appalachia that is at the heart of the human problems of the Appalachian region.

This chapter will treat Appalachian poverty and the region's economic conditions as national problems. The problems of the region are, at root, inadequate social investment in the production and reproduction of its labor force, which the economy no longer needs. Recent political policies have compounded the problems of the region by a form of disinvestment of what little social capital had been previously provided and have produced very disturbing trends of worsening conditions. However, there is also growing evidence of responses from a set of economic reactors: the family, community organizations, the church, and labor unions. While the efforts of these institutions are not sufficient to reduce a growing inequality between the standards of the region and the nation, they are important and provide a basis for implementation of future improved welfare policies.

Appalachia is an American tomorrow in a double sense. First, it provides lessons about the future of the de-industrialized, post-industrial economy and the welfare state. Second, its own future has always been and is now dependent on America's national institutions and practices. This chapter examines briefly the de-industrial and post-industrial economy of Appalachia; it will relate the human needs of the region to these economic changes, and examine the prospects for public policies and private initiatives to address the needs of the Appalachian region. Among the private initiatives, this chapter places a special emphasis on the role of the family, community organizations, the church, and the unions.

DE-INDUSTRIALIZATION AND APPALACHIA: FEWER JOBS

It is important to understand that the Appalachian region has industries—steel, coal, and textiles—that were the early elements of our Industrial Revolution; they continue there even as the national importance of those first industries declines. In 1980, Appalachia had only 7.7 percent of all Americans employed—but 73.7 percent of all Americans employed in coal mining, 28.1 percent of all employed in textiles, 20.3 percent of all in primary metals, and 18 percent of all in apparel. But in 1980, the major industries of Appalachia—with the exception of mining—employed fewer people than in 1975. And by 1990, the major industries of Appalachia—without exception—employed fewer people than they did in 1980; they will employ fewer still in 1995. Between 1980 and 1985, the region lost 310,000 jobs in manufacturing and mining (ARC 1985, 10) and made a net gain of 52,000 jobs or 0.6 percent, compared with a 7.7 percent increase nationally. In 1981 and 1982 alone, the region lost *two and one-half* manufacturing jobs for every *one* it had gained from 1970 to 1980.

Analysts have changed their interpretation of the economy of the

Appalachian region. A study conducted in the mid-1960s described the region as "a good textbook example of a regional pocket which is lagging behind much of the rest of the United States in many categories of economic development" (Saunders 1984, 1). Recent scholarship makes it obvious that the historical form of economic development in Appalachia—and not a lag in economic development—better explains economic conditions in the region today (Billings 1979; Eller 1982; Gaventa 1980; Lewis 1970; and Walls 1977). In a contemporary vein, a study of the Appalachian economy in 1982 related economic development problems to the region's industrial base, which is "relatively mature" (Little 1982, 1).

Appalachia's industries are "mature" in the sense that there is little prospect for growth in domestic demand, and in the sense that the plants have been undercapitalized. These industries are also resource based and labor intensive. They are sensitive to product substitution—for example, oil for coal—and shifts to newer, more efficient production centers with more automation and/or lower labor costs. The Appalachian economy is in trouble because the industrial economy of America is changing. The nation's manufacturing industries are in decline—especially those predominant in Appalachia, steel and textiles. Coalmining continues to follow a pattern of boom and bust, although projections suggest an overall decline in employment.

Figure 1.1 illustrates how the dominant Appalachian industries performed from 1965 to 1981, and shows projections for their growth

Figure 1.1
Employment Growth Rates in Appalachian Dominant Industries, for 1965–1974, 1974–1981, and 1983–1995 Projections (in Percentages)

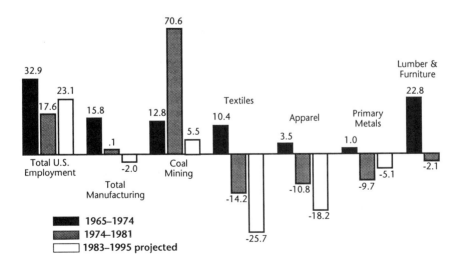

to 1995. In general, U.S. manufacturing industries have had employment growth rates significantly lower than national employment growth rates; and among the dominant Appalachian industries, only coalmining and lumber have had employment growth rates equal to or better than the national figures for manufacturing. Textiles, apparel, and primary metals are significantly lower than the national employment figures for manufacturing. Thus, mature industries mean a decline in employment in most cases.

Appalachia is part of a de-industrialization of America that has deep roots in the American economy. Robert B. Reich (1982), for example, interprets de-industrialization as a normal consequence of institutional investors seeking a healthy show of quarterly earnings. They find these healthy earnings not in long-term strategies of investment in plant and the retraining of workers, but by closing out old plants and locating new plants in areas with lower operating costs or by acquiring other firms whose assets can be either integrated into operations or else liquidated. Practically, this means that Pittsburgh banks invest in steel-exporting countries like Brazil and Japan to compete with American steel; and Exxon shuts down West Virginia mines as it develops the coal reserves of Colombia to compete with Appalachian coal for the European, and even the American, steam coal markets.

The mobility of capital and technology have increased, but the mobility of labor has declined. And this has important demographic consequences. In earlier economic transitions in the Central Appalachian region, people responded by migrating to centers of economic growth and employment opportunity. With decline in the region, people moved to growing economic areas outside the region. Between 1950 and 1970, 3.2 million people migrated away from the Appalachian region (ARC 1981). But between 1970 and 1980, as the economy slowed down nationally, as coal boomed during the energy crisis, and as centers of economic growth appeared at the edges of the region—in Atlanta and in Greenville, South Carolina, for example—about one million people migrated to the region. Since the 1979 recession, however, there are few places to migrate to—anywhere—that offer bright prospects for employment. In addition, the provision of social services have made continued residence in the region more possible. Consequently, despite high unemployment figures in portions of Central Appalachia in the wake of a severe bust in the coal industry, and despite local economies that have not recovered from the 1979 recession to the same extent as the national economy, there is far less outmigration from the region.

Thus, since 1960, Appalachia has had three distinct changes in population related to economic activity. During the decade of 1960 to

1970, Central Appalachian counties of Kentucky, Tennessee, Virginia, and West Virginia lost population as the nation increased population by 13.8 percent. In 1970 to 1980, these Central Appalachian counties exceeded the national rate of population growth. Any return migration to the Central Appalachian region is best understood as a consequence of the decline of employment outside the region as well as the new employment opportunities within the region for parts of the 1970s. Since 1980 the counties of Central Appalachia have lost population. They had been expected to keep increasing through 1995 despite increased unemployment (ARC 1985, 2). The rates of population loss were more than 20 percent in some coalmining counties (Couto 1994, 103–107).

This shift in migration has important consequences for the demographics of the region and its future needs. The working age population—those 18 to 65 years of age—increased during the 1970s. The younger set of workers—those of procreative age, 18 to 44—increased by the far greatest proportion. This suggests that the 1980s would have more people in the Appalachian region who would be looking for work at a time when there were fewer jobs and that there would be more young children at a time of decreased employment and incomes. The other portion of the population to show an increase by 1980 was the age cohort 55 years and older. These people were coming to the end of their working age or had reached it, and represent a population increasingly dependent on social services and provision. Although employment opportunities have declined, despite poor opportunities within or outside the region, and even though much of Central Appalachia lost population, the region is left with larger numbers of unemployed young workers and of older and retired workers, and with the prospect of increased numbers of children—the progeny of a younger work force.

Appalachia is not only related to the de-industrialization going on nationally, but may even serve as its standard. When Robert S. Small, the chairman of Dan River, Incorporated, pinned his hopes for the resurrection of the national textile industry on the emergence of a fewer number of larger and more efficient companies (*Business Week* 1979, 66), he echoed the discussions of union and company officials in the Appalachian coal industry immediately after World War II. Other company officials make their references explicit when they speak of national events today and events in Appalachia yesterday. For example, William Roesch, president of U.S. Steel, compared the problem of dislocated workers in the steel industry today to his experience in the coal industry where he began his career after World War II (DuBois 1983, 15).

The dislocation of workers in a de-industrialized economy will be more moderate in areas where there is diversification and some elements of the economy remain dynamic, according to Daniel Saks in a study that he conducted for the National Planning Association on distressed workers (Saks 1983, 48). The inverse of this is bad news for the Appalachian region where industry is not diversified but concentrated in subregions in a few industries and where, consequently, an industrial decline is more likely to mean prolonged unemployment for dislocated workers. This suggests continuing problems in a post-industrial economy.

APPALACHIA'S POST-INDUSTRIAL ECONOMY: DIFFERENT WORK AND DIFFERENT WORKERS

The Central Appalachian region offers a troubling preview of the post-industrial society. Judging by recent experience there, post-industrial society means different work for a different set of workers at reduced wages, both cash and social. First, there is the example of efforts to maintain heavy industry. On January 11, 1984 in Weirton, West Virginia, 10,000 steelworkers purchased the mill at which they worked. They bought the company out for $386.1 million, assumed $192 million in the company's liabilities (including their own pensions), cut wages 18 percent, and agreed to no wage increase for six years. Even if successful, this effort is a revealing measure of the cut in real and social wages required to maintain employment in the basic industries.

There is other evidence of the decline in real and social wages contained in the pattern of migration. The migration into Appalachia, like every other factor of the region, has had wide variation within the region itself. Southern Appalachia—especially counties in Georgia, North and South Carolinas, and Tennessee—showed the greatest population increases. Table 1.1 illustrates several factors that may account for the lower unemployment in Southern Appalachia, attracting migrants and stimulating the population increase. The table shows a relationship among the following: low union membership, low average manufacturing hourly wage, low unemployment, and high population increases. The data are not all comparable; for instance, union membership and wages are statewide figures, while unemployment and population increases are only for the Appalachian portion of the states. Likewise, different years are used for the measures. Nonetheless, this picture emerges: population increases occurred in larger portions where unemployment was lowest; and unemployment was lowest in states with lowest union membership and manufacturing wages. This association is even stronger if we omit

Table 1.1
**Measures of Social Wage, Unemployment, and Population—Southern
Appalachia**

State	Percent of Non-Agricultural Work Force in Unions*	Average Hourly Wages in Manufacturing	Unemployment		Population Increase 1970–80
			1980	1982	
North Carolina	6.5	$5.37	6.4	9.6	17.2
Rank	1	1	2	2	4
South Carolina	6.2	$5.59	6.2	11.1	20.7
Rank	2	3	1	3	2
Georgia	13.6	$5.77	7.0	8.9	35.7
Rank	5	5	4	5	3
Tennessee	17.1	$6.08	7.9	13.0	19.6
Rank	5	5	4	5	3
Alabama	19.2	$6.49	9.3	14.9	13.7
Rank	3	2	6	6	6
Mississippi	12.7	$5.44	8.3	12.2	15.3
Rank	3	2	5	4	5
Regional Average	20.9	$6.72	8.4	12.5	11.2
U.S. Average	20.1	$7.16	7.1	9.7	11.4

* Figures include the entire state and not just the Appalachian portion.
Sources: Little and ARC.

the exceptionally large population increase around Atlanta, and consider the rest of Appalachian Georgia and its smaller population increase.

In the 1970s, Southern Appalachia epitomized a national economic trend toward employment in lower wage, nonunion manufacturing. By 1982, unemployment in the Appalachian portion of most of these states increased by 50 percent, suggesting that the search for lower operating costs continued. Textile and apparel manufacturing firms were going abroad or modernizing to capital-intensive processes, just as steel and coal did before them.

High tech—the talisman of the post-industrial economy—is best related to recent developments in the low-wage manufacturing sector of the economy in Appalachia. In production processes, high tech is labor intensive rather than capital intensive. And, in practice, high tech is increasingly internationalized. It utilizes low-cost labor in many different parts of the world; indeed, this is how Appalachia has come to be competitive in attracting high tech industry. An Arthur D. Little, Incorporated, study for the Appalachian Regional Commission suggests that a portion of the region's surplus labor from apparel and textiles could be absorbed by high tech industries if there were an aggressive marketing of the lower costs and labor surpluses available in the region coupled with government financial incentives.

> The [Appalachian] region...may represent one of the few areas of the country that can compete with offshore locations for lower cost component manufacturing and assembly operations in the industry. If the United States is to retain these high growth segments under such intensive international pressure, it will be in lower cost, labor surplus production regions such as Appalachia where development incentives and special training efforts will have to be provided to offset the aggressive programs of other nations. (Little, 7)

It is unlikely, however, that high tech will play a major role in the region's future economy. First of all, much of high tech is military related; and proportionately, the region does only a modest military business, especially in weapons. Second, 95 percent of all new jobs nationally will *not* be high tech. Third, Appalachia already has about its proportion of high tech jobs. If it were to gain 9 percent of all new high tech jobs—equal to the proportion of its labor force in the national labor force—it would have about 95,000 new jobs (ARC 1983). This is far less than the 400,000 jobs *lost* in 1981 and 1982 alone. High tech seems to be a possible but limited avenue of economic development for the Appalachian region.

The competitive stance of the Appalachian region for high tech manufacturing suggests two important elements of the region's post-industrial economy. First, the region is part of an increased inter-nationalization of the economy. The region is competing with the Pacific Rim nations and places like Northern Ireland as a place for firms to locate. Wood from the Appalachian region is exported overseas, and furniture made from the wood is then imported to the United States. Similarly, department stores sell "Appalachian Trail" boots made in Rumania. The future of coal is also partly international. A study by the Appalachian Regional Commission on synfuels and the coal market indicates that industry's conversion from coal to oil will depend on the nation's need to reduce its balance-of-payment deficits, the need to increase the security of energy supply for both economic and international policy reasons, and the need to minimize world oil prices (Perry 1979). Another important future market for Appalachian coal will be the export market for steam coal, of which Appalachia now has 90 percent. Appalachia's chief competitor for the European market will be South Africa, which has one competitive advantage; the lower labor costs that are currently inherent in the wage differentials between white and black miners.

Second, as South Africa's competitive position suggests, the other important element of Appalachia's post-industrial economy is the low cost of its labor. Appalachia is competitive for high tech manufacturing and other forms of component manufacturing because it has a large pool of unemployed industrial workers whose labor can be purchased at low cash and social wages.

We must be careful to identify this pool of surplus labor, lest we mistake it for a simple shift of unemployed industrial workers to alternative new employment. It is that—but it includes much more. For one thing, the size of the surplus labor pool in Appalachia cannot be measured by unemployment alone. Unemployment figures are notorious underestimations and do not take into account, at all, labor force participation. These are actually separate but related measures; that is, the greater the unemployment, the more likely that some people will withdraw from the labor force or never enter. Consequently, the surplus labor pool of the Appalachian region has three measures: (1) the traditionally higher levels of unemployment; (2) the dramatically higher levels of unemployment since 1980; and (3) the lower rates of labor force participation. Male rates of labor force participation in 1980 were 71.2 percent in the region, compared to 73.3 percent nationally; both figures represented a decline. The female rate in the region in 1980 was also lower than the national (43.9 and 49.8 percent, respectively) but most importantly, these rates were higher than previous regional and national rates (ARC 1985, 7).

The service sector of the national economy has grown dramatically, and some hope that its growth is an encouraging indication of new employment opportunities. When combined with some parts of retail trade, the growth in service sector employment is staggering. Between 1969 and 1982 this sector gained almost nine million jobs across the nation—an increase of about 60 percent. This increase was 45 percent of all new jobs nationally. Within the Appalachian region there were similar developments. Between 1970 and 1980 the service sector expanded by almost 400,000 jobs or 59 percent. This equalled about one-third of all new jobs in the region. Among the fastest growing sectors were health services and eating and drinking places, as Table 1.2 reports.

This increase in service jobs meant more low-wage jobs with fewer benefits and non-union labor. The simultaneous decline in industry and increase in service has been tantamount to a decrease of middle-income employment opportunities in the region. Because these changes are occurring while more women are entering the work force, they are likely to lead to the increased feminization of low-wage work in the region as well as the nation. This form of genderfication follows from and coincides with the feminization of poverty.

Table 1.2
Service Jobs' Growth in the Appalachian Region, 1970–1980

	New Jobs 1970–80	Percent Change 1970–80	Percent of All New Employment 1970–80
Health Services	177,041	84	14.9%
Eating and Drinking Places	134,754	95	11.4%
Social and Related Services	68,002	71	5.8%
Business Services	62,891	94	5.3%
Food Stores	58,921	58	5.0%
Coal Mining	77,588	76	6.6%

Source: ARC, 1983c.

There are four clear factors to the de-industrial and post-industrial economy of Appalachia. First, we have more jobs than before but they are different. Service jobs insulated from foreign competition grow in number; and the manufacturing jobs that remain are, increasingly, assembly work of foreign-manufactured components. Second, we have too few jobs to absorb new workers and dislocated workers. Third, there is an increase in the labor pool as a result of unemployment and the increased labor force participation of women. Fourth, the jobs that remain require fewer skills and provide less real and social wages in exchange for labor. It is upon these factors of employment that the welfare state must be interpreted and to which we now turn.

CRISIS IN THE WELFARE STATE: THE PRODUCTION AND REPRODUCTION OF LABOR

The present set of problems in the Appalachian region, like those of the past and those predicted for the future, are directly related to the nature of employment in the region. With changes in the nature of employment within a de-industrial and post-industrial economy, there are new problems in the region. This is because the problems of the region are now, as in the past, related to the production and reproduction of a labor force for the regional economy. Perhaps Appalachia makes this relationship uniquely apparent, with its "coaltowns," its "steeltowns," its "milltowns"—that is to say, an infrastructure related to a single industry. The infrastructure includes at least wage employment, education, housing, health, and the environment. Initially, these would frequently come from the industry directly, as a form of social investment to produce and reproduce the local labor force. As private capital investment in mechanized production processes increased, the labor force decreased and so did its capital investment from industry. The state has replaced some of the private capital, with income transfer programs and regional development efforts.

It is the present need for a limited number of workers, with limited skills, that explains the limited capital investment in labor and hence the lower measures of socio-economic well-being that distinguish the region from the nation and that mark the worst portions of the region from the rest. This is apparent if we examine several forms of capital investment for the production and reproduction of labor: education, housing, environment, and health.

Education, for example, reflects changes in the labor force and the amount and nature of employment within the region. From county to county, the differences in educational improvement are directly related to the smaller capital investment in those counties with the largest increases in the surplus labor pool.

Between 1970 and 1980, there were obvious improvements in measures of educational attainment. Low levels of educational attainment decreased, and measures of higher educational attainment showed an increase. However, the regional improvements lagged behind national rates in almost all instances. Moreover, there were important subregional differences, once again, with the Central Appalachian region—which had the highest unemployment in the region—lagging the regional average on all educational measures in 1970 and 1980. Part of the changes in adult educational attainment may be attributed to the immigration that occurred during the 1970s and not to increased social investment. Young adults and pre-retirement workers returned to the region and brought previously invested social capital—their educational attainment—with them.

The increases in educational measures are encouraging, but they have not closed the gap in measures within the region, nor between the region and the nation. That is to say, there is no evidence of increased capital investment in education where the economic problems of employment are most profound. A recent survey found that Central Appalachian county school systems in Kentucky and West Virginia constantly had student scores lower than school systems elsewhere in those states. Coal counties in Virginia had worse student scores than other counties in the same state, as did the easternmost counties in Tennessee. Independent school systems generally reported better student scores than county systems. Additionally, Appalachian Kentucky counties and coal counties in Virginia reported less government revenue in general and a smaller proportion spent on education in particular (De Young 1982).

Housing is another key factor in the production of a labor force. And where we find surplus labor, we find deteriorated housing. This is true not only in comparing the Appalachian region with the nation, but especially in examining the Appalachian counties with the greatest labor surplus. Figures from 1970 indicate that housing within the Appalachian region was approximately 74 percent of the average value of other American homes. While 9 percent of U.S. housing was categorized as deficient in some way, the percentage was much higher within the Appalachian region. Thirteen percent of the housing in Northern Appalachia, 21 percent in Southern Appalachia, and 38 percent in Central Appalachia were categorized as deficient. Seventy percent of the deficiency involved at least plumbing (ARC 1979, 76–80). These ratios dropped precipitously by 1980, primarily because of a change in definition; but the differences among the subregions of Appalachia remain.

Northern and Southern Appalachia increased their housing starts faster than did Central Appalachia, even though the population increased sharply in some sections of Central Appalachia, such as Eastern Kentucky. The increased labor force was housed primarily in mobile homes—a subtle indication of the surplus nature of the work force. A study of the Levisa Fork area in Eastern Kentucky indicated that 85 percent of new housing in portions of that area in 1980 was supplied by mobile homes (Cox 1982, 43). Pat Gish, director of the Eastern Kentucky Housing Development Corporation, reported that 50 percent of the total housing units of seven Eastern Kentucky coal counties were mobile homes. The median value of all homes was $19,400 or slightly more than one-half of the median value of houses in Kentucky. Equally important, one-fourth of all housing in the seven-county area was valued at $10,000 or less (Gish 1983).

A factor often overlooked in the production of labor is the *environment*. Yet, if we look at the experience of the Central Appalachian region, nothing seems quite so clear as that the environment is destroyed where there is little need to reproduce a labor force. The legacy of one hundred years of industrialization and detrimental industrial practices has left the region with substantial environmental costs. The past practice of toxic waste disposal far exceeds our knowledge of its extent or consequences. Old mines in Pennsylvania are filled with noxious fumes and fires. Two million acres of land—of the eight million acres mined—are subsiding and an estimated two million more acres will subside by the year 2000, involving a cost of $30 million per year (HRB-Singer 1975; Merrifield 1980). Finally, nuclear plants operating within the region produce radioactive waste materials requiring tens of thousands of years of care and storage—

and there is a higher concentration of nuclear power plants in the Appalachian region than anywhere in the nation. Symptomatically, the region has not done well in dealing with the refuse of the coal industry. One ton of refuse is generated for every six to seven tons of coal mined. That leaves approximately 50 to 100 million tons of refuse per year. This has been seen as a local problem, sometimes leading to inadequate solutions and disastrous results as was seen in Buffalo Creek in West Virginia where an improper slag dam broke in 1972 and sent a wave of coal slurry down a narrow valley, killing 125 people. Ninety-three percent of the streams in the United States that have been contaminated by acid run-offs from mines are within the Appalachian region—some 6,300 miles of regional streams. Interpretations differ as to the contribution of strip mining to the flooding within the region. However, it is clear that strip mining does have an influence on increasing sedimentation in creeks and rivers. Coal's influence on the buildup of carbon dioxide in the atmosphere may be regulated in the future, and this will certainly have an impact on the coal industry (Seltzer 1979). Moreover, chronic atmospheric inversions in the region compound the problems of airborne contaminants (including $SO+B_2+E$) that result from coal-burning emissions (Cox 1982; Merrifield 1980).

Health is also central to the production and reproduction of labor. But here again we find that the Appalachian region differs from the nation and that there are regional differences consistent with the social investment in the labor force. The rate of infant mortality steadily declined in the Appalachian region between 1960 and 1980, paralleling a national decline. Appalachia's decline lagged behind the nation a bit. Very importantly, there are regional differences in infant mortality rates, with Northern Appalachia—having the greatest amount of past capital investment—generally recording lower infant mortality rates than Central and Southern Appalachia.

Likewise, there are important differences among counties. Thirty-eight counties within Appalachia recorded average infant mortality rates at least 50 percent above the national average. This figure ranged from a low of 22.7 per one thousand births to 41 per one thousand births. Likewise, these figures mask racial differences. While the infant mortality rate within the region is 9 percent higher for whites than the national average, the black rate was even higher. In fact, although blacks accounted for only 11 percent of the births within the region, black children accounted for one-sixth of the total Appalachian infant mortality. Unusually high infant mortality rates in several Southern Appalachian states contribute to the high infant mortality rates for black children (ARC 1981, 27).

A crucial factor impacting health is hunger; and there is evidence that, with the economic recession since 1980 and higher levels of unemployment, there is now hunger in the areas with surplus labor and that the incidence of hunger relates to the changed nature of labor force participation. In 1984, the author and the Center for Health Services of Vanderbilt University conducted a survey on maternal and infant health in four coalmining communities in Central Appalachia (Couto 1986). We asked women, "Are there times when you don't have enough food for your family?" Thirty-one percent of the women in our survey reported being without sufficient food sometimes. Thirteen percent of the women in our survey reported being without food often. Thus, 44 percent of the women that we surveyed reported being without sufficient food for their families at least some of the time.

The distinguishing characteristic of the women who reported inadequate food is their poverty. Clearly, and perhaps obviously, there is a strong correlation between income and hunger. Women in the lowest household incomes reported going without food most often. Almost 90 percent of the women that we interviewed reported household monthly incomes of $750 or less—a rough estimation of the federal poverty guideline. More than one-third of the women we interviewed reported household incomes of $250 or less per month, or approximately $3,000 a year. Of these women, 63 percent reported being without food sometimes or often. Approximately 37 percent of the women with household incomes between $250 and $750 a month reported being without food sometimes or often. Twenty-one percent of the women reporting household incomes above $750 a month reported being without food sometimes or often.

When we look at a profile of our survey families, there are some obvious findings. Families go without food because their incomes are low, and those families without employment income reported the lowest incomes. Inadequate food is part of a pattern of inadequate resources, including employment. The pattern of hunger is not selective in choosing among the poor. The young and old, whites and blacks, and those with varying degrees of educational attainment report being without sufficient food at times.

Our survey results corroborate the increased risk of poverty for women and children living in female-headed households—and consequently corroborate the feminization of poverty, and the financial incentive for women with primary responsibilities for families to acquire employment income. The monthly incomes of female-headed households are lower than households with men. In addition, the lower income of female-headed households is more likely to come from nonemployment income sources exclusively. On the other hand, our survey indicates that female-headed households did not report a statistically significant difference in hunger from the other households. This suggests that, although American social policies still link lower incomes to unemployment, those families with lower incomes are somewhat sheltered from hunger if they have circumstances that preclude full labor force participation, such as being a single-parent household (Couto 1986).

Hungry children and high infant mortality rates are factors in the production of a reduced labor force—that is, the children—and the production of a new segment of the labor force: mothers. This picture is consistent with the very primitive law of supply and demand as Adam Smith applied it to labor in *The Wealth of Nations*. Smith wrote that "the scantiness of subsistence" among "the inferior ranks of people" sets limits to the excessive multiplication of human beings in a civilized society, just as other species have their limits set in nature. The consequence of this civilized limiting is the destruction of a great part of the working class. When the reward for labor is generous, the means of subsistence are less scanty and more children survive "as nearly as possible in the proportion which the demand for labor requires." If the reward for labor drops, then more children perish until the scarce supply of labor increases wages and more children survive, until such time that the market for labor would be so overstocked

> as would soon force back its price to that proper rate which the circumstances of the society required. It is in this manner that the demand for men, like that for any other commodity, necessarily regulates the production of men; quickens it when it goes on too slowly, and stops it when it advances too fast. (Smith, 79–80)

It is precisely the capital investment in the production and reproduction of labor that the welfare state is about. The welfare state represents the substitution of public revenues for private capital where private capital is insufficient or unwilling to provide the necessary social investment. Private capital is most unlikely to provide social investment in the production of a labor force where and when it is disinvesting in the production process itself or otherwise deems the investment to be unnecessary. The substitution of public investment when this private disinvestment occurs is obvious in the case of transfer payments of public money—"welfare"—to some of those who have no employment income. It is also evident in development schemes such as the Appalachian Regional Commission, whose work may be understood as providing social capital for the production and reproduction of a labor force: 2,600 miles of highway and access roads for labor force commuting; 700 vocational educational facilities; 300 new or modernized hospitals; 400 primary health care centers; and

1,300 water and sewerage systems (Newman 1983). But it becomes even more obvious when we look at the distribution of this social investment and find it goes primarily to places where private capital is accumulated but less able or willing to provide social investment— such as in Northern Appalachia—and where private capital is accumulating but has little incentive to provide social investment since its needs are for low-wage and low-skilled labor, such as in Southern Appalachia.

This pattern of providing social capital related to the labor force would suggest a continued serious problem for the Appalachian region in general and the Central Appalachian region in particular. For one thing, the record of the immediate past as well as the projections until 1995 are bleak for employment in the region. The region's share of jobs declined from 8.3 to 7.8 percent between 1980 and 1985. This decline is marked by slower growth than on the national level, and by an actual decline in the number of jobs. Employment declined in the Central Appalachian portion of Kentucky and Virginia by about 1 percent as the nation gained 7.7 percent. West Virginia lost 8.2 percent, and Appalachian Pennsylvania 5.2 percent (ARC 1985, 9). The Appalachian Regional Commission projected a decline in the region's share of the nation's jobs from 7.9 to 6.9 percent between 1985 and 1995. This regional loss hides gains and losses within the region. Almost all of the manufacturing employment gains were projected for Southern Appalachia, consistent with the previous experience of the region (ARC 1985, 14). This suggests, of course, that unemployment rates will be higher within the region in general, and in those counties with little economic diversification in particular.

This decline in employment will have a profound impact on the first factor of the production and reproduction of labor: income. It was projected that the region will see a per capita income decline in relation to national per capita figures. Two-thirds of all the Appalachian counties projected to have a decrease in relation to the national figure are concentrated in the Central Appalachian portions of Kentucky, Tennessee, Virginia, and West Virginia. In addition, Pennsylvania accounts for 34 of the 196 counties expected to lose ground in relative per capita income. The loss will be profound in these areas since the region's average is projected to fall but a majority of counties are projected to increase or remain the same; thus, 196 out of 397 counties will lose ground as the region falls to a level below that of 1965 (ARC 1985, 24–27). Table 1.3 gives the relative per capita income measures for the states most affected.

The outlook for the region is a stark picture of low incomes, low labor force participation, high unemployment, a set of severe human needs, and a depletion of human services. The inadequate social

Table 1.3
Appalachian Per Capita Income Measures—Selected States and Years,
1965–1995

	1965	1980	1983	1995
Kentucky	49.0	64.4	60.9	59.7
Pennsylvania	90.0	92.2	89.6	86.5
Tennessee	na	76.4	76.3	74.9
Virginia	na	73.8	71.6	73.3
West Virginia	na	81.6	78.4	74.6
Region	78.0	82.5	81.2	79.9
Nation	100.0	100.0	100.0	100.0

Note: Data represent per capita income of Appalachian portion of states as percentage of national per capita income.
Source: ARC.

investments of past forms of the welfare state, and the social capital disinvestment of the federal administration in the 1980s, suggest a crisis in a region that even in good economic times lagged behind the nation in measures of well-being.

GOVERNMENT BY THE BOTTOM LINE

It is useful to conceptualize social policies of the federal government along a continuum of public social investment, and to place the policies of the 1980s on the end of the spectrum marked "social capital disinvestment." Talk about safety nets and the worthy poor only obfuscated the nature of the commitment that the administrations of President Ronald Reagan and President George Bush had made to social investment. It was a commitment to provide as little as possible, and was the mirror reflection of its preference to foster the accumulation of private capital through which all social improvements were believed to come. Along with these preferences came a strong belief that the provision of national defense was the major legitimate form of social investment for public capital.

These changes in policy and belief had profound consequences on the Appalachian region, as is evident in the 1982 Arthur D. Little study for the Appalachian Regional Commission. Before 1920, the Appalachian region had been receiving a higher proportion of federal spending on energy, or capital infrastructure, due primarily to the nuclear construction program of the TVA and construction of the Clinch Breeder Reactor. It received its portion of federal spending on social programs and income security. However, it received less than its per capita share for education and employment.

This level of social capital investment declined after 1980, and a redistribution through taxation and public spending occurred by which the residents of the region paid a larger portion of the federal revenues and received a lower portion of spending. The Reagan administration's dual approach of cutting taxes to stimulate economic growth and of cutting federal expenditures on social programs to bring the federal budget in line with reduced revenues offered little advantage to the region. Tax cuts yielded less return per capita in Appalachia than in the rest of the country. It was estimated that in 1983 the average Appalachian resident paid an increased Social Security tax—slightly more than a non-Appalachian—and had an overall tax cut of $86, compared with $114 for non-Appalachians. At the same time, total federal expenditures were cut back within the region by $172 per capita, compared with a decline of $65 in the non-Appalachian regions (Little 1982).

Contributing to the problem of the region's reverse flow of public capital in the 1980s were the numerous federal budget increases for the military. These contributed to record deficits, thus off-setting any government savings from the social service cutbacks already made and exerting new pressures for further cuts in a host of social programs important to the Appalachian region. These deficits also hiked interest rates and inflated the strength of the dollar, making exports—such as Appalachian coal—more expensive on the international market. In exchange, Appalachia received a slight increase in military spending, given the modest fraction of military dollars (3.2 percent) spent in the region (ARC 1985, i).

West Virginia illustrates the consequences of the pattern of spending of the early 1980s. In 1982 and 1983, when West Virginia led the nation in unemployment, the state lost federal aid at the rate of $479 per person—the fifth highest rate in the nation. West Virginia ranked fifth in per capita losses in social services; sixth in per capita losses in health services, rehabilitative services, and wastewater programs; second in per capita losses in Social Security benefits for the disabled; and seventh in per capita losses in food stamps (AFSCME 1984). West Virginia's loss was all the more severe because none of those cuts were in programs connected with federal nuclear projects as they were in some of the states of the Southern Appalachian region.

Accompanying these regional changes in the 1980s were cuts in the development efforts that the unique conditions of Appalachian had fostered. The social and community service programs of the Tennessee Valley Authority—although very modest—were designed in part to provide social capital for the production of labor. Over the years, however, they had been reduced consistently until the TVA's program was almost exclusively related to capital infrastructure, that is, the provision of electrical power for industrial growth—a position that the TVA had moved to before 1980, but without the intention of zeroing out its other programs. Upon reflection, the Reagan era seems but a drastic move along a historical continuum, rather than a completely new measure.

By the mid-1980s, the Appalachian Regional Commission was phasing out its operation. It had a closing agenda of efforts in 60 "distressed counties" with high social investment needs: high rates of infant mortality, low per capita income levels, and high rates of unemployment and of poverty. One important consequence of the end of the Appalachian Regional Commission will be the cessation of its region-specific research. This means that as we were entering an era when the information sector of the economy was a growth sector, the government was producing less information about a region with high needs for social investment. This, as much as anything, signifies the Reagan administration's preference for withdrawing the public provision of social capital—even information.

Changes at the federal level have consequences for state and local government. Fiscal resources are low, given existing assessment and taxation policies; consequently, more effort is required to raise fewer public revenues. The Appalachian states do not get more federal money per capita, but federal revenues represent a larger share of their local budgets. Consequently, federal cuts in aid to state and local governments of 30 percent in the early 1980s meant a greater negative impact on budgets of local government. Local governments in the region had depended on federal grants for up to 15 percent of their budgets (Little, 79–84). Much of Central Appalachia is rural and unincorporated; and thus, county government is the ordinary form of (relatively resourceless) government for most of its population.

The economic recession after 1979 had a substantial impact on some local governments of the region. Gary, West Virginia, is often cited as a small community particularly hard hit by the decision of U.S. Steel to close down its mines for more than a year and then to reopen with approximately one-third of the original work force (Couto 1984). City services, including streetlights, were cut back. Midland, Pennsylvania, is another example of a small community severely affected by economic decline. Its entire budget was based on a wage tax tied to a steel mill. This tax base was lost with the closing of the steel mill (Marchione and Tabac 1982).

Even if increased revenues for public spending existed, the Appalachian region has special needs that are in addition to its need for social investment—needs far beyond the response capacity of local government. In some cases these are related to the disinvestment in the industrial activity of the past. It is estimated, for example, that 6,800 miles of coal haul roads require some $4 billion to $5 billion in repairs. Annual maintenance on these roads alone would amount to anywhere from $66 million to $81 million. In addition, there are up to 13,000 bridges requiring approximately $600 million in repairs and reinforcement (Creighton and Vitale 1979, 10). In the face of such staggering demands and limited resources, partnerships between the private sector and governments within the Appalachian region for building a "viable and enduring policy of human resource development" (ARC 1983a, II) seem unlikely in the future.

APPALACHIA AND THE FUTURE OF THE WELFARE STATE

If this analysis is correct in relating the chronic problems of the Appalachian region to the forms and level of social investment and the relation of this investment to employment, then the future of the region is not bright. This is not merely because social spending levels may remain low. In fact, the Reagan administration represented a departure only in degree from the kinds of public programs of social investment that preceded it. It was a departure that made an important difference in the lives of individuals and communities in the Appalachian region, but it remained a difference of degree. The problems of the Appalachian region will remain so long as social investment is determined by present or future employment and so long as employment is determined by private capital.

The prospects for an alternative welfare state can also be found in the experience of the Appalachian region. The first element of this alternative is to separate income from employment and to guarantee every individual, regardless of employment, some minimum income—perhaps half the national median income. This is not nearly as radical as it sounds and actually would serve to attune the social capital system to the system of private capital. After all, private capital long ago learned to make profits apart from labor. In fact, the problem of de-industrialization is precisely the ability of capital to make profits apart from the production process, that is, disinvestment; and the post-industrial economy is in large part the substitution of capital for labor. As if to illustrate capital's belief that profit is divorced from labor, the stock of U.S. Steel rose five-eighths of a point in active trading on the New York Stock Exchange on December 27, 1983—the day it announced the elimination of 15,400 high-paying, union jobs.

The second element of an alternative welfare state is a public employment program of social investment. This is to say, a public program of employment to provide an adequate level of education, housing, health, and environmental quality where they are lacking. Since unemployment and the lack of social investment coincide, this amounts to a "worst first" strategy.

There are problems with such a program. First, the program is not adequate to reduce severe income inequalities, although the provision of adequate services could alleviate some need for the income sufficient to purchase services not now available. Second, this program is beyond the financial ability of the people with the greatest need to provide for themselves. Capital—presumably public revenues—will be necessary. This will require a renewed public will to address the nation's problems of inequality—a development that seemed unlikely during the Reagan years. But this does not rule it out for the 1990s. The elimination of social investment in the production and reproduction of labor eventually comes to the point of the destruction of labor. But some forms of social capital disinvestment—environmental destruction, for example—are common threats that will eventually have to be addressed or we will destroy everyone. The scenario of two capitalists as the last people left on a devastated planet, haggling with each other over the price of a rope with which to hang themselves is unlikely. We are likely to see mass protest to safeguard some factors of labor force reproduction, such as the environment, and quiescence in patterns of inequality related to differing levels of social investment in employment, income, housing, education, and health.

It is equally likely that we will find this quiescence punctuated by broad social concern over consequences of social disinvestment such as infant mortality and hunger. Perhaps we will acquire anew a vision of one-third of a nation such as Roosevelt offered the nation in his second inaugural address, or perhaps the perception of unrealized deprivation that Kennedy acquired in West Virginia during the Democratic presidential primary of 1960.

However piecemeal or incremental, each opportunity to increase social investment is important to specific human beings, and the experience within the Appalachian region suggests ways of making the most of all such opportunities, as well as creating them. The first step in benefiting from this experience is to examine the economic reactors within the region, that is, the mediating structures that have been dealing with the economic changes within the region. In Appalachia, there are four that come to view: the family, community organizations, the church, and unions.

The role of mediating structure is of central importance in rural, post-industrial economies and it is well-developed in the Appalachian region. *Mediating structure* is a term Berger and Neuhaus (1977) used to describe the supportive institutions and organizations that come between the individual and large-scale social and public institutions and forces. These mediating structures offer individuals access to the large-scale institutions and forces in some cases, and cushion their negative impact in others. It is in this sense that the structures mediate. As liberals and conservatives discuss the potential of such mediating structures in public policy, there already exists in the Appalachian region a set of concrete experiences that display their strengths and limitations. In this regard, as in so many others, the special needs of the Appalachian region have elicited a degree of innovation that is unique and can provide instruction to the nation.

The *family* is the basic unit of the production and reproduction of the labor force, and so it is not surprising that the family reflects the changes that occur in the labor force. The male wage earner has declined in labor force participation and he has fewer high wage employment opportunities. As a consequence, women are entering the work force in greater proportion, but at a time when middle-wage-sector employment is vanishing and the largest employment growth is at the low wage spectrum.

The American family has mediated these economic transitions just as have Appalachian families. A study of the Joint Economic Committee (1985) shows that, from 1973 to 1984, families in all income quintiles lost real income in constant, uninflated dollars. But the lowest quintile lost 34 percent while the highest income quintile lost only 1.7 percent. In addition, single parents headed 24.7 percent of all families in 1984, compared with 16.4 percent in 1973, and female-headed households had incomes at 40 percent the average of two-parent families. Marshall (1983, 6) estimates that only 15 percent of American families are "typical" in the sense of having one male wage earner in a two-parent household. Clearly, there has been a significant change in the family, brought on perhaps by changes in marriage and lifestyle but also fostered by changes in the economy external to the household, including a drop in income (Joint Economic Committee 1986), and to which families are economic reactors.

Some research suggests that women's participation in the Appalachian work force matched or exceeded national rates. Ford's (Ford, Arcury, and Porter 1981) study of families in the Central Appalachian region indicates a decline in the labor market participation of male heads of families, a slight increase of working female family heads, and a dramatic increase of working women in husband-wife households. The rate of the latter doubled from 18.2 percent in 1958 to 38.1 percent in 1976 and increased again by 1985, as we have seen. In other words, de-industrialization and post-industrialization have fostered change in the labor pool. In early industrialization—certainly in the case of Appalachia—there was a change from subsistence agricultural work to industrial wage labor. In post-industrialization, the change is coming from within the family as nonwage workers within the domestic economy are encouraged to enter wage labor to maintain the basic needs of the family in the face of a drop in real and social wages.

The point is that women in husband-wife households have become wage earners in order to provide the family with sufficient income to maintain basic needs—health, housing, education, transportation, and so forth—at a time of decline in the real and social wage and a corresponding decline in social investment. Another consequence of this trend, though, is increased income for families with two wage earners. Even with low wages, two wage earners make it possible for a working class family to rise into middle class consumption patterns. Figures from census data on West Virginia indicate that the 1976 median income for husband-wife households was $12,691. But those households in which the wife and husband were both wage earners had a median income of $15,489, while those in which the wife was not a wage earner had a median income of $10,946. These same figures indicate that the working wives in West Virginia contributed 41 percent to their families' income compared with the U.S. average of 32 percent (Ford, Arcury, and Porter, 79). Thus, wives' incomes in West Virginia had a much greater marginal value, representing a larger percentage of a smaller amount. Their incomes were important in assuring their families' basic needs, as our survey on hunger indicated (Couto 1986). There was no significant difference between female-headed and male-headed households in the report of hunger, indicating the high risk for hunger among all low-income families.

While the attention paid to the increased role of wives in the provision of basic needs for the family is important, it should not serve to obfuscate the continuing inadequacy of employment opportunities for female heads of families in providing basic needs. In 1980 in West Virginia, the median income of families headed by women was $6,504, which was 36 percent of the median income of two-parent families at the same time. Moreover, a female-headed family was four times more probable to have a below-poverty income than a male-headed family: 43 percent of female-headed families in West Virginia were in poverty, as were 11 percent of male-headed families (Hall 1983, 1–2).

Community organizations are another important set of economic reactors in the new political economy of Appalachia. The region encompasses one of the nation's most successful citizens' environmental groups, Save Our Cumberland Mountains; one of the nation's most enduring community-based media collectives, Appalshop; one of the nation's most successful citizens' environmental organizing efforts, Yellow Creek Concerned Citizens; and scores of efforts, large and small, to provide new services to meet basic needs. These include health clinics, housing groups and amalgams of different efforts such as the Mountain Women's Exchange and the Dungannon Development Council.

Even while acknowledging their importance, however, we must remain mindful of the limits of these community efforts. They are necessitated because of the lack of social investment in the region. And their actions often founder precisely because of this inadequacy of capital. Housing construction and repair efforts within the region are chronically beset with a lack of enough private and public capital to support major construction, employment, and training programs. Likewise, some of the successes of these groups come only after the damage from social disinvestment has already taken its toll, as in the case of a remedial education program for adults or a new water system for an area because its usual water supplies are being threatened by industrial toxic damage to the environment.

The community organizations' efforts to improve health care have been the most successful of such citizen group projects in terms of raising enough social capital to remain in operation even in the face of huge deficits related to patients' inability to pay for health care. But even these efforts have had their limits. They have been sustained only by the most strenuous commitment on the part of local residents and assisting professionals. The chronic lack of professionals to staff the health projects may also be understood as stemming from the fact that the lack of social investment is being met only by efforts on the part of local administrators and residents, whose recruitment of professionals and funds for the operation of the clinics represents the fledgling entrepreneurial skills of the formation of scarce social capital.

There are several important points to make about the mediating efforts of community organizations in general. First, they are forms of social investment and substitution. Second, they are not adequate to the task, because they do not have sufficient social capital to replace the lack of investment and the present and past forms of social capital disinvestment. Third, they have demonstrated their competence in initiating, conducting, and maintaining forms of social investment in very difficult circumstances. Fourth, their efforts involve service sector employment for many people, most of whom are women; and thus, their experiences are consistent with a major trend in the economy. Fifth, the most positive aspect of this characteristic of their work is that the employment entails training and income otherwise not available—and very often, career opportunities and professional roles. Sixth and finally, these mediating structures are part of the renewed emphasis on community as a social value extolled by liberals and conservatives alike. The mid-1980s study *Habits of the Heart* (Bellah 1985) and the earlier study of the American Enterprise Institute, *To Empower People* (Berger and Neuhaus 1977), are examples of the renewed emphasis placed on community by both ends of the political spectrum.

The *church* has also shown unusual initiative as an economic reactor in the Appalachian region. There is, of course, the day-to-day administration of relief services, but the church in Appalachia has gone far beyond that and has addressed some of the underlying causes of the human needs for which they provide relief. The Catholic bishops' pastoral letter on Appalachia, *This Land Is Home to Me*, preceded similar statements issued at the national level and is a rundown and critique of social investment within the regional economy. The Commission on Religion in Appalachia was one early example of ecumenical cooperation around economic issues. By the mid-1980s, the commission was already 20 years old and served as the most important regionwide organization because it alone had the capacity to coordinate and communicate with community organizations throughout the region. As social investment has declined over the years, the commission's ability to raise private capital from national Protestant denominations has become a necessary—even if not sufficient—condition for the continuation of numerous community organizations.

It is important to be precise about the role of the church as a mediating structure. It has been most effective in its capacity to produce resources for social investment. This includes money, of course, but it also includes professional staffing for community organizations engaged in alternative social investment. Clergy and lay people with substantial religious commitment have played an important role in providing stable staffs to community organizations despite low and sometimes irregular wages. Another important resource related to social investment that the church can uniquely provide is information gathering, provision, and dissemination. The various church denominations are national in organization, with contacts that extend far beyond the region; indeed, they may be the only organizations in the region with national and global contacts that parallel those of the corporations active in the region. Thus, they are in a unique position to relate economic changes within the region to national and international trends, and they play an important role in doing so. This role increased in importance with the end of the

Appalachian Regional Commission and the decline of public investment in information about the region and its social capital needs.

Unions of organized labor, too, have been important mediating organizations within the Appalachian region. The net effect of their efforts has been to mitigate some of the worst consequences of the region's economic conditions and the nation's policies. Innovative health programs, improved working conditions, and improved wages have resulted from their efforts. Organized groups of former workers have also been active in gaining compensation for the victims of the region's occupational respiratory illnesses, that is, black lung and brown lung. In addition to securing compensation, the unions have also tried to control and reduce the factors that bring on these illnesses. The positive consequences of such efforts accrue not only to the members of the unions, but to community residents and workers in companies without unions as well. Moreover, the unions create a standard for comparison of real and social wages.

The current economic crisis calls for organized labor to assume a new role that is only slowly evolving. Union membership is declining, and major new producers are beginning their operations without union labor. During this time of crisis, management is demanding and acquiring greater control over labor and concessions in the social wages that labor had previously gained. This is all the more reason for organized labor to involve itself actively in the changing economy. At a time of increase in the pool of surplus labor and a decline in real and social wages, unions are very important in slowing the deterioration of labor conditions.

In recent contracts, labor unions of miners and steelworkers have made significant concessions in wages and benefits. Both unions have undergone rank-and-file reform attempts. The most profound reform of a national union began in West Virginia, among the Miners for Democracy, as did the most extensive grassroots and worker campaign to redress and prevent occupational illness, the Black Lung Association. Unions in these industrial sectors will have a major stake in future re-industrialization policies of the nation and provide the only hope for the direct participation of labor in formulating those policies.

Other unions have equally important roles. Unions of textile and apparel workers are negotiating these days with industries that have serious problems and the ability to relocate into new areas with newer plants and lower labor costs. The future of these two unions—and the furniture workers—will have to entail a consideration for the competitiveness of the industry and job security for workers, in addition to wages.

But the future role of unions extends beyond the traditional industrial relations, if they are to respond to the changes in the nature of the work force as well as to the changes in the nature and amount of work. The increased participation of women in the labor force is important, and unions cannot afford to ignore the gender of the majority of labor's new workers. The union membership of women is increasing and concentrated. One-half of all women union members belong to only eight unions, among which are retail clerks and clothing and textile workers. Almost seven million women—15 percent of women workers—were union members in 1978, compared to just under three million women in 1954. Women constituted 24 percent of union membership in 1978. The common ground of unions and women does have its border conflicts, however. Established union seniority systems will do little to improve the job opportunities or situations for women in a tight labor market. Also, despite the numbers of women union members in 1978, only 7 percent of union board members were women (Marshall, 19–20).

The role of organized labor is a necessary but not sufficient condition for improving the increased real and social wage of women workers who are entering the labor market under adverse conditions, as we have seen. The unions' ability to deal with the unfavorable impacts of the internationalization of the economy, and its consequent issues, will be important for women, for example. Women comprise 41 percent of the workers in industries adversely impacted by international trade and 29 percent of those favorably impacted (Marshall, 4). In addition, future employment opportunities in the service and information sectors are likely to be filled by women, and will require organization to protect workers' rights and wages. The victory of the American Federation of State, County, and Municipal Employees in the state of Washington in acquiring equal pay for jobs of comparable value was a direct challenge to a form of sex discrimination that is all too prevalent nationally, and it shows the significance of union efforts to increase the real and social wages of women (Marshall, 20–21). This in turn has profound consequences for the income available to the family as the pattern of female labor force participation and increases in the participation make clear.

CONCLUSION

We have undergone a dramatic change in federal policy since 1980. The role of the federal government during the Reagan administration changed to social disinvestment and the promotion of market mechanisms to meet national needs for employment and the related social investment needs of health, housing, income, and environment. This occurred at a time of private capital disinvestment in the industrial production processes within the Appalachian region and changes in the nature and wages of work and in the nature of the labor force to accommodate the post-industrial economy. The change in federal policy should actually be seen along a continuum of welfare policy options, rather than as a discontinuity with the past. However, its impact was far reaching because the public disinvestment coincided with deficit spending for defense. The national debt may preclude large new federal spending for social investment without some kind of radical change in budget priorities and taxation policies. While the latter are possible, they are not likely in the near future.

But higher levels of social investment are not sufficient to address questions of inequality between the Appalachian region and the nation as a whole, nor within the region. Effective public policy will require an equally dramatic change in attitudes in the public provision of social investment if it is to be adequate in forms and amounts. This means a guaranteed income policy and higher levels of social investment than in the past. Such increases will in turn require a redistribution of wealth from those with more to those with less. Regardless of events at the federal level, it is vital to look at what mediating structures can do with *reduced* federal resources *or* as implementation mechanisms of *expanded* social investment. Churches have an important role in the alternative provision of limited investment capital. Labor unions have the important role of mitigating the social costs of de-industrialization for labor and for improving the terms of new forms of labor, especially for women.

The policies of a future welfare state should include employment programs involving local residents in the provision of social investment, especially housing and environmental restoration. Community organizations have already proven competent in the provision of other forms of social investment—health and education—despite very difficult circumstances. Such policies need to be undertaken with the economic changes in the family in mind.

■ 2 ■
Place for Sale: Repopulation and Change in an Appalachian and a Highland Scottish Community

John B. Stephenson

It is a commonplace that every community is in change and that every study of community ought to be a study of its change. It would be difficult for me to do otherwise, for change is what I have witnessed even in the relatively brief time I have watched the two communities upon which I report here. The change processes I will describe in the two distant geographic settings of Appalachian America and Highland Scotland could be considered, I suppose, examples of rural gentrification or rural invasion and succession. They have to do with the re-populating of the countryside and the cultural repaving of rural areas. These processes are part of a larger pattern in which people search for opportunity, motivated and aided in this search by a variety of commercial and informal brokers. Part of the search is a search for place.

What, one might ask, is the basis for comparison of these two widely separated communities? The place that I call "Shiloh" is located in western North Carolina, the village of Ford in the West Highlands of Scotland. Despite the great separation in distance, there are similarities that invite comparison. Geographically, the West Highlands (the old county of Argyll) and the Blue Ridge section of North Carolina share in common their topography, their beauty, and their shrinking distance from urban centers. They are both peripheral areas within subregions of a country, both less affluent than the urban cores to which they relate, both somewhat culturally different from their surroundings. Western North Carolina is in fact said to have been settled in part by Highlanders and others of Scottish descent in the 18th century, although it would be unwise to press the matter of cultural purity and persistence as far as some do in studies of Appalachia and the South. Both Shiloh and Ford share today a partic-ular form of linkage to the societies of which they are part. There is a peculiar bond between the city and the countryside that finds its expression in these two cases—a bond that, as I have said, involves a search for place. It is the sharing of this bond that is the basis of the comparison drawn here.

SHILOH REVISITED

When I first went to Shiloh, the changes on which I focused had to do with individuals and families in the process of what I then called "modernization," and what I now see as a historically mandated absorption into an industrializing working class. At that time, in 1965, I made note of another change in Shiloh: the arrival of an increasing number of tourists and summer visitors. When I placed this coming-in alongside the then-extensive migration of natives to the cities, I made a note that these twin movements could be captured in the phrase "inside out and outside in." But I did not bring the "outside in" part of the phenomenon to the center of the stage.

In those days, of course, Appalachian out-migration was the big story. I knew of that important trend largely because of the published work of James Brown. I suppose it was because of the absence of published research on tourists and in-migrants that I did not dwell on it as a major theme in my writing on Shiloh. Fifteen years later there was still not much published, but the fact of in-migration was so obvious a fact of experience by 1980 that it simply could not be subordinated to other themes of change in Shiloh.

Shiloh is a cluster of several neighborhoods ranging around a single main road in a rural western North Carolina county. The cluster is sufficiently integrated by kinship, friendship, and economic ties that it is thought of by residents—as well as outsiders—as a whole community. The origin of the community is lost entirely to history. More than likely, it was settled by whites of varied nationality in the 1700s, some of whom would have arrived there by way of the North Carolina Piedmont, though some of whom may have traveled south along the Blue Ridge spine. It is extremely doubtful that this area was ever isolated from the rest of the country in terms of its contacts, although it may have been relatively uninfluenced by what went on elsewhere until the late 19th and early 20th centuries, when timber interest and missionaries moved in to harvest trees and souls, respectively.

Change surged upon Shiloh as a consequence of World War II, when roads were built and improved, schools were upgraded and consolidated, the extent of farming declined, employment in mining and manufacturing began and increased, and communications from the outside grew in quantity and nature as a result of the coming of telephones (in the 1960s) and television (somewhat earlier).

In 1965 I identified the coming in of outsiders as no more important than the passing through of tourists and the occasional summer visitor interested in a second home. These were seen as another source of the "modernizing influence of the outside on the inside of this relatively unknown and nondistinctive mountain place" (Stephenson 1968). On the other side of the ridge there was, I knew, an entire summer settlement of Floridians in a cove named, coincidentally, Pensacola, but I did not foresee adequately what would happen on the Shiloh side of the mountain. Nor did I appreciate what lay behind the resettling of Pensacola and what its effects on local structures and culture were, other than to provide a cultural challenge to "traditional" values and orientation.

When I drove into Shiloh in 1980, however, the first observation I wrote in my notes concerned the real estate billboards decorating the approach to the community. They were new, as was the sign pointing to the campground and recreation area that did not exist on my earlier visits. Driving down the main road, I noticed that a branch office of a national realty chain had opened since my last trip to Shiloh, and that the store had changed hands. I was surprised to see a new Presbyterian church not far from the old one, which apparently was still functioning, and then a brick building that boasted the existence of a volunteer fire department.

A few new homes could be seen from this road, but otherwise the housing looked much like it had 15 years before. When I explored the off-roads, I discovered that what could be seen from the main road was entirely misleading: there were numerous new homes up the coves, as well as new mobile homes and greatly improved older residences of long standing. Farther down the main road I saw signs marking new tract developments, one of which was built around a championship golf course, on the edge of which had been built a new Bavarian restaurant (owned by card-carrying Bavarians, I might add).

With the aid of the son of one of my former key informants, I mapped the entire community, identifying the occupants of every dwelling for comparison to a similar map I had made 15 years earlier. And with the help of the son of another informant, I extracted information on land ownership in the township covering a 13-year span. I interviewed the new realtor and examined the records of property sales in that office. I talked to numerous newcomers and longer-term residents. The story of change in Shiloh in 1980 had little or nothing to do with modernization; it had, rather, to do with the resettlement of the community by persons whose origins were outside the mountains and indeed outside North Carolina altogether.

I found that while my friend John Henry Sommers had moved his household from down on the creek up to the main road, the internationally known concert pianist Lilly Kraus and her physician son-in-law and his family had moved from an eastern city to a place down on that same creek. John Henry was proud of his new location, pointing to the town sign in his front yard and remarking, "You can't hardly get more downtown than *that.*" The Kraus household was equally proud of its new homestead up under the trees and out of sight of the entire community.

I learned that the deaf-mute old man who once made a rockerless rocking chair for me was enjoying life in Morgantown, North Carolina, while his old ramshackle house off the beaten path toward the upper end of the creek had been bought and completely remodeled, complete with white picket fence, by a retired couple from Miami.

I discovered that the store had been bought by a couple from the city of Baltimore who read about the property in a nationally distributed realty catalog. During all his years in the General Electric plant, the man had dreamed about being a country storekeeper, and now his dream was a reality.

Ironically, the farther I drove from the highly visible areas near the main road, the more likely I was to witness the transformation of the community. For people like John Henry, moving to the highway was an escape from marginality and the social class putdowns associated with life down the creek. To the newcomer physician, the attorney, and all the retired couples from the cities, the realization of their anti-urban ideal was measurable by the distance away from the highway. So as the John Henrys moved in closer to what they saw as a progressive, civilized life, the urbanites took their places, both literally and figuratively. Crumbling foundations of old houses were shored up, rusting roofs were replaced, weather-beaten boards were made shiny with paint, and new mailboxes were erected bearing family names unfamiliar both to me and to the natives.

Statistics confirmed what the eye could see. The tax records for 1980, when compared with those for 1968, showed that the total number of parcels of land had increased while the average size of each had decreased. They also showed that the value of the land had skyrocketed over this 13-year period. And they told that the proportion of properties belonging to owners who were not native to the township or the county had grown strikingly.

The tax records showed, for example, that the number of property owners increased from 1,106 in 1968 to 1,521 in 1980 (see Table 2.1). Seventy-five percent of this increase was made up of non-natives. In 1968 the proportion of taxpayers who were natives of the township

Table 2.1
Owners of Taxable Property by Nativity and Residence Category, Shiloh Township, 1968 and 1980

Nativity	1968	1980	Increase	%	% of Total Increase
Township Native	521	532	11	2.1	2.6
County Native	27	86	59	218.5	14.2
Non-Native			[325]		[78.3]
Full-time Resident	59	148	89	150.8	21.4
Part-time Resident	69	171	102	147.8	24.6
Non-Resident	403	537	134	33.2	32.3
Unknown and Other	27	47	20	74.1	4.8
Totals	1106	1521	415	37.5	99.9

Source: County Tax Records for 19678 and 1980, coded by Christopher Chrisawn, native and lifelong resident.

was already low at 47.1 percent; by 1980, the figure had fallen to 35.0 percent.

When the category of "non-native" was broken down, the numbers became even more interesting. The owners were first divided into "resident" and "nonresident," and the residents were further classified as "full-time" and "part-time." The largest percentage increase occurred among full-time residents, followed closely by part-time residents. Far and away the smallest percentage increase was among township natives, who increased their ownership by only 11 properties, or 2.1 percent. To summarize, native ownership was giving way to outside ownership, and the fastest-growing category of new owners were those who came from outside to take up residence.

Who were the newcomers, and for what reasons had they come to Shiloh? Some, of course, were speculators who did not live there and never intended to. They hoped simply to enjoy financial gain. Others had bought property to enjoy for short vacations, sometimes renting out their otherwise unoccupied houses in order to help meet the mortgage payments. Others had built or bought homes to which they would retire; some of them had reached retirement and lived in Shiloh year-round. The remaining category was also made up of full-time residents; these were the year-round dwellers with intentions of permanent residence, who came to work in the vicinity and find a better life for themselves and their families. They were of working and child-rearing age.

The ownership statistics from tax records showed what had already been revealed to me in a visit with the realty office. Sixty pieces of property worth a total of $1 million had been sold by the company since it opened its doors four years earlier. Where were the buyers from? The realtor opened a desk drawer and read off the home addresses of the clients: 23 from Florida; 3 from New York; 2 from Mississippi, one each from Connecticut, Vermont, New Jersey, Ohio, Michigan, Pennsylvania, Illinois, Missouri, Indiana, Maryland, and Lexington, Kentucky. Eleven were from North Carolina, of which five were from the county and only one from the township.

What reasons did people give for buying places in Shiloh? Generally, it had to do with the fulfillment of a dream—not always the same dream, but some kind of imagined improvement in the quality of life. People said they were tired of the city—the danger, the traffic, the noise, the racial situation. People said they had been in places like this while on vacation, and they had in mind to live out their retirement days in a kind of unending extension of long-awaited, full-time leisurely inactivity. People said they came here for solace and retreat, to get close to the land and be with real people. A few people said they came here to help the sick, the poor, the unlettered, the disorganized, and those deficient in high culture. All these people said they liked the place and, in varying degrees, the people, and that they felt at home here.

What they had bought was, both literally and figuratively, a place. (A place, one might say, on Fantasy Mountain.) From whom was the land being purchased? Much of it was in the hands of land speculators and developers. Ironically, most of the so-called spec property was handled by a native son who had sold his father's grocery business to devote more time to more interesting commercial pursuits. This was Craig Bowman, who was exceedingly bright—bright enough to know where the money was, and insightful enough to see exactly what was happening as a result of his own actions.

Craig knows that the land values in this township have risen faster than elsewhere in the country—that this is referred to as the "Gold Coast" of the country. Land sales here have surpassed Pensacola (across the ridge) now, according to him. "Many people," he says, "have sold out to outsiders at what to them is a high price, and have bought over in McDowell County or in Burke, changing their lifestyles." Craig buys land and sells it for a profit. I asked him what the local people think about what he's doing. He says, "The local people always want to know whether the people I'm selling to will be nice people. So far, they've been satisfied." Then he became pensive:

> I would trade all the money for the way it was in the mid-fifties, but it's too late. There's an old saying: don't crap in your own backyard. But we've done it, and I've helped. We all justify land development by saying if we didn't do it, somebody else would. Sooner or later, nobody but a few of us who can afford it will be left here.

As if to prove his point, he later introduced me to a man named Ed by saying, "I want you to meet a member of a dying breed—a native."

The breed is not dying, of course, but it is becoming outnumbered. The natives who have not moved to McDowell or Burke counties—or Charlotte or California—are still finding employment within commuting distance at places such as Baxter Laboratories, American Tread, Hickory Springs, Blue Bell, Glen Raven, Armored Garments, the golf course, the Highway Department, and the Forest Service. They still fish and go to church and observe Decoration Day and visit back and forth in ways reminiscent of Shiloh in 1965.

But the structure of community life is tangibly different, and subtle cultural changes have not gone unnoticed. None but the most hopelessly romantic would deny that these changes represent community improvements for the most part, although there is a great deal of ambivalence expressed by natives. In 1965, Shiloh experienced near-trauma in creating a community improvement organization, because no one would agree to be nominated as chairman. In fact, there were no community organizations except for the churches and a softball team, and the only reason the community improvement group came into being was because of the efforts of a minister from Ohio. Now there is a volunteer fire department, organized by newcomers but run jointly by newcomers and natives. There is a program for senior citizens, organized by newcomers. The new church was begun at the instigation of one man from "outside." A monthly music appreciation group was organized—again by newcomers. Child development and health services have improved because of the initiative of a physician who moved into Shiloh. He has also maintained an imaginative program of assistance to problem families, coupled with housing improvement. Last, but certainly not least, there is now a community center in Shiloh—an unthinkable accomplishment 15 years ago that has since been accomplished mainly because of the efforts of newcomers. (A YMCA-sponsored youth program was the next project in the works; this idea was being promoted mainly by the wife of one recently arrived chiropractor.)

Relations between the newcomers and the natives vary greatly; but in the main, the attitude is one of mutual tolerance, a keeping of distance, a muted disdain. Most of the newcomers expressed the feeling that they were well accepted by the natives, but they admitted that they rarely associated with them except in public places such as the stores and in meetings. They had ideas about local culture that were not especially complimentary. ("Nobody will ever act together down here." "They're not taught things about responsibility and motivation." "They don't know the world outside this little place." "The low level of education is appalling." "I didn't realize the apathy of the people." "They don't know about things so they don't want them." "People are afraid to say anything for fear it will come back on them. We need to introduce the democratic process here.") The newcomers say that people are friendly, but they don't socialize: they do not take meals with natives, for example, and they do not golf with them.

The natives do not hide their feelings well. One man, attempting to put his new neighbors in a good light, said, minimally, "They speak. And I speak to them." Another says that some are better than others:

> Some of these outsiders is all right and others is just plumb hateful. They're unfriendly, don't want you to set foot on their land but want to roam all over yours. I sold a man ten acres above me here; I wisht I hadn't. I needed the money. It's been sold twice since then and I never met the man that owns it now. He might be one of those hateful ones.

Another native talks about how the outsiders stick to themselves. He does have one close friend who is an outsider—he says, "He ain't no smarter than I am"—but as for most of them, he says simply, "The Florida people has about taken over." When I asked Hope Sommers if she knew of any other terms people used for the newcomers, she said, simply, "land-takers."

A retiree from Miami, watching the sun set from his front porch while he broke with local custom and drank beer openly in front of God and his neighbors, said that he had found the local way of life different from his, but not surprisingly different. He said people were easy to get along with: "We don't have any problems. It's live and let live. Nobody sticks their nose in your business." That may be all he asks for, coming from Miami. But I asked him how he thought local people felt about outsiders like himself. His answer was accurate and perceptive: "They like the money from Florida people, but then they resent them."

We see in this one small Appalachian community a case of rural invasion and succession. Local families are leaving Shiloh in search of improved lives in towns and cities, and urban refugees are taking their places in the country, also in search of better ways of living. The machinery of this complex exchange is oiled and operated by a combination of local and outside entrepreneurs—all brokers of one kind or another. And the consequence is an uneasy acceptance of change on the part of natives—an eagerness to take the money and run, coupled with as yet ill-formed questions about messes of pottage. The changes involve getting the community organized, forming more substantial community associations than Shiloh has ever known, and paving over local customs with the thoughts and habits and energy of urban sophisticates who came here to look at the scenery, lift up the benighted, and get away from the high prices and urban confusion they left behind.

While the natives may struggle with ambivalence toward their new neighbors, the newcomers seem on the whole quite happy with their decisions to relocate in Shiloh. While they may be aware of the distance at which they are kept by the natives, that pattern of distancing is nothing new to them, and it is more than acceptable as a part of community life; it is probably even preferred over the alternative. The newcomers *feel* accepted, and they *feel* at home. The full-time residents have made commitments to this place. It is now *their* place. They feel affection for it and love its physical aspects, and they want to care for it and "improve" it.

There can be little doubt that the newcomers' influence on Shiloh is making it a better community in many respects, if we measure community vitality by the degree of locality-based association and mutual problem-solving. If, on the other hand, we were to define the strength of community in terms of shared identity or shared sense of place, the picture in Shiloh is more confusing. My impression is that the newcomers may now have a stronger sense of place than do the natives, who are uncertain what is happening to their place. One native, in attempting to analyze what was taking place in Shiloh, said unsentimentally, "You've got to have progress, but after you reach a point, you lose what you had and you can't get it back."

The place has changed, every native seems to agree. One commented, "Neighborhoods are not as closely knit. Life is faster paced. People don't keep up with each other—they don't care that much." Another, describing what he meant by saying that the pace of life had changed, said, "Decisions are made quickly now. It used to take three days to decide whether to cut your hay. And you don't make deals on handshakes anymore, either." These are people reporting their perceptions of culture change—changes in a place they are not certain is even theirs anymore, a place becoming so filled with outsiders that some of the natives are feeling a bit crowded. Mountain humor, like humor everywhere, often has an edge to it, as when one man said to me, "If you're thinking about moving down into here, I'd say you'd better hurry while you can still wedge in."

As Shiloh changes into whatever it is to become, it will slip quietly into that future with the aid of native land brokers and culture brokers. Craig Bowman is an example of the local land broker who learns to live with his episodic nostalgic urges. Jim Hartley is a culture broker who plays a role in the transition because he understands the old Shiloh. There are California plates on his pickup. There is a surfboard lying in the yard—probably the only one in the county, and it belongs to a native. Jim wants to stay permanently in this valley, but he leaves the door open to opportunities elsewhere, just in case things do not work out here. He could probably live anywhere, make a decent living as a builder/carpenter, and be happy. Everyone—native and newcomer—knows Jim, and everyone likes him. Jim does not suffer from nostalgia; he is not tormented by images of a departed past. He represents the kind of cultural and interpersonal linkage that will make the transition of community identity a relatively smooth one.

THE VILLAGE OF FORD

Comparisons between Shiloh and the West Highland Scottish village of Ford are instructive, although on the surface one would see little reason to seek parallels between them. Their histories are highly divergent, there are important differences in class structure and culture, and their settlement patterns are dissimilar. Even their weather and their topography are different, not to mention the national histories of which they are tiny parts.

Ford is quite small, with 156 people in around 60 households. Its history is considerably older than that of Shiloh. Records make mention of the place in the 17th century, although it was most certainly a human settlement earlier than that. Ford became important as a stopping place and a river crossing for the numerous cattle drives by means of which Highland cattle were delivered to markets in central Scotland. Located at the head of Loch Awe in Argyllshire, Ford grew adventitiously at the intersection of two townships and three then-major estates. Once dependent on these estates for support and employment, the villagers now find employment in diverse settings usually not related to estates: tourism, forestry, hill farming, plant nursery work, fish farming, gamekeeping, and a number of occupations outside the community such as teaching, nursing, geology, and architecture.

Shortly after my arrival in Ford, I was told by an informant that I would have difficulty finding many natives in the village because everyone living there has arrived within their lifetimes. This prediction was not greatly exaggerated. Eventually, I identified seven natives among the 156 people in the village. The native population, it was said, had been dwindling for many years.

Yet the general population in Ford in 1981 was increasing. A look at population figures for the township of Kilmartin (in which Ford is located) showed that until recently the population had been steadily decreasing since 1801. This historical decline paralleled the pattern of population change in the Highlands generally. The infamous

Highland Clearances, begun in the 1770s, resulted in massive forcible evictions, relocation, and emigration so that the native population could be replaced with sheep, which were more profitable to the large landowners. The potato blight, the failure of agriculture in the Highlands to respond to "improvements" and rationalization efforts, and the attraction of employment alternatives outside the Highlands continued this heavy outflow throughout the 19th and 20th centuries.

Entire glens that once might have contributed hundreds of fighting men for some Highland cause are now empty of people. Kilmartin Parish itself declined from 1,501 people in 1801 to 327 in 1971. In one of my first visits to Ford, an informant expressed serious doubt about the future of the village, predicting that it would die within a very few years as other villages had died before it. When I saw the long history of decline in the census figures, I knew no reason to doubt her prophecy.

But Ford was far from dead, as it turned out, both in terms of population and by other measures of community vitality. The Scottish Women's Rural Institute had thoughtfully taken an exact census in Ford village in 1966, a count with which I could compare my own census in 1981, and the comparison showed that the population had increased between 40 and 50 percent. It was clear that this growth was not attributable to natural increase—the young were still leaving Ford just as in earlier generations, and the birthrate had declined, if anything—but rather was brought about by a surge in the number of in-migrants, or "incomers," as they are known in Britain.

Who are the incomers and why did they come to Ford?

Before answering this question, it is important to make a distinction between recent incomers and those who have been residents of Ford for many years. Because the recent surge seemed to begin around 12 years earlier, I chose this as the date by which to distinguish early from recent incomers. Of the 59 present (1981) households in Ford, 33, or 56 percent, were those of recent incomers; 19, or 32 percent, were those of earlier incomers; and only 7, or 12 percent, were those of natives. Now, who were the recent incomers?

They were people such as the Greenshields, retired English schoolteachers, who had traveled earlier in the Highlands and looked for a place like Ford in which to live out their later years.

Mr. Brotherston had an ancestor from the Lothian area (near Edinburgh), so that there was a somewhat remote Scottish connection in the family.

They were people like the Parks, lowland Scots who had worked on the western islands and then moved to Ford where Roger found work on a new fish farm. Roger and Nan say they love the Highland nature, scenery, land lore. They cannot imagine living in the city now. Ford is home.

Bryan Johns is an architect in the nearby town of Lochgilphead. The Johns moved to Ford from Edinburgh. He is a member of the Ford Gun Club, and he teaches bagpiping in the high school at Lochgilphead. When first footing takes place at Hogmanay (New Year's), Bryan is there with pipe and kilt, leading the group from door to door, wishing everyone a happy new year and bringing a small gift to bring good luck as the ancient custom dictates. The Johns like Ford now, although at first they did not feel readily accepted by the village, and they would only move to Lochgilphead or some other town to reduce the inconvenience of country living.

Ian Willis came to Ford from Lancashire (England) to take over a nursery and make a go of it. To the Willises, Ford represented economic opportunity combined with a pleasant countryside environment and comfortable human relationships.

Other recent incomers are teachers, secretaries, nurses, and government employees in Lochgilphead. One is a businessman in Oban; another is a geologist who works anywhere in the world the oil business takes him. Others are shepherds and farm workers and forestry workers. Most came to Ford, like the retired couples, because they knew of the area from earlier travels or from friends, and they always wanted to live in a place in the countryside where the pace was slower, the people friendly, and the scenery beautiful. Others (the shepherds and farmers, especially) came to Ford because of job opportunities.

When you listen to people in Ford talk about why they came there, you realize that they, like their Shiloh counterparts, have come to find a place on Fantasy Mountain. And to give credit where it is due in both Ford and Shiloh, most of them have found it.

For almost all the recent incomers to Ford feel very much at home here. They feel a strong sense of place. Miss Greenshields once said that, whenever she goes on a journey away from the Highlands, when she comes back and sees the mountains she feels that "these are my hills." The Greenshields all voted for Scottish devolution in the 1979 referendum, which made them, by that measure at least, more Scottish than many of their Scottish neighbors in Ford, who by and large voted against it. The MacNays, also English ("born Londoners"), are rooted strongly in Ford, finding there "everything to delight the senses," and good friends and neighbors in the bargain. The incomers are among the most active in the local historical society, and incomers played a vital role in preparing the local history written several years ago. Few of them, incidentally, showed much desire to be buried near their original homes.

The impact of the recent incomers on the village is difficult to overestimate. They express their commitments to their adopted home in a number of ways, including participation in community associations. Mr. Brotherston's sister plays the organ at church. Incomers are active on the Village Hall Committee, which plans a large number of community programs throughout the year. Incomers began a youth program, an exercise program for women, and a new play school. Incomers helped with the planning and installation of the village's television antenna. Some of them are active in the Ford Gun Club, which has been a village institution since at least 1880.

Many recent incomers also participate in pub life at the Ford Hotel, which is the center of village life for the largest number of residents, especially during the winter when the tide of tourists is out.

The incomers have had an undeniably invigorating effect on the village. Although some older community institutions have disappeared or weakened, the incomers have helped bring new ones to life. At the same time that the former urbanites celebrate the virtues of country living and the English celebrate Scottishness, however, they bring change with them. These differences in habit and outlook are not always appreciated by the natives and early incomers. It is as though the olden ways of life are weakened by the very act of glorifying them, or as though what is cherished but not fully understood is smothered in the embrace of affectionate strangers. Whatever is left of native Highland culture in Ford is being papered over with the images of Scottish culture that people bring with them. The culture is reconstructed in accordance with the ideas the incomers bring with them about what village life ought to be like.

New divisions within the community have also accompanied the changes in population. Long-term residents understand something about the nature of invasion and succession, but not all of them like its consequences. A common complaint was, "They come to live here and then tell us what to do." I was told that the incomers are resented because they buy property at high prices that local people cannot afford, which has caused natives to leave. The incomers are described often as unfriendly, superior acting, demanding, aloof, and overbearing. They are referred to as "white settlers," a term usually applied to the English, against whom there is a strong historical prejudice among Scots, but which in this case is applied to a number of urban Scots as well. Some of the incomers are aware that they are thought of as "white settlers," but most are either unaware or choose to ignore it. The resentment is never expressed openly and is never manifested in conflict except when it takes the form of some other issue. The division is there, ever present, but below the surface of human relationships.

The village of Ford is not dying; it is becoming transfigured, but it is alive. In general, if one were to look for signs of community vitality, one might try to uncover evidence of the following:

1. The presence of shared, purposeful activity related to the collective interests of those inhabiting the locality.
2. The presence of locality-based institutions, or organized patterns of living.
3. The presence of shared identity rooted in a sense of place.
4. The presence of at least some minimal degree of authority over part of the decision-making that affects the locality.
5. The presence of shared overall goals and values regarding the community.

On all these counts, Ford shows vital signs. Community associations are reasonably strong, there is evidence of shared place-related purpose and of shared place-related identity. Decision-making autonomy is not strong in any absolute sense, but it is as strong as it could be, given Ford's linkages to larger economic and political systems. Ford is not dying; it is, however, going through another watershed change in its long life.

CHANGING PLACES

What is happening in Shiloh and Ford is no doubt taking place in a number of other settings. Howard Newby (1980, 1987), for example, has published thoughtful studies of the effects of incomers in farm villages of East Anglia. A Scottish anthropologist has almost completed a study of tourists and second-home owners in Sennen Cove, near Penzance, in the south of England. The process proceeds apace—although without benefit of study—along almost the entire Blue Ridge spine in Virginia and North Carolina. It is not unknown in places such as the fringe counties of eastern Kentucky.

Nor is what is happening today a new invention of our time. The surge of movement into the countryside in search of new permanent residences has swelled in recent years, but the precedent has been there to build on for many decades. In the case of western North Carolina, historians track the earliest movement of tourists and second-home owners as far back as the 1820s. Apparently, these were mostly South Carolina planters' families in search of relief from malaria during the summer season. In the case of the West Highlands, travelers' accounts are fairly common from the early 19th century;

and by the late 1800s, the area had been "Balmoralized" along with the rest of the Highlands, with estates given over to sporting pastimes, and the lochs overrun with anglers. (The Game Book from the main estate at Ford showed that in 1903 there were 1,120 birds and 2,370 rabbits shot and 1,162 fish taken from its various lochs.) Loch steamers ferried tourists around the Ford area for about a hundred years beginning in the 1850s. The Ford Hotel is said to have opened in 1864, but inns of some kind were there before that date. The earliest guest book for the hotel I could find began in 1924; it showed visitors from all over Britain and the continent—and one from Arizona—but mainly from England. The point is that many people first learned about Ford by spending summer holidays there, and that second home ownership—if it can be called that—began in the 19th century when wealthy Londoners bought up estates and converted them from farming to sporting ventures for purposes of recreation and personal prestige.

What began in both western North Carolina and the West Highlands of Scotland as exclusively an upper class pattern of extravagant leisure consumption became more available to a nonaristocratic but still "better class of people" before the turn of the century, and gradually has become accessible by large numbers of middle and working class visitors, second-home owners, and new permanent residents.

To return to an earlier point, what is happening in these two communities and elsewhere is not really quite rural gentrification. Today's newcomers are not members of the gentry class. They range from professional class to working class, and the majority are hardworking white collar, managerial, and subprofessional.

Likewise, what is happening is similar to invasion and succession, except that the ethnic and class nature of these invaders is quite different from the classic Chicago case, nor are there anything faintly resembling concentric zones, nor are the consequences of the process anything like what the Chicago model would predict.

If the process must be given a name, I would suggest the simple phrase, place-exchange. It is a process in which rural aspirants to a better life flee to the cities and urban refugees flee to the countryside for the same reason. In both cases, new lives and identities are sought by persons unhappy with their present sense of place. Sense of place lends itself to commodification just as readily as anything else, so that place becomes marketed, brokered, imaged, and hyped just as do rock singers, cigarettes, automobiles, and politicians. Success is promised the young in the cities, and rustic peace is assured everyone who comes to the countryside—peace and a chance to uplift the benighted.

The extent and consequences for small communities of the place-changing process are not fully known; I have only hinted at them in these sketches. Nor can we guess how long the process will continue. Most of the changes are far beyond the means of local communities to control; they can respond only in the same ways that people respond to changes in the weather: they accommodate as best they are able.

In these two instances of repopulation, the transformations have been peaceable, but latent divisiveness remains a subliminal threat to community vitality. The process of in-migration has been at work for a longer period in Ford than in Shiloh, and yet the division is still there, fueling stereotypes, subtly poisoning personal relationships, and making for a good deal of mutually understood—and, so far, amiable—hypocrisy.

The phenomenon of place-exchange will probably continue for as long as there is a general unhappiness with place—a state of being in our world that appears to be quite strong at present. The need for a satisfying sense of place and an identity related to place is not well understood or even recognized, but it is obviously very powerful at times. And where there is a need that can be identified, marketing in- genuity and investment capital are not far behind. My guess would be that we are far from seeing the end of notices in the Shilohs and Fords of the world that announce, in one way or another, "Place for Sale."

■ 3 ■

The Reconstruction of Wales and Appalachia: Development and Regional Identity

Graham Day

Both Wales and Appalachia could be said to be places undergoing crises of identity. The past two decades have seen vast quantities of thought and effort devoted to the examination of what it means to be Welsh or Appalachian, much of it concerned to identify the uniqueness of local history, culture, and contemporary experience. The value of a comparative frame of reference lies in disentangling the truly unique from the general and the shared, and in locating particular experiences within broader sets of relationships. Even the application of labels such as "internal colony," "periphery," or "underdeveloped area" serves to situate a place more precisely, and to make relevant connections. Efforts at comparative regional analysis do, however, raise difficult problems. On what grounds are we to select—and attempt to compare and contrast—pertinent cases?

So far as Wales and Appalachia are concerned, the connection has already been made. It is a feature of the work of scholars working in Appalachian studies that they have been driven to resort to analogies drawn from the "Celtic" fringe of Britain on a number of occasions (Clavel 1983; Lewis 1984; Whisnant 1980b; Caudill 1962). Their understanding of their own society has been clarified by comparisons made with Scotland, and/or with Wales. This is not to say that they have necessarily been right in the conclusions they have drawn; whatever common features may be discerned among the places, there are also very fundamental differences; Hechter's (1975, 1984) well-known study of the British "Celtic" regions fell foul of Scotland's failure to be either Celtic or like Wales. This chapter reviews some of the arguments that have been proposed for seeing Wales and Appalachia as similar and uses the discussion as the basis for an examination of some aspects of regional awareness and action in the two places.

SIMILARITIES OF DEVELOPMENT IN WALES AND APPALACHIA

The 1960s witnessed a corresponding pattern of state intervention in Wales and Appalachia. Given prevailing ideas, this could be interpreted as a mopping-up operation in which the successes currently enjoyed in the wider society—full employment, "affluence," and a sense of confidence in the future associated with the post-war boom—were being extended to areas that had so far failed to share fully in them. Within Britain, Wales was regarded as one of the deprived or backward regions scheduled to be assisted by new forms of regional policy that state agencies such as the Welsh Office (established 1964) and the Mid-Wales Development Corporation (established 1967) were charged with executing. In the United States, Appalachia was the forgotten America, "discovered" by John F. Kennedy in his 1960 campaign trip to West Virginia, and shortly thereafter the target of President Lyndon Johnson's War on Poverty and of the Appalachian Regional Commission, or ARC, which began meeting in 1965. The theory and ideology of regional planning was broadly the same: the areas required "modernizing" through increased integration into advanced economic and social relations, with corresponding cultural change—what Lewis (1984) refers to as the drive to "mainstream" the regions.

Underpinning the intervention were arguments that the problems stemmed from fundamental economic deficiencies, which were traced in turn to peculiarities of the social, political, and cultural organization of the local people. These arguments were to be taken up and reinterpreted by others who rejected the conclusions drawn from them by the various officials and planners designing the policies for regional change.

Wales and Appalachia display certain economic resemblances, the most obvious being the historical significance to both of the *coal industry*. It is quite reasonable to expect such a distinctive industry, and "extreme" occupation, to generate its own typical effects in relation to community structure, gender divisions, and social and political organization (Bulmer 1975); insofar as Wales and Appalachia are regions dominated or shaped by coal, they will tend to be pulled in the same direction.

However, neither is nor has been totally governed economically by the one industry. If they were, it would be easier to identify their character as "regions." In the case of Wales, the dominance of coal has been concentrated in the valleys of South Wales and, to a lesser extent, the quite separate North Wales coalfield. Many assertions about the industrial history of Wales, the militancy of its labor force, and the strength of its socialist and labor movement history and class consciousness generalize unduly from the specific features of South Wales; thus Lewis (1984) makes a number of claims about Wales that would be strictly accurate only for this more restricted area. At the time when the industry sustained more than a quarter of a million miners and their families densely concentrated into a small geographical area, it did produce a remarkable and resilient social structure with social, political, and cultural attributes very much its own—elements that certainly provide one definition of what it is to be Welsh (Francis, Smith and Frost 1980). Yet at the present time, miners account for less than 2 percent of the Welsh labor force; coal had a marginal place in the modern Welsh economy, and increasingly this fact is sinking in to people's perception of Wales.

Similarly, in Appalachia the boundaries of the industry do not, on most definitions, coincide with those of a region. "Official" Appalachia—a 13-state territory with a population of over 20 million—was assembled into some sort of entity by the attractions of federal money disbursed through the Appalachian Regional Development Act. In 1970 it contained slightly less than 8 percent of the U.S. labor force, but 74 percent of its coalminers (Couto 1984). Even so, many Appalachians can grow up never seeing a mine or meeting a miner. The industry is concentrated in Central Appalachia, a "subregion" defined by ARC to include 85 counties located in eastern Kentucky, southern West Virginia, southwestern Virginia and northeast Tennessee. Among the Central Appalachian population of 2,100,000, employment associated with coal remains preeminent.

Broadening the focus a little, we can establish that the two regions have a common history as *resource-centered economies*; the greater part of their economic development until recently has been accounted for by a combination of extractive (mineral, especially coal) and agricultural activity. This description must be qualified more for Wales than for Appalachia, but is broadly accurate. In each case, industrial development was launched from a foundation of rural, small-farm, family production. In Wales, the iron, coal, and slate industries drew their original labor force from a near-peasant society and continued to have links into rural society at least to the beginning of this century. Appalachia was renowned for vast stocks of timber, and then for coal (in 1970 still a quarter of the total U.S. reserves, and 70 percent of production), oil, and gas. These have been developed within a society that remains characteristically rural. The whole of Appalachia is described by ARC as "a region of small towns and rural areas" (ARC 1985), and the description fits Central Appalachia especially well. Despite the centrality of coal production and ancillary activity (railways, trucking, repairs and servicing), it is an area of dispersed population, with few towns—most of which originated as coal camps and company settlements—scattered around rugged and difficult terrain. Agriculture itself continues to be a significant part of the economy; the number of farms has been declining steadily in recent years, and their average size has been increasing, but produce from small holdings and gardens continues to be an essential part of the household economy for much of the population. Three-quarters of the inhabitants of Central Appalachia are classified as "rural," mostly "rural nonfarm" population, in official statistics.

Agriculture in rural Wales (as in all other parts of the developed world) has undergone similar change: the number of agricultural units fell by 41 percent (from 55,402 to 32,495) between 1951 and 1971, while those larger than a hundred acres rose by 17 percent (Williams 1980; Rees 1983). Naturally, the type of agriculture differs markedly between the two areas, with sheep and cattle virtually monopolizing Welsh farming, while tobacco and food crops are staples in Appalachia; but most agriculturalists in both are small-farm, low income, and marginal producers working poor and geographically demanding land. Aspects of a rural, small-community way of life are extremely important in each region, and extend across the divide between farming and other forms of economic activity. The mining communities of South Wales have also been focused around relatively self-contained, and small, pit villages. However, the life of the coalfield and the society of rural Wales have grown apart over time; and it is much easier to draw a distinction, both socially and geographically, between the urbanized, industrialized, and working-class Welsh of the South Wales valleys, and their rural counterparts, than it would be to do the same among the Appalachians of Central Appalachia.

On the basis of these economic features, one can construct a case for treating Wales and Appalachia as analytically alike. Their status as problem regions within their respective social formations can be attributed to the particular kind of economic specialization they have experienced. As resource-based economies, they have lacked the secondary and tertiary activity that, through value added in manufacturing and services, makes for economic health; this has undermined their self-sufficiency, leaving them dependent on exports, and therefore vulnerable to fluctuations in demand from markets beyond their control. Appalachian coal has been sent out of the region to fuel the U.S. steel industry, to supply electricity generators, and to meet foreign demand; 90 percent of U.S. coal exports to Canada and Europe in 1970 came from Appalachia, and the mines of the Appalachian heartland now compete directly with those of Poland, South Africa, and Latin America. West Virginia was the third-largest exporting state in 1984, sending not only coal but the chemical products of the Kanawha Valley to external markets (David 1984). Wales for a long time held a position as a major exporter, the rhythms of its economic development owing more to the Atlantic economy than to internal factors (Williams 1982). The *dependence* arising from this level and type of integration into the wider system has been stressed by those in both regions who have employed concepts of "underdevelopment" and "internal colonialism" to typify their situation (Day 1979; Lewis et al. 1978; Hechter 1975).

The aim of the interventionist agencies that became active in the 1960s was to correct excessive specialization. According to their analysis, the economic answer was *diversification*, chiefly through the introduction of manufacturing industry. Both areas could be viewed as suffering from special problems of industrial decline. The traditional heavy industries of Wales (coal, steel, docks, railways) were either obsolete or in need of modernization and could not be relied on to provide a secure economic base; hence it was necessary to attract in more advanced forms of production, and to shift employment toward more technologically sophisticated and skilled jobs. In rural Wales, high levels of out-migration threatened the entire social fabric, and this was held to require efforts to industrialize through the creation of small businesses. The strategy involved the identification of "growth centres" in which new economic development could be concentrated, the provision of infrastructural investments (motorway building, industrial estates, subsidized factories), and the payment of regional premiums as incentives for business to locate within Wales (Welsh Office 1967; Beacham 1964). The policy pursued by the Appalachian Regional Commission was much the same. The longstanding economic deprivation of the region had been magnified by the collapse of the coal industry in the 1950s: a drop in demand was partly responsible for this; but more crucially, the industry was being technologically transformed, the Mineworkers' Union having endorsed a program of mechanization. Unemployment levels rose and massive loss of population followed as the number of Appalachian miners fell by 58 percent during the decade. Vast numbers had no option but to leave the region: more than two million did so during the 1950s, and a further million in the next ten years. The states suffering the heaviest losses were Kentucky, Virginia, and West Virginia, the core counties of Central Appalachia.

Appalachia registered on the American consciousness as a national disgrace. In 1960 a great swathe of counties stretching across the region had poverty levels exceeding twice the national average. Income levels in the late 1960s in rural Appalachia, and in the 60 coal-producing counties, rarely exceeded half the national figure. The poorest counties in the whole of the United States were Appalachian, with eastern Kentucky at the bottom of the heap. In the restrained language of the ARC, "In 1964, Appalachia's profile was down-scale: a remote, inaccessible, worn out mountain land, destined to stagnate in the ups and downs of coal" (ARC 1985). This was a degree of deprivation and degradation not experienced in Wales since the 1930s; but the official explanation was quite similar: a declining industrial base, in a region already somewhat backward and neglected, which had to be brought quickly up to modern standards.

The ARC singled out as the decisive problem the *isolation* of the Appalachian region—a view that it adhered to throughout its 25-year history:

> Appalachia...was isolated from the mainstream of American economic life by poor roads. And in the second half of the 20th century, isolation is another word for stagnation. (ARC 1985)

This was not a new problem, since "Appalachia existed for generations as a region apart, isolated physically and culturally by its impenetrable mountains." This rudimentary analysis led readily to a solution: build roads! The principal achievement of ARC was in building a number of "Appalachian corridors," opening up the region for jobs and for industry. The major beneficiary has been the coal industry, which uses the new routes to haul vast quantities of Appalachian coal out of the region; the highway plan shows greater correspondence to the requirements of coal operators than to any objective analysis of growth potential (Bingham 1983).

While the stress laid on the remoteness and inaccessibility of Wales has not been so great, the same thinking lies behind many of the recommendations of regional planners. In the less expansive geographical perspective of British policymaking, Wales is a marginal area, difficult to get to and from; and the main development efforts have been aimed at its edges, with new roads and communication links to the more prosperous parts of England.

In both areas, considerable success is claimed for the program of regional regeneration. It has undoubtedly become implausible to envisage modern Wales as the primary producing region of the past: Table 3.1 gives some indication of the changes in employment in manufacturing and in service occupations. Much of the growth has been concentrated in the area surrounding Cardiff, and along the route of the M4 motorway. But the rural districts of North and West Wales have seen some of the highest rates of increase in new forms of economic activity—admittedly starting from very low levels. The result is a very considerable diversification of the economy, and a rather complicated spatial arrangement of the various sectors and industries (Cooke 1981)—a transformation sufficient to prompt claims that

Table 3.1
Occupational Distribution—Wales, Selected Years, 1948–1986

	1948	1951	1961	1971	1981	1986
Agriculture, Forestry	4.2%	3.6%	2.4%	2.4%	2.4%	2.4%
Mining Quarrying	16.0%	15.0%	11.0%	5.0%	4.0%	—
Manufacturing	28.0%	31.5%	31.5%	35.0%	25.0%	23.5%
Services	32.0%	21.0%	36.0%	40.0%	54.0%	64.5%
Transport, Construction	19.0%	18.5%	18.0%	17.0%	14.0%	10.2%

Wales had more or less caught up with general British patterns by the 1970s, as part of a process in which regional differentiation was becoming less marked.

Equally, in Appalachia, it has been argued that the enormous discrepancy between regional conditions and national norms has been reduced. An extra half-million jobs were created during the 1960s, broadening the activity profile with additional manufacturing and service occupations. Gains were made even in the most depressed sections of "hard-core Appalachia": in eastern Kentucky, manufacturing employment increased fourfold. The ARC points to improvements in income levels from 78 percent of the U.S. average in 1960 to 85 percent in 1980, over the region as a whole. In the 1970s, following the oil crisis, demand for Appalachian coal soared, and migrant Appalachians returned in large numbers to work in the coalfields. It is difficult to judge how far the state policies were responsible for these changes. To a great extent they reflect either market shifts outside the control of ARC, or the continuation of trends already under way in the late 1950s. While ARC could point to the decrease in the number of counties whose income per capita fell below 60 percent of the U.S. level—from 79 counties to around 40 (ARC 1985)—this still left Central Appalachia deeply afflicted by poverty. At the height of the coal boom, in the center of production (the Big Sandy) only half the population were economically active, and 40 percent were in poverty. In the early 1980s, statements from ARC concerning "distressed counties" in Appalachia indicated the limited progress made in affecting the essential condition of Central Appalachia; they confirm the comment on the Commission's achievements that the impact "on the lives of Appalachia's poor, the people it was really supposed to serve, will have been little more than a ripple in the stream of Appalachian life" (Bingham, 1983).

The 1980s witnessed a sharp downturn in the fortunes of both areas. In Appalachia the first three years of this decade saw a loss of more than twice the number of manufacturing jobs created in the preceding ten years. The coal industry was also hit by the national and worldwide recession, with falling demand for steel and electricity. Couto (1984) provides information on income levels for Central Appalachia in the late 1970s: the subregion as a whole had reached just under 68 percent of U.S. rates, with rural districts and Kentucky doing no better than 64 percent. By the end of the decade, unemployment throughout the region had risen to 16 percent and reached 30 percent in the coal counties. Equivalent figures could be given for Wales since the recession, and high levels of redundancy in major industries such as steel and coal once again underline the economic weakness of the region. In the former mining valleys, and even in parts of urban Wales, unemployment often exceeds 20 percent. As for rural Wales, like Central Appalachia, it finds itself thrown into competition for jobs and income-generating activity with large numbers of similarly vulnerable areas not just in the advanced economies, but also in the Third World. Such evidence of economic revitalization as there is rests uneasily on a base of low wage, nonunionized, insecure, and frequently female labor. In Lipietz's (1980) general classification of types of region within the spatial division of labor, both Wales and Appalachia would straddle the categories of "reserve low skill labor" and "depopulated tourism."

IMPLICATIONS FOR THE CONCEPTION OF "REGION" AND REGIONAL IDENTITY

We have seen a number of points of similarity between Wales and Appalachia with regard to their economic development. In neither case is it as easy to generalize as might at first appear; although a broad-brush picture accentuates the gross similarities, they often fall apart under more detailed examination. The exact units being compared become uncertain. It is Central Appalachia—also widely described as "hard core," or the Appalachian heartland—that most resembles Wales. But then it is difficult to speak of Wales without paying attention to distinctions between rural Wales, industrial South Wales, the still-prospering belt around Cardiff, and so on. Brown's (1972) description of Appalachia as "a loose collection of counties with very diverse characteristics which function in a variety of systems and subsystems" is backed by Duncan and Tickamyer's (1983) analysis of the sharp differences between coal counties and noncoal counties in eastern Kentucky and aptly describes the industrial restructuring and new forms of spatial division of labor within Wales (Day 1980; Cooke 1982). Even if before these changes the two areas had presented a clearly homogeneous and distinctive set of characteristics, that unity would have come under increasing pressure. At the economic level, at least, *regional coherence is problematic*. A major intellectual concern of the 1970s became the attempt to clarify what, in fact, bound the regions together. This gave rise to a strongly convergent body of theoretical work, underpinned by the efforts of intellectuals and activists to come to grips with the common *marginality* of the two regions. Since this has played an integral part in regional advocacy as well as analysis, it provides a suitable bridge to the examination of political and cultural processes.

Whisnant pinpoints the essential theme of the debate in Appalachia when he notes:

> a shared perception that Appalachian people are struggling against an attempt by mainstream America and its powerful vested interests to contain, subjugate and destroy a region, its people, the few remaining fragments of their culture. Whether this perception is accurate is not important here. People are united by the perception, nevertheless. (Whisnant 1973, 125)

As a reaction to the policies being carried out, and to the ideas that lay behind them, people began to develop alternative interpretations of the nature of the region, its intrinsic value, and its possible future. Almost routinely, Appalachia came to be referred to as a colony, emphasis being put on the "exploited" condition of the region, the extent to which it had been subjected historically to external direction and control (of which the War on Poverty was viewed as merely one more example) and the way in which a prolonged outflow of profits and resources had left a rich region populated by poor people. This implied the rejection of the thesis that the source of the problem was "isolation"; it also involved a struggle against various derogatory stereotypes of Appalachian culture and ways of life. Lewis's (1970) article on "Fatalism or the Coal Industry" set the tone for much of the work that followed, and helped stimulate the growth of "Appalachian Studies" as a field of academic and political activity. Although the concept of Appalachia as an internal colony was eventually dispensed with, it was replaced by a variety of related notions designed to encapsulate the basic condition of the region, and to define its political economy (e.g., Walls 1978). In the same way, Welsh enthusiasm for the internal colonial analogy waned as commentators took up theories of development and applied new models of regional analysis (Lovering 1978; Day 1979). The period was less fertile for academic growth and development in Wales; but even so the creation of school and university courses in the Sociology of Wales, the activities of bodies such as the British Sociological Association Sociology of Wales group, and Coleg Harlech, and a tremendous flowering of research into modern Welsh history and Labor history (under the aegis of *Llafur*, the Welsh Society for Labor History) made the nature of Wales the object of intense interest. The period culminated with two major television series devoted to exploring this issue (Smith 1984; Williams 1985). In both places, definitional problems had become a major preoccupation.

This in itself militates against any assumption that regions, and regional identities, have a natural presence or objectivity that forces itself into social consciousness. Although there have been many attempts to establish the existence of natural areas, whether conceived of as "rural," "urban," or "neighborhood" units, and to show how they exert a causal influence over social arrangements, these ecological approaches tend to be unavoidably reductionist and inadequate. It is extremely difficult to establish convincing general criteria for such natural areas, and the failure to do so leads to endless definitional wrangles (Warde 1986). Because of this, many theorists have come to discard "the region" as a fundamental category, and to turn instead to study those sets of social relationships and types of organization that may form themselves into spatially distinct configurations. Although it may be difficult to arrive at unambiguous specifications of "regions," it is still possible to demonstrate the *regional distribution* of various social characteristics, and to analyze the contents of *regionalism* (Markusen 1980; Simon 1984 vis-à-vis Appalachia; in Britain, the work of Urry 1981; Massey 1979 and others).

The idea of regionalism, in particular, directs attention to the way in which regions are constructed within various forms of discourse and social practice. The literature on both Wales and Appalachia is replete with statements that point this way; for example, Walls writes, "The naming and redefining of Appalachia appears to have no end. Clearly there is no ultimate definition, only delineations that serve particular social, political, organizational, or academic interests" (1977, 75). The point has been discussed at length by authors such as Whisnant (1983) and Shapiro (1978). It is equally possible to comprehend "Wales" as shorthand for (many kinds of) diversity.

To approach the problem from this angle might occasion some alarm. Emmett (1983) has voiced her disapproval of what she regards as an exaggerated—even idealist—emphasis on the social construction of reality. Concern with the ideological and subjective meanings of region and place can lead, she contends, to phenomena such as "Wales" and "Appalachia" being dismissed as figments of the imagination, or even as tricks played on some social groups by others. She compares the presence of a social entity such as Wales with that of a mountain: it can be appreciated and understood in a variety of ways, but it is massively *there*. This argument tends to miss the point that it is in the context of debates with those who are *too* inclined to take objective reality for granted that the need has been felt to accentuate the importance of social interpretations. Even with a mountain, there is room to dispute just where it begins and ends; and it is the variety of meanings bestowed on it (geological, aesthetic, recreational) that makes it interesting to us. Examining how social reality is constructed need not blind us to the objective contents and raw materials involved nor discount the material reality of the resulting constructs. Emmett's own definition of Wales as a historical and geographical entity that is contained within a frontier and consists of "people, land, and mountains" is too vague to tell us what to expect of this Wales in its current concerns or future development. Her comprehension of a culture that is "continuously and emphatically Welsh" would tell us more, but would involve her in sifting and sorting the relative significance of often conflicting and contradictory versions of Welshness (cf. Day and Suggett 1985).

In neither context is there a shortage of those ready to argue a fairly undiluted version of environmental determinism, in which the character and way of life of the people is derived directly from the physical geography they inhabit. Upland countryside, narrow valleys, and inhospitable mountain ridges create the setting in which, it is argued, communications are difficult, population is thinly spread, life is hard, and family and immediate neighborhood form the principal boundaries of everyday concerns. The result is an inward-looking, strongly traditional, and very distinctive form of culture. Insofar as the regions have lagged behind others in the speed and direction of development, the culture may be seen as partly responsible.

Such conceptions have played an extraordinarily powerful role in the case of Appalachia, where claims have been advanced over a long period as to the basically intransigent and exceptional quality of local values. The Appalachian mountaineers have been typified as "our contemporary ancestors" (Frost 1899) and as "yesterday's people" whose customs, attitudes, and even language preserve the traits of their 17th-century British ancestry (Weller 1965). The conventional account identifies Appalachian values as individualism, religiosity, fatalism, passivity, family centeredness, lack of ambition, inability to cooperate and organize. Even where the aim is to speak for local people and their needs, the same broad image of their character is often endorsed (Caudill 1962; Jones 1975). A set of negative and demeaning qualities is attributed to people, and this attribution then serves to justify intervention into their conditions of existence; as "dumb hillbillies," incapable of helping themselves, Appalachians either need or deserve to be told by others what is best for them, whether these others are radical Appalachian volunteers wishing to rouse the mountains in a fight against poverty or technocratic planners eager to place their superior rationality and expertise at the service of the region. Not surprisingly, local people find it difficult to identify with an image of themselves that is almost wholly disparaging. Even those aspects that seem more positive—independence, individualism, self-reliance, and so on—are unhelpful when it comes to resisting unwelcome change, since they tend to confine action to narrowly personal means.

A good deal of the thrust of analysis from within the region has been concerned to correct or replace this image of the culture, and to discount it as an explanation for the region's problems. The main contention has been that, insofar as they have any validity, these cultural traits represent consequences, and not causes, of Appalachian development. They reflect the way the people of the area have accommodated themselves to a situation in which they have consistently been valued primarily for the material assistance they could give others in making their fortunes. Successively this has entailed the appropriation of their timber, their land, their coal, and their labor. Furthermore, this has been carried out at the behest of economic forces vastly more powerful than those within the region.

From early in this century, the main forces shaping the development of the area have been corporate enterprises such as U.S. Steel, International Harvester, the Ford Motor company, and the great railway and coal combines. These have disposed of massive resources in order to open up the region and transform it in the interests of corporate profit; this involved the displacing of the relatively self-sufficient family farm, the gathering of workforces into settlements designed to meet the needs of production, and when these had outlived their usefulness, the removal of support from them. The social and political circumstances that have shaped the culture have to be seen therefore as almost totally constrained by the dictates of interests eager to extract maximum returns from the region (Eller 1982; Gaventa 1980). The poverty that besets Appalachian communities is the creation of this long history of exploitation, yet those interpretations that proclaim the helplessness of Appalachians faced by nature's forces—the wild, dangerous, unmanageable environment—are curiously blind to the impact in the region of such huge man-made concentrations of power.

Obviously, this drastic reorientation of the way the Appalachian past is understood has had far-reaching contemporary political implications. Aimed above all at the myth that Appalachians are violent, irrational, primitive folk completely outside the American norm—a "strange land and peculiar people" (Shapiro 1978)—the approach seeks to show that whatever peculiarities they display are a rational, intelligible response to exceptional conditions. The academic contributions that make this point now form simply but one part of an intense and convoluted interrogation of the concepts of "Appalachia" and "Appalachian culture."

The discussion has its counterpart within modern Wales. Although one has to go back to the 19th century to find comparably thoroughgoing vilifications of Welsh culture (at least in public commentary), the feeling of a beleaguered way of life subjected to intense destructive pressure is widely expressed, particularly from within Welsh-speaking Wales. Much space is devoted in the media to examinations of Welsh, Anglo-Welsh, English, and British identities and culture. With a longer history and a more developed institutional base, a sense of Welshness can be upheld with far greater confidence and aggression than seems possible in Appalachia. Indeed, many Welsh people would vehemently object to the use of the term *region* to refer to what they would insist is a *nation and people*, separated from the English by history, tradition, race, and culture. Appalachian identity has an altogether more ghostly existence than Welshness. Many who live in the mountains would not use the term, Appalachian, and would identify themselves more readily as "hillbilly," "mountain folk," or as Kentuckians, Virginians, and so forth. The term *Appalachian* has gradually become more familiar in recent years as the result of the "Appalachian identity movement" (Whisnant 1980a), but it is not a term in everyday use. By contrast, "Welsh" and "Wales" are thoroughly normal parts of the everyday vocabulary, attached to virtually the whole range of activities and institutions; calling oneself "Appalachian" would almost certainly be done to make a point.

Nevertheless, Welsh identity is insecure, given the colossal presence of English (and Anglo-American) culture, and given the alterations taking place in those social arrangements and institutions upon which Welshness has traditionally rested. The place of the Welsh in the modern world is uncertain. Indeed, it has been asserted that "Wales and the Welsh, as distinctive entities, cannot survive the capitalist mode of production in its present historic phase....If capitalism in the British Isles lives, Wales will die" (Williams 1979). Thus the Welsh and the Appalachians can be presented plausibly as peoples under threat, whose very existence is at stake.

Postwar efforts to reconstruct the two areas have undoubtedly had far-reaching cultural and political consequences; their significance as regions has been laid open to question. Their experience in this respect is far from unique, since it forms part of a much wider tendency toward the "delocalization" of production and, to a lesser extent, consumption, which has undermined many of the social meanings attaching to place and locality (Castells 1983). Given that among the people of Wales and Appalachia there are many who show "strong attachment to the land and profound sense of place" (Eller 1982), one could anticipate a high degree of resultant mobilization, and it is indeed the case that, as places, Wales and Appalachia have become increasingly politicized, as have Appalachian and Welsh "identity." As well as being a potent political *resource*, in each case this identity is also a considerable political *problem*—an unresolved tension that complicates and confuses the mobilization of interests.

THE POLITICS OF PLACE

Comparison between Wales and Appalachia shows that, while there are underlying similarities in developmental paths, the manner in which these become expressed in action owes a great deal to the particular and divergent political traditions and institutions that exist in the two areas. A crucial consideration is the way in which the transformations that have been described penetrate everyday concerns. Invariably they are experienced *locally*, and the immediate response tends therefore to be localized, parochial, concrete—a series of limited battles and debates over problems specific to particular "communities," (however these are defined), which for those concerned amounts to a fight for control over "one's own space."

Local and Regional Politics in Appalachia

A characteristic form of organization to tackle local issues in Appalachia involves groupings of "concerned citizens." In 1983 no less than 62 such groups were listed as active in eastern Kentucky alone, according to *Mountain Life and Work* magazine. A wide variety of incidents and fears stimulated collective action, for example, dumping of toxic waste, proposed pumped storage schemes, and highway construction. According to local perceptions, each involved the destruction of homes, land, and environment with direct consequences for the ordinary life of those who regarded the affected place as theirs, by right of occupation and family ties; usually the threat arose at the instigation of external agencies that did not share local values and aspirations. The great majority of specific problems related to the plans and activities of bodies linked to the coal, energy, and tourist industries, for whom the environment was primarily a resource for commercial development. For example, when in 1980 it was discovered that a plan existed to secure federal funds to relocate the town of Beauty, Kentucky, ostensibly to eliminate flood dangers, local people formed the Concerned Citizens of Martin County or CCMC, which began to gather support and create a formal structure for community involvement. As discussion of the plan took off "it became a real battle of who was actually going to determine the future of the town—national political forces, possible outside landowners, local officials, planners, or the people who actually lived in the house" (CCMC 1980). The real purpose of the proposal was believed to be a trial run for ARC relocation of 3,000 families from the Tug Valley area to allow the sinking of a new mine. Protest about lack of public consultation led to withdrawal of federal approval for the plan.

There has been a proliferation of such grassroots organizations, each capable of producing a local leadership; but the form of action poses genuine problems of continuity and capacity to generalize beyond the immediate crisis; single-issue groups are likely to be shallow and short lived (Plaut 1979). To survive, they have to become involved in a process of building toward a wider sense of context and a greater linkage of concerns. CCMC did so, as the action it mounted brought increased awareness to many who had previously played little part in public decision making. Large numbers of such people became active, and took stock of what their community meant to them. They came into conflict with a power structure, typical of the region, which was determined to decide on behalf of people it regarded as unimportant or stupid. CCMC found itself pushed forward, in confrontation with powerful local political forces, into electoral campaigning, provision of community facilities, and eventual engagement with a statewide movement to bring about basic tax reforms. A similar learning process has occurred elsewhere, for instance in the campaign waged by Yellow Creek Concerned Citizens or YCCC, to combat pollution from a tannery in Middlesboro, Kentucky. From a community action group, it has also moved to take on a political role, challenging local control (Staub 1982).

Such developments can generate contacts with other groups within second-level organizations, often identifiable by the title of "coalitions." YCCC was actively involved in the formation of a Southeast Regional Toxics Coalition, containing some 30 constituent organizations (*Mountain Life and Work* March 1982). One of the most effective bodies of this type has been the Kentucky Fair Tax Coalition or KFTC, a direct membership organization with more than 1,200 members based in county chapters in eastern Kentucky that aims to rectify the situation whereby the major economic actors in the area make miniscule contributions to local finances (KFTC 1982). These groups take as their frame of reference particular local units of government—a community, county, or state. Perceptions of problems mostly remain limited, and the way in which they are related to wider issues is somewhat accidental and tentative: local groups have to discover (or rediscover) for themselves the common ground they share with others who have similar worries. The target of action generally stays ill-defined or close to home.

Neither political parties nor trade unions in Appalachia provide much help toward extending the pursuit of ends from the immediate to the general. In this respect, the differences between Wales and Appalachia are sharp. People in Appalachia must act within a political order that is peculiarly integrated and oppressive; it represents an extreme form of corporate capitalism, aided and abetted by the local political system (Gaventa 1980; Arnott 1978). Parties operate locally as channels for patronage and brokerage within a tight system of political domination. Community groups struggling with the effects of economic and political power can hardly turn for help to institutions so deeply embedded within the prevailing order; instead, activists tend to see party politics as a lost cause. Unions also—despite an often bloody history of industrial struggle—rarely take up broader community issues.

Because the labor movement and organized parties do little to unify grassroots struggles, definitions of territorial identity take on special significance, as do groups that propagate a regional dimension to politics. Popular struggles sometimes yield an awareness of the breadth of the underlying problems. Anti-strip mining organizations indicate this by their choice of titles: in Knott County, Kentucky, a determined battle was fought by the Appalachian Group to Save the Land and People (Hoffman 1979) while in Tennessee action has been coordinated by Save Our Cumberland Mountains. But since the definition of regional interests is contestable—rather than given—such movements are prone to significant internal tension. This is apparent both from the record of the longest-lived regional body, the Council for the Southern Mountains, and from the more recent experience of the Appalachian Alliance. In each, we find very different individuals who claim to be "authentic" Appalachian persons, as well as conflicting views about the way the region should be developed. The Appalachian Alliance is the closest approximation to a regional political organization yet to appear; it aspires to be a "third-level" organization that will transcend local concerns, bring different issues together, and address itself to the underlying character of the region. Its publicity material states:

The Appalachian Alliance is grounded in the belief that community, state and regional groups can forge a regional network that will link people and issues, develop leadership, and involve community people in planning for political, economic and social change. (Appalachian Alliance 1978, 1982)

This interaction of regional and local organizing has not, however, been adequately secured, and the files of the organization reflect a constant uncertainty about how to achieve it—indicating a state of some disarray. We can contrast the statement of objectives proposed in 1979 by the Urban Appalachian Council of Cincinnati—which recommended the Appalachian Alliance should

work towards a mass based movement with some organizational roots that will legitimize a united Appalachian voice on issues that affect the lives of all Appalachians....The time for the birth of an Appalachian identity movement with national significance, public recognition, and political clout has already begun—

with the more recent reflection of one key supporter that

I am still left with a sad notion that organizations and activists in the region...claim to speak for a great number of people when, in reality, they can only justifiably speak for themselves.

Community and Nation in Welsh Politics

Whereas the attempt to give political expression to Appalachian identity is novel, and as yet lacks depth, the corresponding project has been part of the political agenda within Wales for well over a century. Yet when in 1979 the people of Wales were given the chance to assert their distinctiveness, they decisively rejected it; not only were proposals for a Welsh Assembly defeated by an 80 percent majority, but the Welsh electorate also followed the British general election trend in transferring support to the Conservative Party. This was interpreted as "the elimination of Welsh peculiarities...Welsh politics had ceased to exist" (Williams 1985). No such simple lesson can be drawn, since the 1979 referendum confirmed that the fragmentation of the economic and social structure of Wales had real political bearing: it concentrated the ambiguities and contradictions of Welsh identity in that it was impossible for all the diverse sections of Welsh society to arrive at a common view of what devolved government might mean for Wales; their reasons for rejecting it were quite distinct (Balsom 1985).

Electoral and party politics constitute a far more dominant feature within Wales than in Appalachia. Much of the "networking" and tentative coalition building that occurs in Appalachia takes place inside the Welsh political parties, each with its formalized structure of local membership, regular meetings, and conferences, and its privileged access to the media and to influence at Westminster. Although a party must work to maintain popular support, it can do so according to a well-tried model of political activity. In general, the population shows a high level of trust in existing political arrangements and in the efficacy of parliamentarism. Like other parties within Wales, the nationalist party Plaid Cymru is primarily concerned with winning votes and will seek to incorporate various local struggles within its perspective. Arguments about regional or national identity quickly become caught up in intraparty disputes, especially within Plaid Cymru and the Welsh Labour Party.

Much concern with defending local ways of life and established social relations inevitably takes the form of protectiveness toward the Welsh language and the cultural framework it supports. "Welshness" has been seen as under attack from a variety of external forces, wherever the Welsh community is threatened. Thus the 1954 Liverpool Council scheme to flood a valley at Tryweryn in order to supply the English city with water stimulated a considerable mobilization of opinion and action, which was followed by similar battles to stop other reservoir schemes. Action was given a clear Welsh dimension when the Welsh Language Society or Cymdeithas yr Iaith Gymraeg, began its campaign of agitation, civil disobedience, and minor sabotage from 1962 onwards—aimed at securing official recognition of the Welsh language—but was also concerned with developing a consciousness of the kind of society within which a minority language could flourish (Williams 1977).

Both Cymdeithas and Plaid Cymru have advanced a conception of Wales as a "community of communities" in which strong identification with locality can be combined with a sense of nationality. Plaid Cymru made the maintenance of communities the prime aim of its 1970 Economic Plan for Wales, reversing the thrust of prevailing policy, which had sacrificed community to economic calculation. Elements within the nationalist movement have also propounded a more exclusivist version of this position, in which part of Wales would be set aside for a totally Welsh-speaking population rid of all Anglicizing influences, including the presence of non-Welsh-speaking Welsh people (Llewelyn 1986). Such an objective is not, however, designed to gather much sympathy among the people of South Wales, particularly when combined with an emphasis on rural rather than industrial economy.

Although there have been few strong local movements of resistance to economic and social transformation, there has been a generalized grassroots awareness of the need to defend and preserve "community" (Wenger 1982). In a number of cases, as in Appalachia, local people have looked to cooperatives and small-scale development projects as the way to secure the existence of their town or village— invariably with limited success. In rural areas, local bodies concerned with creating jobs or providing houses may opt to work through the Welsh language, or to favour Welsh speakers (e.g. Cymdeithas Tai Gwynedd; Antur Alhaearn). Rural hostility to tourism and to second-home ownership is overlain by anti-English sentiment. As in Appalachia, illegal measures are sometimes adopted to extirpate such influences: more than a hundred houses have been burned down, because they belonged to (mostly) English people residing outside Wales. The extent of tacit support for such action is gauged by the failure of the police to solve more than a handful of such incidents. Other local struggles in rural Wales have been able to accommodate the interests of non-Welsh speakers alongside Welsh-language factions. In the early 1970s attempts to explore sites to dump nuclear waste brought together a wide range of local opinion in mid-Wales; large public meetings and rallies were held, critical posters were widely displayed, and direct action against surveyors coupled with veiled threats to Forestry Commission plantations led to the eventual abandonment of the explorations.

The perceived identification of explicitly nationalist groupings with the Welsh-speaking area and culture has tended to restrict their impact in the most populous part of the country, South Wales, where other problems are more pressing. The 1970s and 1980s have seen the continuing erosion of working class communities in South Wales; the decline of basic industries, rising unemployment, and the increased need to travel to work have undermined the functions that first brought the communities into existence. Recession has even revived the arguments of the 1930s that wholesale relocation might be the best answer. It was against the background of this kind of thinking that the South Wales miners during 1984–1985 fought the most determined battle in defense of their existing communities yet seen (Rees 1985; WCCPL 1985). The prolonged strike inspired the formation of a network of support groups throughout Wales—comparable to those that have arisen in Appalachia during similar struggles around the coal industry—uniting activists from several parties, from a variety of nonpolitical organizations, including churches, and from different community backgrounds. The formation of the Wales Congress in Support of Mining Communities crystallized many of the currents of territorial politics in Wales of the previous two decades.

Plaid Cymru and Labour, Welsh-language and non-Welsh-speaking, urban and rural fragments were able to work together within a broad umbrella organization that had community as its focal concern. According to a spokesman for the South Wales National Union of Mineworkers or NUM,

> In South Wales we rediscovered...that we are a part of a real nation which extends northwards beyond the coalfield into the mountains of Powys, Dyfed and Gwynedd. For the first time since the industrial revolution in Wales, the two halves of the nation came together in mutual support. (Howells 1985, 147)

Orchestrated by the South Wales NUM and the Welsh Communist Party, the congress also represented a spontaneous convergence of interests that had been developing for a long time. In no other part of Britain did the miners' strike produce such an outcome. The arguments within the congress as to whether action should be confined to the interests of miners or extended to cover the future of communities throughout Wales (Osmond 1985), and the talk of "alliances" and regional solidarity, would not have seemed alien to a member of the Appalachian Alliance, although the undercurrents of competition and mutual suspicion between factions looking for party political gains would have been more surprising. The congress also resembled the Appalachian Alliance in assembling activists and leaders without cementing rank-and-file loyalties; and ultimately its capacity to transcend the divisions within Wales between parties, and between sections of the population with different conceptions of what it is to be "Welsh," was strictly limited.

CONCLUSION

It has been said that the political meaning of local struggle depends crucially on the way in which issues and demands become linked together within an effective ideology (Laclau and Mouffe 1985). The examples of Wales and Appalachia illustrate this very well: neither has followed the "normal" path of development of the larger societies within which they are embedded; and in both, as a result, conceptions of "regional" identity and distinctiveness have assumed an unusual political significance. For many people in both areas, the identities that are experienced as most meaningful remain close to home, rooted in their specific communities. However, few such local communities have escaped being seriously disrupted by recent economic and social change; and it is here that a variety of political organizations, leaders, and theoreticians have intervened—with varying degrees of effectiveness—in an attempt to weld local communal identifications into something larger that will make sense of the frequently contradictory experiences of recent development, and to mobilize those affected in common action. An examination of their activities shows how, in the process, they are compelled to become involved in constructing and contesting, different versions of what it is to be "Welsh" or "Appalachian." Each version provides a way of drawing together a particular range of interests and concerns, but at the same time is likely to exclude others. Given the diversifying effects of recent changes, which have created new divisions and contrasts within both areas, it becomes harder rather than easier to win support for any one definition.

NOTE

This paper arises from the award of a James Still Fellowship at the University of Kentucky, Summer 1985.

■ 4 ■
The British Coalminers' Strike, 1984–1985: Class and Regional Inequality in Post-industrial Economies

Richard A. Couto

Americans have some difficulty in understanding the British coalminers' strike of 1984–1985 and its significance. The media in the United States gave it scant attention. Televised coverage, in particular, was sparse. Totaling less than an hour of all the evening news broadcasts on all three major networks combined during the 51-week period of the strike. Much of the news was reported in 10- and 20-second segments. The dominant theme of the coverage was violence with scenes from the conflict of police and miners at Orgreave shown throughout the year. Inevitably, as with most issues in American politics, the strike was reduced to a personal power struggle between Arthur Scargill, president of the National Union of Mineworkers, or NUM, and Prime Minister Margaret Thatcher. The larger significance of Britain's longest strike ever, and the complex issues behind it, were not reported well.

This is especially disappointing because the issues of the strike bear a marked similarity to issues in the Appalachian coalfields that brought on the longest strike in the history of American miners in 1977–1978. This chapter examines the important parallels between the British peripheral coalfields and the Appalachian region. It examines the background and causes of the strike—rather than its conduct—and compares those causes to conditions in the United States. The discussion proceeds with a summary of events in the United States; an analysis of changes common to the peripheral coalfields of Britain and the United States; the policy options with which to distribute the benefits and costs of changes in the coal industry; and the unresolved questions of inequality, unemployment, and the conduct of industry that are asked in the coalfields of Britain and America. The premise of this work is that the issues of the strike are central to industrial workers in the post-industrial economics of advanced capitalism.

AMERICAN COALMINERS: CHANGE AND CONSEQUENCES

American coalminers, like their British counterparts, had to deal with a decline in traditional markets for coal as well as with competition for the new market of selling coal to electrical power stations. This competition meant changes in production techniques. The new production techniques included mechanization whereby fewer workers produced the same amount or more coal. They also included increased strip mining—which employed fewer workers, and those workers held different loyalties to the miners' union. Changes in the use of coal affected American coalminers in other ways as well. The quality of coal demanded by power stations was lower; and so production shifted away from the established coalfields with higher quality seams, which were more costly to mine, to new coalfields, often with lower quality seams but always with less expensive mining costs including—as has been noted, surface (or strip) mining. Like their British counterparts, American miners cooperated with many of these changes in coalmining. John L. Lewis, president of the United Mine Workers of America, or UMWA, during the time of mechanization and massive layoffs, even took credit for the changes in the American coal industry that were producing fewer, larger, and more efficient mines (Finley 1972, 171).

The munificence of mechanization did not proceed as Lewis envisioned; and many unintended, adverse consequences were suffered by the American coal miners. In general, since World War II, the American coal industry has witnessed a shift from deepmine production to surface mine production; from established coalfields in the East to new coalfields in the West; and from a work force represented by one strong union—the United Mine Workers of America—to a work force with several unions and a very significant unorganized segment. These changes followed upon several other events including the changed ownership and management of the American coal industry. Oil companies bought coal companies; energy conglomerates bought the oil companies; and multinational conglomerates—without specific economic concentrations except for the production of profit—bought the energy conglomerates.

These changes in production and capital have fostered different relationships between the UMWA and the major coal companies over time. The union cooperated with management from 1950 to 1972. After that, the union entered a period of reform and renewed militancy that ended with an unsuccessful strike in 1977–1978—the longest in the union's history. Since that time, the union has been in search for new strategies to deal with the changed structure of capital in the coal industry (Couto 1987). In the late 1980s, the UMWA was shadowing changes in the make-up of the coal industry by leading a boycott of Shell products because of its coal operations in the apartheid nation of South Africa and by discussing merger with another union in the energy sector of the economy.

The changes and consequences in the American coal industry are many, but underlying them are the root issues of the British miners' strike in 1984–1985. Specifically, the strike dealt with social consequences of changed technology in the use and production of coal. This issue is part of larger questions of class inequality compounded by regional inequality and the transition of the British and U.S. economies from an industrial base to a service base. This transition and a corresponding shift in profit centers of the economy exacerbate forms of inequality in regions dominated by a single industry in transition, like coal. Within the Appalachian region and the peripheral coalfields of Britain, we have seen a decline in work opportunities in the dominant industry; no significant increase in alternative employment; lower wages within and outside of the coal industry; changes in the make-up of the labor force with more participation of women; and a decline in social investment in the work force as a consequence of these combined factors. The preservation of existing forms of work in regions of economic decline has profound social consequences, and it was this relation of work to social stability and change that was the essence of the strike.

REGIONAL DIFFERENCES IN TECHNOLOGICAL INNOVATION

The British coalminer, like his American counterpart, has dealt with new forms of production and new uses of coal. Demand for coal declined as other fuels competed for its traditional and new markets. The traditional market of the railroads was lost to oil, and domestic heating was lost to natural gas. Coal competed with oil and nuclear power for the supply of energy to electrical power stations. Coal's share of Britain's inland energy consumption declined from 90.8 percent in 1947 to 35.6 percent in 1983 (Digest of United Kingdom Energy Statistics 1984); concurrently, the share of coal production consumed by electrical power stations increased from 13.1 percent in 1947 to 74.0 percent in 1983. The total amount of coal dropped from 186 million tons in 1947 to about 90 million tons in 1984. New forms of mechanized production meant large increases in productivity, so that fewer miners could produce as much or more coal. These labor-saving production techniques came at the same time as the declining demand for coal—which increased the unemployment caused by the higher levels of productivity. Consequently, although total production of coal dropped by almost 50 percent between 1947 and 1984 in Britain, employment declined by almost 75 percent in the same period, and the number of pits declined by 81 percent. The British coal industry, like the American coal industry, changed in the direction of fewer, larger mechanized pits with higher labor-productivity rates that produced coal primarily for electrical power stations.

This broad picture of change in production disguises variations that are most important in understanding the issues facing coalminers. First, the changes in the British and American coal industries were concentrated in a decade—the 1950s for the United States and the 1960s for Britain. In these decades, mechanization and unemployment proceeded at their fastest pace. Second, these changes were not uniformly distributed, because investment and disinvestment were not uniformly distributed. Capital investment was made in coalfields with grades of coal that had the greatest marketability and in which the seams could be worked at the lowest cost. Consequently, geological conditions and the quality of coal played a large role in decisions of investment, the development of coalfields, and hence the distribution of benefits and costs of the changes in the coal industry. In practice, this means that the British National Coal Board, the NCB, invested more in pits to produce power-station coal, thus serving its largest market. Some coalfields became peripheral to this investment and development, and others became central.

The peripheral coalfields are in Wales, Scotland, the Northeast of England, the Northwest and Midlands, and Kent. These coalfields were the earliest ones developed by private capital; their coal has the superior B.T.U. content that stoked the furnaces of the steel industry and of transport, both ocean and rail. In a sense, this coal was too good for the market of the 1970s and 1980s power stations. But these peri-pheral regions were at another disadvantage as well. Production costs were high because the easiest, most profitable seams had already been developed and extracted. In addition, the high production costs of pits in these areas were, in part, a consequence of the costs related to previous development—flooding and roof support, for example. Table 4.1 indicates the changes in four factors of production among the coalmining regions of Britain, and the differences among the regions. Statistics for Kent are omitted because they have not been reported uniformly since 1947 and are not easily extrapolated.

Table 4.1
Changes in Production Factors among British Coalmining Regions—Selected
Years, 1947–1984

Production Factor	Regions						
	Scotland	Northeast	Yorkshire	Notting-hamshire	West Midlands and Northwest	South Wales	TOTALS*
Saleable Output (000,000 tonnes)							
1947	22.8	36.0	37.6	34.7	30.4	22.6	186.0
1980	7.8	14.2	31.6	37.7	11.3	7.7	110.3
1984	5.3	10.9	26.1	31.9	9.1	6.6	89.9
1947–1984 Difference	-17.5	-25.1	-11.5	-2.8	-21.3	-16.0	-96.1
% Change	76.8%	69.7%	30.2%	8.1%	70.1%	70.8%	48.3%
No. of Miners (000s)							
1947	81.1	156.0	138.5	94.6	119.3	115.6	711.4
1980	19.8	32.0	63.3	62.2	22.2	25.3	224.8
1984	13.8	22.9	54.0	52.7	18.5	20.1	181.4
1947–1984 Difference	-68.0	-133.1	-84.5	-41.9	-100.8	-95.5	-530.0
% Change	83.8%	85.3%	61.0%	44.3%	84.5%	82.3%	74.5%
No. of Mines							
1947	187	213	117	102	135	222	912
1980	15	24	62	55	21	34	211
1984	9	16	53	48	16	28	170
1947–1984 Difference	-178	-197	-64	-54	-119	-194	-742
% Change	95.2%	92.5%	54.7%	52.9%	88.1%	37.4%	81.3%
Output per Manshift (tonnes)							
1947	1.10	.93	1.18	1.53	**1.06	.79	1.07
1980	1.92	2.07	2.42	2.82	2.35	1.40	2.32
1984	1.95	2.23	**2.59	**2.88	2.44	1.57	2.43
1947–1984 Difference	.85	1.30	1.41	1.35	1.36	.78	1.36
% Change	77.3%	139.8%	119.5%	88.2%	125.9%	98.7%	127.1%

* Total does not equal regions because Kent is not included.
•• Estimate.
Source: NCB (various years).

Table 4.1 makes clear that the six reported regions all underwent similar changes in the direction we have already indicated; fewer mines, fewer miners, less production, and increased productivity. But the degree of these changes varies greatly and importantly. Some coalfields—Scotland, the Northeast, the West Midlands and Northwest, and South Wales (the peripheral coalfields)—have very comparable declines in production, the number of mines, and the number of miners. The figures of these coalfields far exceed those of the central coalfields, Yorkshire and Nottinghamshire.

It is important to note that productivity increased in all the coalfields and that, overall, the British coalminer is now more than twice as productive as in 1947. Most of that increase came in the single decade of 1960 to 1970. The Northeast shows the greatest increase in productivity, while Scotland shows the lowest. South Wales's increase in productivity was greater than that of Nottinghamshire. However, these increases in productivity did little to change the rank order of the areas. The Northeast increased its standing among the areas, and Scotland decreased its standing. South Wales remained with the lowest productivity measure, and Nottinghamshire with the largest. This is important to note because it demonstrates that increases in worker productivity may be necessary, at times, to improve the competitive position of a coalfield, or a plant, but it is not sufficient to assure successful competition. Single-solution proposals for competitiveness based on the increased productivity of workers overlook the increases that have already been made and the myriad of other factors that determine whether or not a product, pit, or plant is competitive.

The changes in productivity in all the coalfields came about for very different reasons in the different coalfields. Productivity increased in the peripheral coalfields primarily because pits with low productivity were closed. Thus, productivity in the peripheral coalfields increased because larger numbers of miners were made redundant, more pits were closed, and production declined. Investment in new technology did occur there, but in smaller amounts than at other coalfields; and this investment was a secondary factor in increasing productivity. In the central coalfields, productivity increased primarily *because* of investment and the introduction of new technology. Table 4.2 reports new capital expenditure from one region to another and indicates the apparent differences in capital expenditure that began just after 1960 and continued thereafter.

The pattern of investment affected the amount of coal production that was mechanized and the rate that power-loading was introduced in each coalfield. In 1950, only 3.7 percent of all of Britain's underground coal production was machine loaded. After 1960, investment and closures were targeted to increase power loading production.

Again, gains in peripheral coalfields were made primarily by closing pits, and in central coalfields by new investment. By 1970, a full 92.2 percent of coal production was power loaded—which was still about the industry level of 1984. However, in 1970, Scotland, the Northeast, and South Wales all had levels of power loading below 90 percent; and Yorkshire, Nottinghamshire, the West Midlands, and the Northwest all had levels higher than 90 percent. Table 4.3 indicates the changes in power loading that occurred from 1950 to 1970.

The figures on power loading indicate the dominant trend in the industry but, once again, not an important variation in that trend.

Table 4.2
Capital Expenditure in British Coalmining Plant, Machinery, and Vehicles—
By Region, Selected Years, 1950–1984 (in millions of pounds sterling)

Year	Regions						
	Scotland	Northeast	Yorkshire	Notting-hamshire	West Midlands and Northwest	South Wales	TOTALS*
1950	1.84	3.94	3.19	3.58	2.39	1.61	17.85
1960	5.00	7.26	9.12	7.84	9.91	7.32	46.73
1970	5.10	7.40	13.80	17.10	7.00	7.10	58.40
1980	2.17	4.63	25.04	17.30	4.85	3.56	57.55
1984	3.10	3.90	38.10	13.60	6.20	2.40	67.30

* Total does not equal regions becuase Kent is not included.
Sources: U.K. Ministry of Power (various years, b); NCB (various years).

Table 4.3
Profit or Loss per Ton of British Deepmine Coal—By Regional Average,
Selected Years, 1947–1983 (in pounds sterling)

Year	Regions					
	Scotland	Northeast*	Yorkshire*	Notting-hamshire*	South Wales	TOTALS*
1950	.98	3.38	2.80	10.72	.57	3.74
1955	6.38	6.35	9.76	16.30	4.00	9.80
1960	32.43	31.12	33.00	61.80	24.40	38.20
1965	72.83	67.89	85.04	87.18	58.19	30.70
1970	86.41	82.82	95.73	97.19	85.33	92.20
1975	90.30	85.40	94.59	98.17	93.33	93.60
1980	93.00	75.40	93.68	97.40	93.90	92.60
1983	92.70	78.00	93.05	96.15	94.30	92.60

*Average for areas within each of these regions.
Source: U.K. Ministry of Power (1972; various years, a; various years, b).

Appalachia in an International Context

Immediately after the embargo by OPEC—the Organization of Petroleum Exporting Countries—fuel prices, including the price of coal, went up. In the "boom" from 1974 to 1978, new profits were available in the coal industry. In Britain, the NCB reported net profit. However, productivity in both Britain and the United States declined at this time of higher profits. In addition, the degree of mechanized production also declined. The United States displayed sharper declines in both instances than did Britain (Couto 1987). The point is that the coal industries of both nations enjoyed a period of greatest profit at a time of higher marginal labor costs, declined productivity, and a drop in mechanized production. Obviously, the competitive position of coal is not determined entirely by the factors of production within the coal industry.

Another change in production that occurred to improve the competitive position of coal in both countries was the increase in surface-mined coal. This change was more drastic in the United States where stripmine coal was more than 60 percent of coal production in the 1980s, compared to Britain where it has never exceeded 15 percent of total production. But the proportion of opencast production varies among mining regions at vastly different rates, especially since 1975. In Britain, as in the United States, established coalfields with less

Table 4.4
Amount and Proportion of British Opencast Coal Production—By Region, Selected Years, 1947–1984

Years	Regions						
	Scotland	Northeast	Yorkshire	Notting-hamshire	West Midlands and Northwest	South Wales	TOTALS
1947	.7	3.94	3.19	3.58	2.39	1.61	17.85
% of Deepmine Production	3.1%	5.3%	5.6%	7.5%	6.6%	4.4%	5.5%
1960	.3	2.6	1.0	1.0	1.1	2.3	7.5
% of Deepmine Production	1.7%	7.5%	2.7%	2.9%	3.6%	10.3%	4.1%
1970/71	1.4	2.8	.8	.8	.2	2.4	8.3
% of Deepmine Production	12.4%	14.7%	2.3%	1.9%	1.4%	20.5%	6.2%
1980/81	2.8	3.7	1.7	2.9	1.9	2.2	15.3
% of Deepmine Production	35.6%	26.1%	5.4%	7.7%	16.8%	28.6%	13.9%
1982/83	2.7	3.8	1.1	2.8	1.9	1.5	13.8
% of Deepmine Production	40.9%	30.6%	3.6%	7.6%	17.6%	21.7%	13.2%

Source: U.K. Ministry of Power (various years, a; various years, b).

capital for the mechanization of deepmines compete with better capitalized coalfields by turning to surface mining. Table 4.4 indicates a great increase in opencast mining in Scotland and the Northeast between 1947 and 1984, slight decreases in Yorkshire and Nottinghamshire, and unchanged amounts in the Northwest, West Midlands, and South Wales. Because the total amount of coal in each region also changed, the amount of opencast coal as a proportion of total production increased far more in the peripheral fields than in Yorkshire and Nottinghamshire. In other words, these fields saw less investment in underground mining and a shift to opencast mining as a means to increase productivity and regional profits.

THE DISTRIBUTION OF THE BENEFITS AND COSTS OF INDUSTRIAL CHANGE

The broad changes in the production and use of coal that have occurred since World War II are common to both the United States and Britain. What is very different is the manner in which these changes were managed in the two countries. The British coal industry is a national industry, and the National Coal Board—now British Coal—combines the social function of the state and the economic function of an industry. The state may meet its social function along a political continuum that ranges from redistributive policies that reduce the difference of wealth, privilege, and influence among social classes to redistributive policies that increase these differences. In general, most public policies are regulative and distributive with incremental consequences for equality and inequality. This continuum of redistributive policies exceeds the differences between the Conservative Party and the Labour Party, but helps identify them on a political spectrum. The Labour Party is generally associated with public policies to reduce inequalities, and the Conservatives with policies to increase or maintain inequality. Similarly, industry may function on a spectrum of management styles from enlightened self-interest with an element of long-term planning that includes a broad analysis of costs to a much narrower self-interest based on profit and loss and in which long-term planning is dedicated to conforming to a free market where the producer with the lowest price establishes industrial behavior.

The National Coal Board, the NCB, has combined its state role and its industry role in various ways over time; but in general, from nationalization to the Thatcher administration, the NCB worked within what Miliband (1978) calls the Settlement of 1945. This term refers to a set of assumptions that were common to public policies after World War II. The state was to promote economic growth through state intervention in the economy and to protect workers from involuntary unemployment. One primary mechanism for doing this was national industry. In addition, the state would make public investment in social overhead capital by removing essential services from the market forces as much as possible. These services included health, education, and, to a lesser extent, income, transportation, and housing (Miliband 1978).

The American coal industry underwent its changes with a very different set of assumptions. John L. Lewis, in 1950, entered into an agreement with the largest producers of coal to mechanize the industry, to increase productivity, to decrease total employment, to increase wages for those workers left in the industry, and to force producers without sufficient capital to leave the industry. The social costs of these changes were to be financed by industry revenues, were to be arrived at by collective bargaining, and were to include increased benefit and retirement plans for retiring or disabled miners. Lewis had consummate faith in a strong, expanding American economy to absorb displaced coal industry laborers (Baratz 1955; Finley 1972).

Lewis devised this strategy at the end of World War II when the American government was changing its role in the coal industry. The government had administered the industry during a large portion of the war, and Lewis had made substantial wage and benefit gains when coal was a state industry. Events after the war indicated that the Truman and Eisenhower administrations would not continue the state's wartime generosity (Seltzer 1985, 55). Lewis preferred the private ownership of the mines, and in the management of the large coal corporations found unprecedented cooperation to bring about change in an industry facing substantial competition from other fuels for traditional and new markets. In summary, during the 1950s Lewis worked for an industry with far fewer producers with union labor in larger and mechanized mines. The proceeds from the industry were to finance the transition of older workers and an expanding economy was to provide new employment for younger workers.

There was an important consensus within and between the NCB and the NUM against the Lewis strategy. Lord Robens, who at the time was chairman of the NCB, visited John L. Lewis and then distanced himself from the labor leader for his lack of attention to the social consequences of the changes in coal production (Robens 1972, 43). Robens described himself as being to the right of center of the Labour Party (40), but insisted that part of running a national industry—in contrast to a private industry—was the conduct of that industry in light of social benefit and not merely profit and loss. He called this a "total sum approach" (297).

To say there was British consensus against the Lewis strategy is not to suggest that there was total agreement between the NCB and the NUM. In fact, the relationship of these parties changed with time, as did the relationship of the UMWA and the American coal company managers. From nationalization to 1960, the NUM cooperated to make nationalization work and to preserve the industry. From 1960 to 1969, while the industry underwent both drastic decline in total production and mechanization of the production process, the NUM continued to work with the NCB to maintain a humane form of capitalism. The primary mechanism of this humane capitalism was the National Power Loading Agreement, the NPLA, which created uniform job descriptions and wages throughout the industry (Kreiger 1983). In a sense, this 1966 agreement distributed the benefits of mechanization by increasing the wages of workers in unprofitable pits to the level of workers in profitable pits. It was regarded by leaders in the NUM and the NCB as a benchmark in industrial relations (Robens 1972; Paynter 1976).

From 1969 to 1974, the NUM expressed new militancy, which Robens did not understand and probably could not have handled had he remained chairman of the NCB. This militancy expressed itself in two national strikes, which were, in part, calls to change the terms of the 1945 settlement and to provide the miners more for their part in the economy (Miliband 1984). After 1974 and up to the time of the Thatcher administration, the NCB and NUM worked unsuccessfully for national plans for the coal industry. Part of their failure is manifest in the Area Incentive Plans, which undermined the NPLA of 1966 and reintroduced different wages based on pit productivity (Paynter 1976). Despite the differences of the NCB and the NUM during this time, there was still an agreement between them about the goals of the state and of the industry—goals very different from those that John L. Lewis espoused.

This is important because the strike of 1984–1985 was preceded by movement of the British government and the leadership of the union to new opinions about national industry and the state. Arthur Scargill, who became president of the NUM in 1981, still rejected the Lewis strategy and staked out a position that the NCB absorb additional social costs in the production of coal. Ian MacGregor, who became chairman of the NCB in 1983, represented the views of the Thatcher administration and—more specifically—the experience of the American coal industry. The policy preference of the Conservatives after 1979—and which was pursued vigorously after 1983—was a Lewis strategy of fewer, more efficient, more profitable pits, with as few social costs as possible incorporated into the coal industry (Lloyd 1985).

This was a very great change. The NCB had traditionally balanced the losses of some regions with the profits of others to minimize the deficit of the industry or to achieve profit. From 1960 to 1970, the NCB invested in centers of profit and ran down the loss centers. This was done both among the coalfields and within them. This move came after almost a decade and a half of profit-making by the industry nationwide, despite losses within individual regions. By 1970, the NCB was reporting modest profits per ton of coal produced, and continued to do so until the effects of the energy boom wore off in 1978. These modest profits occurred at a time of wage increases won by the NUM in the national strikes of the early 1970s. By 1978, the NCB began reporting a loss per ton of coal produced. These losses increased staggeringly from about £1 per ton in 1980 to more than £6 per ton in 1983–1984. These latter figures may reflect changes in accounting and management and a deliberate attempt by the government to discredit national industries, as suggested in the 1978 Ridley Report (Benyon and McMylor 1985). Table 4.5 reports profit and loss per ton of coal over a number of years and shows vast regional differences for 1980 and 1983 similar to those of 1960 and 1965.

The NUM was far less disposed to participate in another rundown of the industry, as it had in the 1960s, for several reasons. First, there would be no humane face to capitalism with the Thatcher administration and Ian MacGregor. These officials trusted the free market, as had John L. Lewis, to provide for workers displaced by the move to create fewer, more profitable mines. Second, the capitalism of the NCB in the 1960s—while much more humane than the decline of the

Table 4.5
Profit or Loss per Ton of British Deepmine Coal—By Regional Average, Selected Years, 1947–1983 (in pounds sterling)

Year	Regions						
	Scotland	Northeast	Yorkshire	Notting-hamshire	West Midlands and Northwest	South Wales	TOTALS
1947	1.5	-4.0	.4	4.4	.5	-9.7	-1.0
1960	-12.0	-2.4	8.2	9.8	-.8	-5.8	1.8
1965	-4.1	-2.5	-.3	6.3	-4.7	-11.0	-1.0
1970	-.6	-.3	.2	.4	.2	.0	.2
1975	-.7	.5	.4	.6	-.9	-.9	.2
1980	-3.3	-2.0	-1.7	1.9	-1.2	-9.0	-1.0
1983	-10.3	-5.4	-2.2	-.5	-.8	-16.4	-3.1

Sources: U.K. Ministry of Power (various years, b); NCB (various years).

American coal industry in the 1950s—had severe adverse consequences that could only increase with another rundown. In particular, the peripheral coalfields had seen drastic unemployment and a shift to environmentally destructive opencast mining. Third, the policies of the administration emulated the American model that had proved particularly adverse for peripheral coalfields and for the UMWA. The NCB had traditionally mitigated some of the consequences in the production of coal—which were obvious in much worse form in some peripheral coalfields in the United States—despite very similar pressures from changed markets and competition. In particular, British coalminers witnessed less unemployment, disinvestment, surface mining competition, shifts to new coalfields, dual unionism and union busting, reversion to labor-intensive technologies, and erosion of safety and health procedures than did their American counterparts.

The NUM, like the Thatcher administration, proposed new standards for the conduct of the coal industry. Figure 4.1 represents these standards on a matrix and delineates their differences. The NCB operated on the "National Industry" segment up until 1979 when its

Figure 4.1
Matrix of Industrial Conduct and State Policies

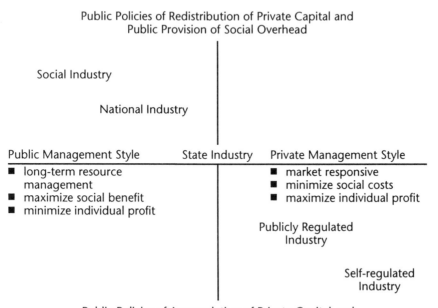

style changed to "State Industry" and with a preference for "Publicly Regulated Industry." At the time of this change, the leadership of the NUM changed its position to one of "Social Industry." This would require the state to take new steps to conduct the coal industry in a manner integrated with other national industries—electricity, oil, and nuclear power—and to promote social goods such as maximum employment and income redistribution to the peripheral coal regions. In contrast, the United States had never achieved a "National Industry" in coal; the shift had been from "State Industry," during and just after World War II, to operation along the segment "Publicly Regulated Industry," with a trend toward lax enforcement of regulations or de facto "Self-regulated Industry" (Miernyk 1980, 33).

At the time of the 1984–1985 strike, the National Coal Board was a state industry in which the state policy was redistributive policies to preserve, if not to increase, class differences, and the industry policy was one of narrow profit and loss with a long-term goal of conformity with the free market. In time, the NCB emulated the American model of management embodied in Ian MacGregor and his experience as head of Amax, an American mineral corporation. Simultaneously, within the National Union of Mineworkers at the time of the strike there was a well-articulated view of a National Coal Board that combined the functions of industry and the state in precisely the opposite fashion. In this view, the state functioned to reduce class differences and industry functioned according to enlightened self-interest and with a broad analysis of costs, especially social costs (Lloyd 1985). Each party to the strike had moved in different directions on the axis that suggests the mix of state and industry policies.

CONTINUING CONSEQUENCES AND UNRESOLVED QUESTIONS

In the wake of the American and British miners' experiences, there are several important and unresolved matters. Some of these apply to other industries as well as coal, and some apply with special importance to regions that are dependent on a single, declining industry. The first set of matters deal generally with industrial change to achieve a competitive position, and the second set deal with efforts in regions of economic decline to deal with the consequences of that decline. We are not dealing with the matter of whether to adapt to competition or not—the miners did that. We are dealing with a matter of degree: how much adaptation is enough. In addition, we are concerned with the state's role in establishing and maintaining new social relations entailed by the changed economy—how the sacrifice and benefits of adaptation should be distributed.

CREATING AND ENFORCING NEW FORMS OF INEQUALITY

Competition

A host of complex factors determine the competitive position of a coalfield. It is not a simple matter of technology or the market. It is especially not a simple matter of increased worker productivity because, as we have seen, all the British coalfields witnessed increased miner productivity and the British coal industry enjoyed prosperity at the time of the OPEC embargo. At that time the ability to make profits encouraged a decrease in productivity, especially in the United States (Couto 1987). Part of the competitive position of a coalfield relates to what costs producers absorb or ignore. This is true of coalfields within a country and perhaps even more true of coalfields of different countries. Advantage accrues to American coal over those countries that incur higher production costs because of stricter health, safety, and environmental standards. Advantages accrue to South Africa and Colombia because a combination of low labor costs; new and appropriate technology in production, handling, and transportation; and lower quality coal result in far lower production costs and increased marketability.

Coalfields become "peripheral" as advantages accrue to other sites of production. Workers in those peripheral coalfields can compete by rolling back the wage and benefits for their labor and continuing to use less productive technology. Such workers may also remain competitive by state regulation of the diffusion of technology, the allocation of the historical costs of the industry, and the distribution of benefits and costs within an industry. A coal company severed from the history of its industry, or the coal industry of one area or country severed from the industry's history in other areas or countries, carries with it fewer social costs from the past and consequently a better competitive position.

There are competitive advantages to coal companies that divorce themselves from the historical, accumulated costs of the industry. In particular, such a company may claim no responsibility for the pensions and benefits of former workers and their dependents. This reduces labor costs. Left on their own, producers will minimize the past social costs of an industry. The ability of one producer to do this creates pressure for all producers to do the same. Expenses related to disabled miners, retired miners, and dependents of former miners are part of the social costs of coal production—part of the competitive position among new and established coalfields, and a cost of production that new centers of profit attempt to eliminate or minimize (Schnell 1977).

The lack of history means a lack of labor tradition as well. New coalmining areas are more likely to have a work force without the tradition of miners' unions. This is obviously true in the United States where the new coalfields in the West have little UMWA representation and avoid payment to union and industry funds for the social costs of the industry's past, that is, pension and health care for former workers. In addition to where coal production takes place, how it occurs is also important to tradition, history, and cost. Surface miners in the United States—like their counterparts in opencast mining in Britain—share less with deepminers and more with heavy machinery engineers and operators (Miernyk 1980, 47). The social consequences of divorcing new industrial activity from the past is clearer in the eastern coalfields of America than in Britain because the passage of the American coal industry to new areas in the West, to the new techniques of stripmining, and to nonunion labor has been relatively unimpeded.

Distributing Costs and Benefits of Change

The role of the state is obviously central in auditing and allocating social costs to regions and industries that incur them. How the state carries out this role affects the competitive position of an industry and the creation of production and profit centers within an industry. This introduces the second unresolved matter related to the 1984–1985 strike. How should the benefits and costs of change be distributed? Clearly, change is inevitable. And for most of its history, the NCB sought to balance the changing needs of the nation for coal at competitive prices with the needs of the areas that produced it. Or at least, it attempted this balance to a far greater extent than the United States did. The British strike was essentially a dispute over a new balance in light of changes in the industry and their consequence for coalmining regions. The NUM suggested that benefits should be distributed with emphasis on the workers and regions that bear their costs. The NCB suggested that benefits should be distributed with emphasis on centers of profit where the accumulation of capital was possible.

In addition to this very large question about the distribution of costs and benefits within the coal industry, there is also the matter of balancing the costs and benefits among coal and other fuels. The position of coal has been traditionally undersold by successive campaigns for more attractive and less expensive fuels. Oil and nuclear power achieved their share of the energy market in part because they were "cheap" or related to other national purposes such as the nuclear arms program (Hall 1981, 1986). Subsequently, their prices have increased with changes in international politics, shifts in the international market for energy and the history of accidents at nuclear power plants.

The relation between coal and other fuels touches on the matter of long-term management of resources. The decline of pits in the peripheral coalfields means the deterioration of mining conditions in those seams and the improbability of recovering coal from them later. In addition, pit closures and unemployment mean the dissolution of a labor force that was accumulated initially at great cost and maintained with great tension and conflict, a labor force which cannot be replicated without great expense at some future time.

State Enforcement of Inequality

A third major issue that was part of the miners' strike was the management of dissent, unemployment, and inequality in a time of declining industry. President Harry S. Truman used the power of the courts and his office against the UMWA in an unprecedented manner to shift the coal industry from a state industry to a publicly regulated industry. The British miners' strike likewise evoked strong action on the part of the state. The strike cost the state £7 billion. No private enterprise could have withstood the financial burden of the strike as the British state did. It was able to do so because it had public capital it could draw to pay for the expenses of the strike, including the huge costs to the Central Electricity Generating Board, the CEGB, which substituted oil for coal to maintain electrical production. This required the CEGB to operate £1.7 billion in the red for 1984–1985.

Similarly, miners in the United States have encountered coal companies that are subsidiaries of larger conglomerates and that can devote capital from other activities to "invest" in the strike in hopes of achieving long-term savings in labor costs (Craypo 1979, 197). Clearly, the state in Britain, and perhaps American corporations, have now achieved an integration of industries sufficient to pursue policies related to the concentration and accumulation of capital. They have exercised that power, thus far, to restore the style of private management and on behalf of private capital.

Miliband wrote insightfully on the management of dissent, and anticipated a platform of the Conservatives to repress "desubordination" in Britain, which implies state policies of public management style and for greater redistributive policies. According to Miliband, part of the Settlement of 1945 was a reduction of class tensions, if not class differences, about the redistribution of wealth and the conduct of industry. The militancy of the miners in the late 1960s was an early indication of new class tensions and that the state would have to bear higher costs to reduce them. But it was not only the miners who were changing. Miliband suggested the Conservatives would be more "firm":

> With greedy workers, picketing strikers, presumptuous trade unions, subversive teachers, noisy students, tiresome blacks, welfare scroungers, sinister Marxists, misguided libertarians and everybody else standing in the way of national renewal by way of 'free enterprise' and the working of the market. (1978, 409)

The changes in British law that restricted civil liberties and previous labor behavior, and the militant practices of police preceding the strike and applied to the miners (Benyon and McMylor 1985)—and other workers as well—are a measure of state requirements to enforce modified terms of the Settlement of 1945. These terms are more along the lines of the state and regulated industries of the United States and may entail state violence and repression to enforce new forms of inequality in Britain, as they are required to maintain forms of inequality in America.

Peripheral Coalfields and the New Inequality

Some of the consequences of the decline of industry and attempts to achieve new competitive positions are very severe in coalmining regions. This is because the regions had a dependence on a single industry; with the decline of that industry, the amount, nature, and terms of employment changed drastically. In addition, factors that support and reproduce a work force and contribute to the quality of life of an area—social overhead—deteriorated with the decline of the coal industry. As the contribution of the industry to this social overhead declined, the state's contribution to social overhead—health, housing, education, and family income—also declined. This disinvestment of social overhead by the industry and the state has spawned new forms of community organizations to mitigate the negative consequences of industrial decline. These changes in the coalfields are important measures of the adequacy and efficacy of the welfare state policies of both Britain and the United States. Events in the British peripheral coalfields specifically entail the Settlement of 1945 in two ways—first, the conduct of national industry; and second, the development of regions with low socio-economic characteristics—and thus offer a measure of changes in the British welfare state.

Changing Forms of Work and Workforce

Residents in the peripheral coalfields of the United States and Britain are faced with changed prospects for work. The decline of the coal industry in these regions means less and different work in the coal industry. In some cases, there is employment in much more mechanized, safer, and more productive pits for fewer men. On the other hand, marginal producers continue to compete in unmechanized, riskier, and less productive mines employing small work crews. In the United States, the increased proportion of nonunion coal in the East and the number of attempts on the part of producers to undermine the industrywide UMWA contract also mark this turn of events (Couto 1983; Finley 1972). These developments may eventually mean the increase of hand-got coal in the peripheral coalfields and the increase in private mines employing miners at lower wages in Britain. In addition, the peripheral coalfields in both nations have witnessed an increase in the production of surface mining for coal. This form of mining entails a different set of skills from deepmining, and represents a different work force without links to the NUM in Britain and with fewer links to the UMWA in the United States.

These changes in production have adversely affected the membership of major unions in both countries and have coincided with management's attempts to introduce new unions. These developments have increased the supply of coal available during strikes of the major union of mineworkers in both countries. Consequently, union miners in peripheral coalfields of both countries have seen the strength of their collective action diminished.

The changes in work in the coal industry are only part of the changes in work that have occurred in the coalmining regions of Britain and the United States. Studies of mining communities in Wales (Town 1978; Sewel 1975) suggest a set of developments that parallel events in the Appalachian coalfields. There is less work available in general and the work that is available offers minimum wages, few benefits, and a lack of organization of the work force. In the Appalachian region, for example, low-wage component assembly and manufacturing offers employment opportunities, as do services—for example, retail and cashier clerks, and the like (Couto 1984a, b).

The change in work opportunities has meant a change in the work force as well. In the Appalachian region, the decline of traditionally male high-wage employment opportunities has required many women to join the wage economy to supplement family income. This development has meant the formation of two pools of surplus labor that work to depress the terms and wages of labor. First, there is a pool of young men without disability. This labor group competes for the work opportunities left in the coal industry and for other, better work opportunities. The second pool of labor includes older men, some of whom have disabilities, and all women (Town 1978). Workers in this group compete for employment in the secondary economy of lower wages, fewer benefits, and less protection through worker organizations. In the United States, these developments have meant a decline in family income and reports of increased hardship, including hunger (Couto 1986; Smith 1986).

Capital Investment in Social Overhead

With changes in the nature of work and the work force, there are profound changes in the factors that produce, reproduce, and reward a work force. These factors include health care, family income, housing, education, and the environment. Private capital provided many of these factors of social overhead in the initial development of the coal industry. Thus we had "coal towns" or "mining villages" in the United States and Britain, in which the companies provided and controlled social overhead factors and investment. After World War II, Britain attempted to provide much of the social overhead through public capital, that is, state programs. In the United States, after World War II, the UMWA and the industry attempted unsuccessfully to provide these through private capital. The American coal industry was inadequate to meet the capital costs of adequate social overhead in the Appalachian region and, beginning in the mid-1960s, that region became grounds for state programs to meet human needs: the Appalachian Regional Commission and the War on Poverty.

Peripheral coalfields like Appalachia and those in Britain illustrate that a decline in a dominant industry means less investment in the communities and people related to that industry. As less workers are needed, less capital is invested in social overhead (Holland 1976). When one measures income, educational investment, housing standards, health care, and health status in Appalachia or in Wales, one finds differences between the region and the nation. Equally important, however, one finds differences within the region related to coal industry. That is, the more dependent a region is on a declining industry, the less capital—private or public—is invested in social overhead and the worse are the measures of well-being. This is less true of health care in Britain than in the United States because the National Health Service represents continued public capital investment in that form of social overhead. But with changes in the National Health Service, it is likely that inequalities in the access to and quality of health care and the differences in health status that exist in the

Appalachian region will appear in the British peripheral coalfields. Housing is another indicator of the decline in social overhead that comes with declining industry. In the coalfields of Wales, the National Coal Board leases 15 percent of the housing, but 50 percent of the dilapidated stock (Welsh Office 1976, 58).

Compounding the problem of declined social overhead investment is the disinvestment in social overhead that also occurs. In both the Appalachian region and the peripheral coalfields, surface mining represents an attempt to compete within a changed coal industry. It also represents an attempt to acquire a subsidy for its operation by disrupting the ecology of an area. The bedrock of social capital is the environment on which residents depend for basic factors in the continuation of life, including water, soil, and aesthetic values. The rate at which the environment is discounted and run down seems in direct relation to the unemployment, migration, and poverty of the residents of a region. Opencast mining and stripmining are best understood as forms of disinvestment from the social overhead of an area and as part of the decline of an industry.

Intermediate Organizations

The National Union of Mineworkers in Britain and the UMWA in the United States are important labor organizations to guarantee that workers acquire as much benefit from their work as possible and that the social costs of industrial conduct are met. The success of the union is important for workers in the coal industry and for others in the coalmining regions as well. The standards of the terms of labor in union mines influence other workplaces, both in the coal industry and outside of the coal industry. With the decline of the union, the standards of the terms of labor may decline as well. This decline may not be obvious as some coal operators in Appalachia, and in the United States generally, offer coalminers higher wages than union standards—sometimes—to work in a nonunion setting. But such terms, like alternative unions, are available only because of the dominant union, and they will diminish with the decline in the strength of the labor union from which they derive.

There is an increase in intermediate organizations to take on some functions of the union and to mitigate the consequences of economic decline. *Intermediate organizations* is a term used to describe organizations (such as a labor union) that mediate between an individual and larger forces or institutions (Berger and Neuhaus 1977). In the United States, the most prominent intermediate organizations in peripheral coalfields are the church and voluntary organizations. The Catholic bishops of the Appalachian region issued a pastoral statement on the economy of the Appalachian region that is critical of the conduct of American industry there. The Protestant churches have cooperated in the conduct of programs—programs that include many Catholics— through the Commission on Religion in Appalachia, which started in 1964. Much of the practical work of these church efforts is focused on the attempts of community organizations to provide improved employment opportunities in the face of the declining coal industry. Most importantly, however, the largest portion of efforts among community organizations is directed specifically to improve health care, housing, and education and to preserve the environment from destructive industrial practice. In other words, the community organizations are attempts to provide social overhead where public and private capital have failed and are insufficient.

These efforts are especially important to women and children who, in the United States at least, are the most vulnerable to the post-industrial economy. Women have found it increasingly necessary to enter the wage labor force because family incomes have declined with the decreased terms of labor in the region and the changed employment opportunities for men. Women in households with a male wage earner have always participated in large proportions in the wage labor force of the secondary economy of the region. There are more such women now, as the number of female-headed households increase. In addition, women with male wage-earners present are also under pressure to enter the wage labor force in order to maintain family incomes despite the changed status of the male. The services that community organizations provide—such as health care, child care, education, and arts and crafts production—offer some women employment and offer other women the services necessary to permit them to work outside the home (Smith 1986).

The importance of the support groups during the 1984–1985 British strike, and the prominent role of women in them, suggest parallels to the history of intermediate organizations in the Appalachian region. First, the church in the British peripheral coal-fields was prominent in attempts to mediate between the NCB and the NUM and in criticisms of the conduct of the NCB and the state in the strike. In Wales, the church had expressed itself in economic affairs previously through the work of Ty Toronto in the aftermath of Aberfan (Ty Toronto 1977). Second, the support groups provided an alternative source of social overhead—food, housing, and other necessities to sustain life—during the strike (Massey and Wainwright 1985). In addition, pre-dating the strike, voluntary associations such as the Sierra Club and its local affiliates were conducting action to oppose the continuation and expansion of opencast mining.

CONCLUSION

These efforts of intermediate organizations in Appalachia and Wales are important in themselves and for the people of the region in which they take place. But they must be kept in perspective in light of the experience in the Appalachian region. This experience suggests important grounds on which to draw parallels between the British and American peripheral coalfields, summarize similar events in both, and suggest common existing problems. First, the efforts of intermediate organizations are necessary in light of inadequate private and public capital investment in social overhead. Second, social overhead declines with the decline of industry and with the increase in a pool of surplus labor for limited employment opportunities—conditions that preclude the necessity of producing an adequate labor force or enticing workers into wage labor. Third, there are forms of disinvestment of social overhead, including lack of regard for the environment, which intermediate organizations act to curtail. Fourth, new forms of community organizations emerge as the strength of organized labor as an intermediate organization is challenged or subsides. Fifth, these intermediate organizations are particularly important for women because the decline in the peripheral coalfields, especially in the Appalachian region, has decreased family incomes and prompted many women to enter the wage labor force at a time of declining opportunities and diminishing terms for labor. Sixth and finally, while these community organizations are necessary responses and defenses of local residents to mitigate the consequences of industrial decline, they are not sufficient to provide adequate amounts of social overhead or sufficient employment opportunities.

It is this last point that entails the essence of the strike of 1984–1985 in Britain and the web of issues that bind the American and British coalfields. How does the state address new forms of inequality and unemployment that stem from industrial change? This question is common and paramount to American and British coalfields.

The seemingly "appropriate" answer is undoubtedly related to one's place of residence, employment, income, and advantage. From the perspective of the peripheral coalfields, and of the industrial workers (along with their families and communities) who are becoming increasingly peripheral, the appropriate answers to new forms of unemployment and inequality are state policies of redistribution to reduce inequalities and to promote intermediate organizations in the direct provision of social overhead, as well as industrial policies to promote employment. The political strategy to achieve that answer requires new coalitions of labor organizations and the integration of labor organizations with intermediate organizations concerned directly with working for the welfare of families and communities. The strike of British coalminers in 1984–1985 articulated well the issues of inequality, unemployment, and industrial change. The state imposed an end to the miners' action, but not a resolution to the perplexing issues behind their action. In this manner, the strike is most likely a precursor of action yet to come to provide a satisfactory answer to the problems obvious in the peripheral coalfields and endemic in the industrial sector of the British and American post-industrial economies.

■ 5 ■
Local Development Activities in Newfoundland and Central Appalachia

Nelda K. Pearson

Groups with very similar economic and community problems can take different routes to resolving these problems—some more effective than others. Interviews in Lethbridge, Newfoundland (held in the summer of 1985 and funded by the Canadian government), and in Dungannon, Virginia (held in the summer of 1986 and funded by Highlander Educational Center and the Lutheran Church), give us some information on how effective various self-help projects might be. In Lethbridge, a branch of the Women for the Survival of Agriculture, or WSA—the Goose Head Farm Women's Association, or GHFWA—was formed primarily to push for government assistance for agriculture. In Dungannon, Virginia the Dungannon Development Commission, or DDC, was formed to promote economic and human development principally through the development of local infra-structure, such as a clinic, a water system, a community center, and currently a sewing factory. The two organizations have confronted a very similar problem—poor economic conditions, with very little government support—in very different ways leading to different types and levels of success. The differences in how problems are defined and solutions are implemented in the two groups tend to reflect the attitudes of the prime initiators in each group. These different attitudes in the Canadian and American initiators reflect differences in the cultures of Canada and the United States.

COMMON PROBLEMS AND DIFFERENT SOLUTIONS

Both Lethbridge and Dungannon are geographically and politically isolated communities. Lethbridge lies on the east coast of

Newfoundland in a small cove. It is nearly an hour from its nearest urban center, Clarenville, and about three hours from St. John's. Its isolation is attested to by the fact that it lies adjacent to Terra Nova National Park and is off the main highway. Not only is Lethbridge, as part of Newfoundland, isolated from mainland Canada and thus suffers the problems common to the rest of the province, but it is also isolated from Newfoundland's most populated region and suffers the usual problems of such an isolated community: poor roads, limited opportunities, and substandard housing, sanitation, and water supply. This also means that Lethbridge is politically isolated. As one woman stated, "The Canadian government thinks the country ends at North Sydney [Nova Scotia] and the Newfoundland government ends at St. John's." Most GHFWA women interviewed felt that neither the provincial nor federal government knew or cared about their local economic problems.

Similarly, Dungannon, Virginia, is a small community nestled in the mountains of Scott County—the far southwestern tip of the state. Lying in the central Appalachians, Dungannon—like Lethbridge—is isolated from both the rest of the United States and from the more prosperous regions of Virginia. Dungannon is situated between two major highways, each of which is an hour away by car on a narrow mountain road that becomes nearly impassable in winter. Dungannon has no supermarket, a substandard water system, and— until DDC was established—no clinic, no fire station, no community center, and no bank. People in Dungannon feel that they are neglected by the rest of the county and the state. As one woman explained, "We're small and we don't have many votes. To get something done we have to make a big noise and embarrass everyone." This statement refers to the exposé that Dungannon residents gave to a national newspaper about conditions at their school, in order to embarrass county officials into helping upgrade the building.

Another similarity is that both Lethbridge and Dungannon have been heavily dependent on a single-product economy that has declined. Lethbridge has been heavily dependent on the fishing industry, a seasonal industry that has declined. Currently, fisherpersons and their families are taking "pokie money"—that is, UIC or unemployment insurance income. This economic decline has led to a host of other problems associated with underemployment and unemployment, such as alcohol abuse, spouse abuse, delinquency, increased school dropout, and outmigration. Similarly, southwestern Virginia has been heavily dependent on coal production—an industry that has been in decline in the mountains since 1926, with the exception of World War II and the 1970s oil embargo (Eller 1982; "Coal: Saver of a Region" 1981). Two other sources of income in the mountains have been tobacco and textile mills/sewing factories. Both of these opportunities are also in decline. Tobacco allotments have declined more than 25 percent since 1980, and the price per pound of tobacco has also declined. The textile industry in general in the United States has been in trouble, and the sewing factory in Dungannon—the sole industry—first went bankrupt and then closed completely due to a fire. The same problems of spouse and drug abuse, school dropout, delinquency, and outmigration have occurred in Dungannon as have occurred in Lethbridge.

Both communities see economic diversity and some degree of self sufficiency as necessary to their survival, yet both communities are involved in an economy of affinity, that is, doing what they already know how to do—namely, farm and sew. This is frequently seen as continuing a way of life. The farm women of Lethbridge see farming as a "good" way of life, especially for their children who are not so easily exposed to the temptations of idle adolescence that they see in the town. Similarly, the women of Dungannon are proud of their sewing ability and speak forcefully of their craftsmanship and their ability to turn out a quality product—even sewing for designer labels. But in both communities, those women who extol the virtues of their particular lifestyle, do not, in fact, work on the farm or in the factory—a problem we will explore below.

Finally, both Lethbridge and Dungannon suffer from official and unofficial government policies of neglect. In Canada, the 1976 DMIO Task Force Report encourages the phasing out of small family farms by 1990 (National Farmers Unions 1979). Further, the National Policy of 1978 put a high tariff on the movement of manufactured goods from the Windsor-Montreal corridor to the hinterlands, while keeping a low tariff on natural resources from hinterland to heartland—which increases costs for machinery and other goods in Newfoundland. Further, Newfoundland's government policy—while overtly encouraging agricultural production—ignores agriculture as a viable occupation on the island. In fact, unofficial government policy encourages outmigration of all the Maritimes whose general economies have been in decline since the turn of the century (Kresl 1982).

Similarly, Dungannon—like the rest of Central Appalachia— suspects it is being abandoned by both the federal and state governments. In the late 1980s, the Appalachian Regional Commission was being systematically defunded by the federal government. The Lacy Commission Report does not encourage state incentives for economic growth in the county; rather, it suggests that the state concentrate on already thriving communities by encouraging private enterprise there. The official policy toward Appalachia in the 1920s and 1930s was to encourage outmigration (ARC 1985a). It is widely believed that both the federal and state governments will once again encourage this policy through decreased incentives for investment, decreased funding for highways in the region, and a limiting of funds for social services.

The two communities under study have very parallel problems: (1) they are geographically and politically isolated; (2) they suffer from dependence on a single-product economy that has been in decline for quite some time, creating a chronically depressed economy; (3) both are attempting economic diversification into areas that are not perceived by outsiders as likely to be successful, and in fact are seen as doomed to failure by most; and (4) both areas are suffering from official government policies that discourage further investment in the region.

There are also parallels in the solutions. In both Lethbridge and Dungannon, community members have organized to deal with the problems. In both, it has been the women who have established and maintained these organizations. And the main concern in both cases has been to deal with economic issues.

There are also some differences that have affected the direction and success of solutions. A major difference is the role of outside leaders and the general approach these leaders have brought to the problems. This has significantly affected the "philosophy" of the group, the problems they address, the tactics they use, and the style they adopt. Lethbridge's GHFWA has adopted a very political stance, which requires that local leaders groom themselves or be groomed as good lobbyists. This has been encouraged by the founder of WSA, of which GHFWA is a loose affiliate, and has been part of WSA's general thrust. The approach tends to concentrate on activities that will work for the common good; although certain individuals can become "stars," this is not likely to translate into individual careers as stars. Dungannon has involved itself more in local fundraising and the upgrading of individual women's educations through programs that provide access to formal education. This approach reflects the concern of several well-educated newcomers and tends to reflect their own concerns with formal education as a vehicle for enhancing the self-worth of the individual. This has, however, tended to create stars who, whether intentionally or not, are using the community development program as a vehicle for their own careers.

The differences in approach do not merely reflect differences in the needs of the two communities but also differences in the values and world views brought to the problems by the mentors in each case. In Lethbridge the low concern with formal education reflects the view held by D.H., the founder of WSA, that anyone can learn what one needs to know to get the job done, with or without a degree. In Dungannon much energy has been put into upgrading the formal education of women in the community, regardless of the usefulness of that degree for the community leader. This reflects the leadership style of community leaders we have labeled "familiar outsiders," who have been instrumental in the development and direction of DDC. These two differences in approach perhaps reflect a broader cultural bias in the two nations. The United States sets great store in individual success, and in education as a vehicle to that individual success (Bellah 1985) while Canada has always been a nation with greater concern for the common good (Craig 1982). Canada's people are more likely to look to their government as more benevolent and dependable than are Americans, and are more likely to trust government leadership (Horowitz 1966; Lipset 1970; Arnold and Tigert 1974).

A second difference in the organization of the two self-help groups affects outcomes. WSA and GHFWA have no paid positions or staff and all work as volunteers. Any glory that accrues to the individual has little chance of being translated into economic gain. Although jealousy might arise toward the stars and toward "glory grabbing," in the end all the women have to work either on or off farms to survive economically. In the Dungannon Development Commission, on the other hand, locally recruited leaders have become paid staff members. This means that funds raised either locally or through grant writing go to pay their salaries. As their leadership skills are enhanced and they gain more credibility with funding agencies, their incomes also have a potential for increase. Their leadership becomes an individually motivated career and the danger of funding to promote individual careers becomes a real possibility. In a community of scarce resources, this becomes a serious problem for community support and cohesion. Once again, the two situations reflect cultural differences between the United States and Canada. In the United States, much emphasis is placed on credential attainment through formal education and it is expected that those who attain these credentials will be suitably rewarded (Davis and Moore 1945). Although this approach has been attacked and there is much evidence that equality of education does not translate into equality of opportunity (Jencks 1972, 1979), it still remains a central belief of American folkwisdom, as witnessed by the extremely high university enrollment in the United States compared to Britain (four times higher) and Canada (two times higher). Himmelfarb and Richardson (1979) indicate that most Canadians do not expect individuals in the middle income ranges to be university educated, and have set up their community college system as a terminal degree especially designed for these mid-range occupations.

Both groups have been successful on a variety of levels but their overall direction—and the difficulties they must deal with because of those chosen directions—have led to very different solutions. These directions and the problems they create will be explored below.

LETHBRIDGE AND GOOSE HEAD FARM WOMEN'S ASSOCIATION

Newfoundland is a rocky island off the east coast of Canada. Its soil is extremely thin, very acid, and stoney, requiring both lime and fertilizer to allow farming. Only 0.3 percent of Newfoundland is judged suitable for farm production, and of this, only 7.9 percent is used for commercial production. Nonetheless, this low percentage of land provides 39 percent of all the food consumed in Newfoundland ("Farm Production" n.d.).

To promote agriculture:

> The provincial Government has a program for identifying and preserving the province's scarce agricultural lands. The program first involves detailed study of each region to assess the land capability, present land use, land ownership and social economic status related to agriculture. ("Farm Production" n.d.)

Fourteen "agricultural development areas" have been designated in Newfoundland. Regulations controlling each of these areas have been developed:

> The main intent of the regulations is to preserve and protect the land from conflicting uses that irreversibly remove it from agricultural production. ("Agriculture in Newfoundland and Labrador" n.d., 16)

From reading government pamphlets such as those quoted above, it would appear that the Department of Rural, Agricultural, and Northern Development has an active program of promoting agriculture on the island. Interviews with members of the Goose Head Farm Women's Association present a very different picture.

There are 400 farms in Newfoundland, widely scattered into four main areas, St. Mary's Bay, Lethbridge, Wooddale, and Corner Brook. The farms near Lethbridge are primarily small truck farms—specializing in broccoli, cauliflower, potatoes, and strawberries—and dairy farms. GHFWA has "about twenty members," with five or six (primarily the executive committee) most active. Nine of the twenty members were interviewed in depth through the unstructured focused technique, including all members of the executive committee.

The farm women interviewed saw several problems specific to

agriculture in Newfoundland: (1) the need to fertilize and lime the soil at heavy cost; (2) inadequate hay and fodder for farm animals due to the lack of cleared land (necessitating importation from the mainland); (3) high freight costs (increasing costs of production); (4) limited funding for land clearance; (5) lack of marketing boards for all commodities; (6) widely spaced processing plants and markets (increasing marketing cost); (7) lack of basic inspection and processing plants for some commodities (e.g., there is no red meat inspector in Newfoundland); and (8) moose damage to crops.

Given these problems, why pursue agriculture in Newfoundland? The women interviewed gave two reasons for pursuing agriculture. First, they felt that Newfoundland should be less dependent on the rest of Canada. Second, they believed that farming in Newfoundland can and does generate badly needed employment for nonfarmers. Although farm women were definitely concerned with the farm providing a decent living for themselves and eventually their children and their families (although in only two cases were the farms successful enough not to require off-farm wages), a real concern exists for a better way of life for all Newfoundlanders. This involves Newfoundlanders' awareness of the stereotype of "Newfies" as a backward lazy people, as well as the belief that agriculture can solve unemployment problems. It was felt that the development and expansion of farms would generate more jobs, if only seasonal ones. Currently, if individuals can find work for ten weeks, they can then collect unemployment benefits (UIC). As one Goose Head woman pointed out, "There are a lot of government 'make work' projects so people can collect UIC. If we could expand our greenhouse and root crops we could employ people so they could get UIC when the season's over." Another woman said, "It's a sin, really, seeing young people wandering around looking for work. If we had the market, we could expand and employ them." The president of Goose Head pointed out that farm production generates other farm-related jobs such as washing, grading, and packing produce. These jobs in turn mean people can "buy other things, more trucks, more gas, buy a new chesterfield rather than making the old one do." This, in turn, generates more off-farm jobs. The goal of these women is to improve economic conditions for themselves first, but also for the general community. For this reason they believe that government should support them in their efforts.

Most of the women felt the government was unresponsive to them and their efforts. In fact, there was a wide belief that the government actively ignores or discourages agriculture. They believe that agriculture must be made more visible to both the government and the consuming public. In general, the government was seen as more "blameworthy" than the consumer in its lack of response to the farmers' concerns. The president of Goose Head said she heard "third- or fourth-hand" that a Newfoundland government official at a meeting on Prince Edward Island had stated "there were maybe a few part-time farmers in Newfoundland." Statements such as this were repeated to me with great indignation.

An especially sore point with these women was the fact that Agriculture was part of the Rural Development Department and that this department had little knowledge or interest in agriculture. One woman stated:

> Those people from St. John's come out and they don't have time for us—they don't know one end of a cow from another....
>
> Their attitude is, you get a job [in government], you're getting paid, why do something when it takes less energy to do nothing? If somebody comes in with a bit of energy and wants to get the job done and gets things done, they say, "Slow down buddy, you're going to make everybody look bad."

The number-one concern is to make agriculture visible to government, "to let them know we're here." Although these farm women recognize that farming represents a small percentage of the Newfoundland economy, they feel that united they are "a strong voice and the squeaky wheel gets the grease."

The main policy that these farm women would like to see government enact is some method for encouraging Newfoundlanders' to "buy Newfoundland," that is, home-produced agricultural products. Several specific policies, some hotly debated, were suggested to promote agriculture and this buy-Newfoundland policy. These included: (1) a law mandating that suppliers first purchase Newfoundland commodities so long as a commercial quantity of the commodity exists on the island; (2) the subsidizing of freight rates on items such as hay that are production related, thus using the higher freight on off-island food as a tariff; (3) higher subsidies for clearing arable land; (4) doing away with the leasing of land and a return to land grants; (5) the establishment of a Department of Regional Economic Expansion (DREE) agreement with the federal government; and (6) UIC for farmers and their families during the off-season—a benefit that fisherpersons and their families now enjoy.

Clearly, these women have defined their economic problems as primarily political in nature. They see the solutions as political and have organized specifically for political action.

GOOSE HEAD FARM WOMEN'S ASSOCIATION AND
WOMEN FOR THE SURVIVAL OF AGRICULTURE:
HISTORY AND ACTIVITIES

The Goose Head Farm Women's Association was formed in Lethbridge, Newfoundland, in 1984. This group formed in response to a felt need on the part of farm women in the area for a higher visibility of farming and farm issues in Newfoundland. The president of the GHFWA stated, "We're not a women's organization and we are not involved in women's issues. We are a farm organization." Why form a women's farm organization? Responses from the women in GHFWA indicated that they felt the men had tried but "didn't make much headway with it." Several reasons were offered for this. First, the men were felt to be already overburdened with farm work and therefore had little time to devote to a farm organization. Second, the women had more experience with organizations and groups such as PTA, the church, Girl Guides, and figure skating competition. Third, women were regarded as more likely to share their problems "over tea" and not see it as a threat to their abilities and egos if they disclosed problems to others. Fourth, it was believed that the men were more likely to fight among themselves.

GHFWA started with five or six women and expanded to about twenty active members. The initial impetus came from the combined efforts of the local Agricultural Representative (a woman) and one of the current executive members who had attended a province-wide meeting of Women for the Survival of Agriculture, on Prince Edward Island, a group that GHFWA is modeled on and loosely affiliated with. Since its inception, the group has sponsored workshops on public speaking, farm management, and estate management. These skills are seen as necessary to build credibility when representing farm interests to urban government officials and the public. They participated in the Agricultural Field Days in 1984 and 1985 and sponsored the first ox pull on the island. They sponsored their own provincial farm women's conference in Gander in May 1985. As a result of this conference, three other farm women's groups were initiated on the island. At the time of the interviews, their main concern was to find sponsors in order to send a delegation to the Second Nation Farm Women's Conference on Prince Edward Island in November 1985. It was very important to these women that they be represented at the conference so that Canada "would know about them."

Women for the Survival of Agriculture, the group that GHFWA is loosely affiliated with, was formed in Winchester, Ontario, in the mid-1970s to meet the incipient farm crisis being felt throughout North America. GHFWA models itself along the guidelines set by

WSA, which encourage self-education in order to educate the government and the public. D.H., the "mother" and primary organizer of WSA—also interviewed in the summer of 1985—firmly believes that anyone can learn what is needed to be politically active; she believes in empowerment, and encourages each group to educate itself to its own specific agricultural needs and government. D.H. was the guiding light of the group for its first ten years, and only in the mid-1980s did she step down as president. Her main concern has been to develop credibility in the eyes of the nonagricultural community. This credibility includes: (1) knowing the facts, data, and issues (and to that end, WSA or its affiliates have initiated several sophisticated studies of farm issues); (2) having the ability to speak publicly; (3) developing small group leadership skills; and (4) presenting a positive and sophisticated image in dealing with the public. Although D.H. encourages these skills in all group members, she admits that she and others select and "groom" women as leaders for the group—women who will be particularly effective. This grooming includes "everything"—general grooming, clothing style, body language, and intonation of voice. Not only is it believed that the women must know their stuff, but that they also must appear credible to the urban eye and ear. D.H. has been both the prime motivator and the mentor of this group and its affiliates, and her philosophy of creating effective lobbyists for agriculture has been incorporated into these groups.

This approach *has* stressed education, but not in the sense of acquiring formal degrees or credentials. Each winter—the off-season for farmers—WSA sponsors workshops through local community colleges that will provide the specific skills farm women need. Most of these courses are provided by professionals but are set up to meet the stated needs of local women. For example, with regard to the crucial problem of self-presentation, in one course the women were videotaped while making a speech. This tape was then criticized, as one woman put it, "on everything," including tone of voice, use of language, style of delivery, body stance, gestures, eye contact, as well as general grooming. Other skills contracted for include courses on estate and farm management, bookkeeping, home computers, and leadership skills.

This approach to the problem tends to encourage individual women to empower themselves to act effectively in their community and their government. One of the main impacts of GHFWA membership the women reported was that they now had more self-confidence and did not feel inferior to their urban sisters—a very sore point with most farm women ("Farm Women through the Eyes of Their City Sisters" 1985). As one woman stated, "We want to let everyone know we're here and we're not stupid. Everyone has a negative image of the farm woman as too dumb to do anything else, that they have manure on their shoes." The president of Goose Head stated, "It surprises people we can get on television and speak the way we do and I say, 'Oh, my dear, you'd be surprised what we can do!'" As one dairy farm woman stated, "There's a lot more to farming than shoveling shit." These women have organized and educated themselves to be effective lobbyists for agriculture and through this have empowered themselves. This approach reflects the woman who is the driving force behind WSA and represents her style. It is clear that this stress on self-empowerment through self-education reflects the values and world view of D.H., the mentor of WSA and its affiliates.

D.H. dedicated more than ten years to the establishment and development of WSA in Canada, and from that she earned nothing. This does not mean that WSA has not sought funding. On the contrary, it has been very active in obtaining government grants and support from sponsors in the private sector. In all but limited situations, this funding has gone to group projects such as leadership conferences, province and national farm women's conferences, and studies on the plight of agriculture and the farm woman. Funding for the individual is obtained only to defray expenses when traveling for the group. Often this means that individual WSA members must canvas sponsors to obtain this funding. D.H. herself estimates she has donated more than $100,000 of her time to the group. Her own income comes from her husband's off-farm job, the farm, and a column she writes for a farm magazine, plus incidental income from serving on government commissions. D.H. and other leaders in WSA and GHFWA see themselves as farm women first and agricultural lobbyists second. Although they are proud of their accomplishments, they do not think of these activities as a career or as an income opportunity.

DUNGANNON AND THE "FAMILIAR OUTSIDER"

Until the 1950s, Dungannon had been a thriving rural community. Now it has dwindled to a village of about 340 people with few commercial establishments. Lying on the banks of the Clinch River and along the route of the Norfolk and Western Railway, it was a natural center for the exchange of freight for coal and a terminal for rail passengers. At one time it had its own switchyard, Miller Yard, and was the site of a prison and the regional boarding high school, and was the source of electric power for the region, due to its river-driven turbine. Although not a coalmining community itself, Dungannon had been dependent on coal—and before that, logging—in its role as a transportation center. With the demise of coal in the 1920s and the increased dependence on highway transportation in the 1950s, Dungannon slowly reverted to a combined economy of hunting and gathering, subsistence farming, cash cropping of tobacco, and intermittent employment in the secondary labor force either at the local sewing factory or in the nearby cities of Gate City, Kingsport, or Bristol. A typical family might see very little "cash-money" and be only marginally dependent on it for taxes and utilities, especially if living on inherited family property. Currently, men hunt out of season in order to stock home freezers with meat. Women and children gather wild berries both for home use and preservation and also to sell to city people, earning as much as $40 to $80 per week in season. Gardens are large and a good deal of food is "put up." One interviewee stated that she cans around 1,500 quarts of food every summer. Those who have tobacco allotments grow tobacco for cash, but even this reliable source of income has declined since 1980, with a 25 percent decrease in allotments and a lower price per pound. In the 1950s many community members left the region (as was common throughout Central Appalachia) for Northern urban centers. Some found work in the textile mills and sewing factories that sprang up in the rural South after World War II. In Dungannon, the main employer was a small sewing factory run by a "New York Jew." The factory was nonunion, paid by piecework, and employed about 100 women from the community. Dungannon's history parallels that of much of Central Appalachia—starting with a subsistence barter economy prior to the 1880s, moving to a wage economy between 1880 and 1930, with a slow deterioration into a mixed economy from then on (Eller 1982; Daley and Kobak 1990).

After the John F. Kennedy presidential campaign and during the subsequent War on Poverty, the spotlight shone on Central Appalachia and many well-educated and well-meaning "outlanders" flocked to the region to "help" (Carawan and Carawan 1986). The Appalachian Regional Commission was formed to help funnel federal money into the region, especially to provide a badly needed infrastructure. In theory, this infrastructure was to encourage economic investment and diversification, but in practice, it has not. Despite all these efforts, Central Appalachia—especially the southwestern counties of Virginia and the eastern counties of Kentucky—have remained among the poorest counties in the United States. Trends in the 1980s indicated an abandonment of programs in the region and a withdrawal of federal funding (Caudill 1982).

Part of the immigration of well-educated newcomers into the region during the 1960s was a group of people who stayed in the region, bought up land, built or refurbished homes, and became part of the community. We have identified these people as "familiar outsiders" (Daley and Kobak 1990)—people who became part of Appalachian communities and wanted to help those communities while maintaining extensive social, economic, and cultural links to the outside world.

In Dungannon we identified at least four "familiar outsiders." These outsiders do not have an overt agenda to change the mountains, nor do they have a stereotypical preconception of mountain people as backward and lazy. As a result, they were more likely to be welcomed into the community than were former "missionaries," and were more likely to be accepted as community members. Similarly, the outsider is likely to see himself or herself as merely "helping" the community and individuals to realize their own potential. These outsiders tend to deny their role as reformers, which in fact they are, and in doing so, they deny their own power and responsibility in the community. It is clear from interviews that these outsiders have a covert unarticulated agenda—a conceptualization of how they would like mountain life to be lived and how they would like to live their own lives in the mountains.

The familiar outsider has come into the mountains to "escape" the emphasis that the dominant culture places on success—especially material success and individualism—and to find a life of community and service and commitment. But as Bellah and his co-authors in *Habits of the Heart* (1985) indicated, our culture encourages either an attitude of taking care of "number one" or the formation of special interest groups around individual needs. Rather than being committed to a community's set of values, more and more individuals do "what is right for them" or "what feels right." The standard of evaluation is the individual, not the group nor an abstract principle. But there are no easy mechanisms for exchanging or replacing the "first language" of our historical cultural heritage—namely, radical individualism—with a "second language" of community, service, and commitment. The familiar outsider does wish to replace this radical individualism, this first language, with a sense of community, the second language, but they are products of their culture and have neither fully articulated this transformation to themselves nor have they sought out mechanisms for this transformation. In their relationship to the community, they tend to fall back, through lack of alternatives, on mechanisms and techniques from the dominant culture that perpetuate some of the very behaviors they wish to escape or change.

The familiar outsider has several characteristics that make them distinct from indigenous populations. First, they are from outside the region. Second, they are well educated, having advanced degrees beyond the bachelor level. Third, they are not economically dependent on jobs within the community for their livelihoods. Fourth, they all are motivated to stay in the mountains in order to be part of the community. These outsiders are both part of the community and not. For example, all the familiar outsiders travel extensively both within the United States and in foreign countries. Their homes are different both in having more modern conveniences—such as jacuzzis, home computers, and extensive stereo systems—and in style, with custom-built rooms and additions as well as unique furnishings and artwork. Despite these obvious differences, the familiar outsiders do not flaunt their economic independence in their daily lives. All lead lives that are, to them, "just like" those of their neighbors. They plant gardens, put up food for the winter, go to the local church, and attend local community social functions. They are also willing to help with local economic development efforts. From their point of view, they *are* creating the second language of community and service and commitment. To the indigenous population, however, it does not seem that these people are "in the same boat" as themselves. In fact, one community member went so far as to suggest, that if these people *were* in the same boat as everyone else, then the proposed sewing factory that the DDC is currently working on would already be a reality.

THE DEVELOPMENT OF THE DUNGANNON DEVELOPMENT COMMISSION AND THE ROLE OF THE "FAMILIAR OUTSIDER"

In the summer of 1986, all the paid staff of DDC, the board of DDC, plus community leaders and outside technical consultants associated with DDC were interviewed (18 individuals), using the unstructured focused interview. These interviews provide both an oral history of DDC and a subjective interpretation of "what was going on." From the above discussion of the familiar outsider, it would appear that the familiar outsider would be the one to initiate and lead the development of the Dungannon Development Commission. This assumption would overlook the fact that the indigenous community members had their own agenda and saw the familiar outsider as a resource in realizing that agenda (Daley and Kobak 1990). The DDC was initiated and developed through the conjoint needs and desires of both the community members and familiar outsiders. For example:

> C.N. [a community member] and several other women kept talking about getting that depot, getting the train station for the community, for the community center and getting the railroad company to give them that. So she latches onto A.L. [a familiar outsider] and uses A.L. to do stuff that she wants done and A.L. is very eager to be used that way.

However, due to their greater sense of empowerment and their greater access to resources, the familiar outsiders played a mentor role both in defining the problems and how these problems were to be handled. They also played mentor roles in that they recruited and "trained" indigenous community members for staff positions in the DDC. The familiar outsiders tended to define the problems and solutions in the first language of radical individualism rather than community involvement, despite their belief that they were doing otherwise. Solutions tended to be individualistic solutions and tended to promote individual careers.

DDC was initiated by the community's Women's Club in 1979 to deal with the loss of jobs created by the bankruptcy and burning of the Apollo Sewing Factory, the single industry in the town. Late in the 1970s, A.L. had worked with other community leaders to form the Women's Club as a community service organization. The group had formed to obtain the abandoned railway depot that was being offered by the railway as a community center. The women formed the organization because the town council—made up predominately of men—had maintained it would be impossible to obtain the $8,000 needed to move and refurbish the building. The railway company gave the women a year to raise the money. This they successfully did with A.L. as president of the Women's Club. After the building was moved, A.L. encouraged the club to apply for a CETA grant to both employ local people and to refurbish the Depot, as it was called. This project was also successful. A.L. had also helped the community successfully build and develop its own health clinic, and she was now approached by the town to help obtain funding for a new water system. Due to this activity she became town manager. In these two roles—as president of the Women's Club and as town manager—she was approached by women who worked at the sewing factory and asked to deal with their labor problems. This was not surprising. As another outsider stated, "She's running Dungannon, just about." A.L. called a meeting to discuss the problems at the sewing factory; out of this, the Dungannon Development Commission was born—a nonprofit corporation with A.L. as chair of the board. The same outsider stated that "it [DDC] was probably A.L.'s idea because she had formed something similar to that [elsewhere] in Appalachia."

Although A.L. was not the only familiar outsider who was active in helping develop the DDC, she clearly had a key role. This role tended to have very clear individualistic rewards for her, both as a job (town manager) and as a source of personal power and influence (her executive positions on both the Women's Club board and the DDC). Other familiar outsiders also profited, however, in how they formed the goals of the DDC. One major thrust of the organization was to upgrade the levels of education in the community. In fact, two of the four paid staff members dealt almost exclusively with education. The DDC encouraged the local community college to offer classes at the Depot in order that townspeople could obtain everything—from G.E.D.s to Associate of Arts (A.A.) degrees—without the long commute to the community college. It is obvious that this helped the people of Dungannon—particularly the women—who were the primary consumers of the course offerings. First, the program benefited these women in that it provided them with some income through Pell grants. For one woman, the only money in her family of four was the $35 per week she earned at work-study. Second, several community women received both a G.E.D. and an A.A. degree. One woman went from less than an eighth grade education to an A.A. degree in two years and then developed a community literacy program through the DDC. Third, the classes led to another benefit for these women, employment as staff at the DDC. All paid staff members had gone through the DDC's educational program. And this points to a benefit to the familiar outsiders. Three of the four familiar outsiders taught in the DDC's educational program. This not only provided them with income and enhanced their careers but it also made them more visible as mentors in the community and gave them a forum to shape the beliefs, values, and attitudes of potential DDC staff members.

At the time of the interviews in the summer of 1986, the DDC had accomplished a great deal, including getting a new town hall, firehouse, and elementary school, and implementing the initial steps of establishing a new sewing factory, the Phoenix. From the townspeople's point of view, the factory would be their most important achievement because it would re-employ the 100 women left out of work by the demise of the Apollo. Several men who had shown little interest in other projects were very active in offering their support for this project. The familiar outsiders, on the other hand, seemed less enthusiastic and one stated—which seemed to be the attitude of all four—that, "Phoenix, frankly, is not a big interest of mine, whether there's a factory or not." Whether their lack of interest was causing problems or not, the project had been floundering. A hired technical assistant saw the situation as very confused and disorganized; it was only through her efforts and the efforts of the former manager of the sewing factory that the project had gotten as far as it had in the summer of 1986. At that time the building was going up and was scheduled to be completed by November. But funding—not only for the factory, but to pay the DDC staff—was drying up, and there was little hope among both staff and board members that the capital for a factory could ever be acquired. Outside technical assistants who had been called in to deal with various specific problems, both organizational and technical, were highly critical of how funds had been handled, how inadequate the planning had been, and how poorly the board and staff functioned together. The president of the board called the project an "awful mess" and felt there was no way out of the situation. Other board members echoed these sentiments, and accusations of nepotism and mismanagement were made. The community itself had divided into various camps as to "what was going on" and "who was getting their unfair share." Several felt that A.L., who had resigned all her positions in Dungannon to pursue a career as a therapist, had "seduced and abandoned them," while most felt that if she were to "come back," she could "straighten things out."

How had this happened? How had a community that had progressed so far fallen apart so badly? How was it that the very clearly excellent skills of the familiar outsiders who had initiated these projects had not been translated into workable skills for the staff they had mentored? From the interviews, it can be concluded that a major cause of the current problems was the definition of Dungannon's main problem as lack of formal educational credentials and the definition of the solution as individual career development through the DDC.

As indicated above, the familiar outsiders tended to be well-educated individuals who enhanced their own personal careers through community service. And despite their commitment to the community, they tended to develop individualistic solutions. As mentors they tended to model the individuals they recruited from the community after themselves, to encourage these women to obtain formal educational credentials and convert these credentials into careers. A.L., for example, encouraged N.R. to become a leader. N.R. stated:

> She [A.L.] taught potential leaders. She saw potential leaders in the people themselves. I was one of those people. I did not know what she was doing until she had done it....Had she not seen the potential in me, I probably would not be sitting here today....Changed my life. Now, I develop potential leaders myself....I train people myself....I delegate a lot of responsibility.

As Daley and Kobak (1990) point out, this new local leader has the personal support and encouragement of her mentor to obtain credentials and further her career, but she does not have access to the technical skills and resources that the familiar outsider possesses. It appears that the familiar outsiders—whose own expertise and sense of empowerment have come from a variety of sources in addition to their own formal education, including family background and class of origin (Jencks 1972; 1979)—have assumed that it *is* their credentials that give them this expertise and empowerment. Rather, it is the other way around; it is their class of origin and their family background that has given them their expertise and sense of empowerment, which in turn has given them their credentials. One individual who had offered technical assistance pointed out that the familiar outsiders always feel that everything will turn out for the best, while the townspeople tend to fear the worst. This reflects class of origin. The familiar outsiders come from upper middle class homes where things generally do turn out. Even when there is a tragedy, money and influence can ameliorate the pain inflicted. For poor people living constantly on the edge, things rarely turn out. As this interviewee pointed out, this tends to create different feelings of empowerment, different feelings about what you can expect from life and what you can accomplish. The familiar outsiders assume that their credentials empower them and assume that when the townspeople acquire credentials, they are similarly empowered.

This is not necessarily the case. For example, the DDC had taken out a loan, using some land as collateral. Every year they paid only the interest on the loan at the inflationary rates of the late 1970s and rolled over the loan. When an outside technical assistant asked why the loan had not been renegotiated, the staff both lacked the knowledge that this was possible but also did not feel they had the power—the "right"—to approach the bank with such a suggestion. This does not show lack of credentials, but rather, lack of experience with banks and a conception of them as all-powerful institutions.

Furthermore, the familiar outsiders had encouraged the staff to make the DDC their career. In a very real sense the DDC now functions in a large part to keep these women employed. Funding of staff comes first and completion of projects has become a second concern. The board president in 1986—a familiar outsider—saw nothing wrong with this. For example, she commented that it was the staff's job to obtain funding and part of that was to fund themselves:

> If someone says your goal [funding yourself] is less important—we're going to let your salary run out—that's just not how you do it around here....Well, what's he going to eat in the meantime? Is he going to write his own proposal?

Another familiar outsider stated that, although Dungannon did not have enough jobs to absorb more workers with A.A. degrees, nonetheless the A.A. program should continue because grants could be written to provide funding for the students' employment:

Some of this stuff could be funded by tax money I think, like some of the education programs....So in a sense you're getting into the set of redistribution of monies in the same way that money comes in to pay schoolteachers and health workers and things like that.

The familiar outsiders see nothing wrong with perpetually funding oneself through grant writing and tax-free institutions because they have promoted their own careers through various nonprofit organizations such as FOCIS (Federation of Communities in Service), CREC, Appalshop, and Highlander Educational Center. In fact, academic backgrounds tend to encourage this kind of career building.

In summary, the familiar outsiders were recruited by local community members to deal with local economic problems. They were seen by the community as people with resources and abilities that the community could use. But the familiar outsiders—because of their own cultural background—were instrumental in defining and resolving economic problems in individualistic ways. Although the problems they solved undoubtedly benefited the community as a whole, the mechanisms for solving those problems stressed individualistic solutions, relying heavily on attainment of formal credentials and the creation of individual stars. Thus, individual careers become the covert but nonetheless most salient priority. The mentors did not intentionally choose an individualistic approach. Rather, they simply modeled new indigenous leaders along lines that reflected their own success patterns. If the Phoenix sewing factory ever comes into existence, the staff women of the DDC—all, at one time, factory workers—have no intention of working in it, no matter how steady the pay.

SUMMARY AND CONCLUSION

From the above discussion it is clear that the cultural background, education, and self-perception of the mentor affects how the mentor defines and decides to how solve the problem. In Canada, the belief on the part of the leaders of WSA that it is the government's responsibility to promote the welfare of its citizens created a political definition of the problem in Lethbridge. This combined with their own experiences led them to develop a solution that created dedicated and effective political lobbyists. In this solution, education was a key factor, but not formal education in the sense of attaining credentials. Rather, the emphasis lay on providing specific skills that would both create effective political actors and at the same time empower the individuals. Since these individuals were all volunteers, none could make her activities into a career except outside the organization. Stars did emerge in the organization, and there was jealousy. But the jealousy was limited to feeling that some people like to "grab the limelight" and did not become the basis for believing that individuals were subverting the organization to their own ends.

In Dungannon, however, it seems that the familiar outsider mentored by encouraging the new local leaders to follow in their own (mentor's) footsteps, without empowering them. This rested in the familiar outsiders' belief in the efficacy of a formal education and the importance of developing individual careers. As we have seen, this did not develop empowerment and in fact created staff members who lacked the resources or skills to get the job done and who therefore came to rely heavily on others—especially paid and volunteer outside technical assistance. The DDC accomplished its goal as long as the familiar outsider was involved and had the resources and skills necessary for accomplishing those goals. When familiar outsiders withdrew their support or when their interest declined, the weakness of their dependence on formal education to empower emerged.

From the analysis it can be concluded that the differences in solving economic problems between Lethbridge and Dungannon do not merely reflect differences in the personalities of the mentors, but in a real sense reflect a difference in cultural backgrounds of Canadians and Americans. Canada—although generally seen as more conservative than the United States—is much more likely to define problems in terms of the public good and the responsibility of government to promote that good. On the other hand, the United States—although generally seen as more liberal—is much more likely to see social and economic problems as individual responsibilities, and to encourage individual solutions. The most common approach tends to assume that if we upgrade individuals' educational levels, they can solve the problems for themselves.

The implications of these findings are that mentors shape groups but also that cultures shape mentors. Further research is necessary to examine the mechanisms used by mentors in defining problems, in recruiting leaders, and in training leaders, and how these mechanisms impact on the effectiveness of the group. This research would be of great practical value to all community action groups.

■ 6 ■

Regional Resurgence: The Case of Industrial Catalonia in Spain

Glenn A. Mitchell

Catalonia in northeastern Spain has, like Appalachia, emerged as a minority region within a modern industrial nation-state. It has a distinct economy, language, and cultural identity, but has lacked political control. Comparing Catalonia with Appalachia provides a perspective on the long historical political and economic processes that structure minority regions. It also provides a model of a successful grassroots movement for regional political and cultural autonomy and economic redevelopment, led by a coalition of workers, intellectuals, and business people.

While Appalachia is primarily rural and contrasts with the urban and industrial character of Catalonia, the minority positions they both have within their respective states points to the fundamentally political nature of regional issues everywhere. At the same time, the urban industrial base of Catalonia does not fit Third World models of internal colonialism versus regional self-sufficiency that have been used to analyze Appalachia. Regional economies are interdependent within the modern global economy, and international perspectives are necessary for developing strategies for the future.

Changes in the world economy since 1970 have restructured the traditional textile economy of Catalonia, as they have Appalachia's coal and textiles industries, leaving high local unemployment and cuts in social services. Yet in the midst of the global crises of the 1970s Catalonia became the center of a successful movement to transform the Spanish state from a dictatorship into a democracy, and to gain regional autonomy and self-determination. It has been able to support its unique language and cultural heritage and develop local strategies for redevelopment of the region's economy.

THE ORIGINS OF CATALAN CULTURAL IDENTITY

The identity of a region is defined by its political and economic role in history. As the particular modes of production of its economic base develop over time, different classes, elites, and subordinated groups—within the region and outside—come into conflict over political control of the economy and society and determine the form of the state. It is through these conflicts that the region becomes ideologically defined for those inside and outside the region.

The Economic Formation of Regional Culture

Catalonia today is a well-defined economic, political, and cultural region in the northeastern corner of the Iberian Peninsula, centered on the regional capital of Barcelona. It covers almost 32,000 square kilometers (12,500 square miles) with a population of six million. Its somewhat triangular shape is bounded on the north by the border with France along the Pyrenees Mountains, on the southeast by the Mediterranean Sea, and on the west by roughly the Segre and lower Ebre river valleys. The region is integrated by river valleys that drain southward from the Pyrenees into the Mediterranean. Since prehistoric times, they have served as routes for early settlement, transhumance, and trade. They also provided a base for industrial development, tying limited coal, iron, and other minerals—and subsequently, hydroelectric power—from the mountains, together with agriculture from the valleys, into ports along the Mediterranean, and creating an integrated region centered on the metropolitan capital of Barcelona.

The modern identity of Catalonia has its origins in the historical commercial and industrial character of its economy, and in its conflict with the central Spanish state. Catalonia first arose as a culturally distinct region in the 13th century. It was a medieval trading center in the western Mediterranean with a distinct Romance language, Catalan, which emerged out of the Latin of the Roman empire. Catalonia, like other regions in Europe, then declined in the early modern period. It was subordinated under the hegemony of the rising Spanish empire. With the discovery of the New World and the shift of world trade from the Mediterranean to the Atlantic, Catalonia's economy declined. The New World was claimed for Castile, the core region of the emerging Spanish state (Hechter and Brustein 1980); and Catalonia was excluded from the colonial trade. Catalonia reemerged however with industrial capitalism, which grew out of its commercial agriculture of wine and grains in the 18th century (Vilar 1962).

By the mid-19th century, the region was one of the centers of the textile industry in Europe, and a true industrial bourgeoisie and proletariat had formed. The region became defined by a typical bourgeois nationalism. This was led by a conservative high bourgeoisie of large industrialists in conflict with the Spanish state over tariffs to protect their domestic industrial markets. Catalans identified themselves with their distinct Catalan language and their *seny*, their practical common sense, which reflected their commercial and manufacturing way of life. Popular cultural consciousness was defined and expressed through folk dance associations, poetry, and modernist architecture.

Increasing class conflict between the bourgeoisie and anarchist workers by the end of the 19th century undermined the conservative nationalism of the high bourgeoisie. The petty bourgeoisie of small business people, professionals, and intellectuals then led a new, left-republican, Catalan nationalism. In alliance with the socialist and anarchist working class, it challenged the existing social order of growing inequality and repression by the state and called for radical change and regional autonomy.

Appalachia by comparison is defined by its mountain character, with the high ranges and valleys running north and south tying it into industrial centers in the Northeastern United States, but cutting off east-west communication that might integrate the region. While Appalachian culture does not have as deep roots in its present location as European regions do, what is considered contemporary Appalachian culture also emerged with modern capitalism in the 18th century as the rural populations in the semi-periphery of Europe were dislocated by increasing commercialization and industrialization, and emigrated to North America. Arriving from Scotland and Germany through Philadelphia, they settled southward along the Great Valley of the Appalachian range, and in the process integrated their own traditions and survival strategies with those of the colonial English and Native Americans into what is called traditional Appalachian culture. It is an upland frontier agrarian subsistence base organized through strong values of self-reliance and family solidarity (Zelinsky 1973).

As in Catalonia, it was also late-19th-century industrialization that defined the current role of Appalachian regional culture within the larger political economy of the United States. Unlike Catalonia, Appalachia became a rural periphery providing primary resources and cheap labor for urban industrial centers outside the region. The lumber and mining industries extracted resources for construction and steel production elsewhere. Textiles and tobacco production expanded into the mountains from centers in North Carolina and South

Carolina. Finally, with the global economic boom following World War II, Appalachians left the mountains in massive numbers and provided the labor for industrial centers in the Midwest. Appalachian class relations have been defined by its extractive industries, with local subsistence farmers, miners, and lumbercutters in conflict with external elites, the large outside land and mine owners, and their local agents over control of land and exploitation (Eller 1982). Appalachian culture became defined through its forms of resistance to outside control, its family and community solidarity, and its self-reliance.

The Politics of Regional Definition by the State

The political context that defined Catalonia was a product of the form of economic development outside the region—of Spain as a whole—which determined the form of the Spanish state. In the 19th century, Spain recovered from the collapse of its former empire with the rise of export agriculture. Its economy was based on a mode of production centered on commercial agriculture in such products as sherry, which was organized through free trade, foreign investment, and state development projects in railroads and irrigation. The dominant class was an agrarian bourgeoisie with aristocratic titles, supported by a dependent, bureaucratic middle class of lawyers and clerks, over a subordinated mass of poor peasants and landless agricultural workers (Linz and Miguel 1966; Carr 1966).

With this base, Spain emerged as a modern state with a typical authoritarian form of government (Moore 1966; Hechter and Brustein 1980). Labor was controlled repressively and economic development was carried out from above through the state. Weak democratic reforms did not confront the structural changes necessary to accommodate a changing economy and society, so control of labor and regional nationalism remained repressive.

After a decade of dictatorship in the 1920s, an electoral alliance of working class anarchists and socialists, and bourgeois left-republicans and regional nationalists, succeeded in forming the Second Republic in 1931. But in the midst of world economic crisis, social and political conflict became increasingly polarized and led to the military uprising of the right and the Spanish Civil War from 1936 to 1939.

Under the Franco dictatorship that followed, the traditional authoritarian form of the state—with its centralized role in economic development and social control—continued for almost 40 years until 1976. The state built irrigation and hydroelectric projects, set up government-run industries in everything from automobiles to fertilizers, and regulated production and trade. Fascist-styled, government-run syndicates or vertical unions of both management and workers controlled the society. Free unions, independent political associations, strikes, and demonstrations were illegal.

In Catalonia, development in textiles, machinery, and construction in the 1950s and 1960s brought an economic boom and labor migration into the region. Migration came primarily from Andalusia, the region of large estates and poverty in the south. Small Catalan towns became working class suburbs of Barcelona, the regional capital. Neighboring cities such as Terrassa and Sabadell were surrounded by immigrant barrios cut off socially and culturally from their middle class Catalan centers. The class structure became ethnically divided by language and custom between a Catalan bourgeoisie and an Andalusian proletariat, and class and ethnic conflict intensified. The city of Terrassa, for example—located about 30 kilometers from Barcelona and specialized in wool textiles—grew from 58,800 in 1950 to 118,000 in 1965 and 165,000 in 1975, with the greatest immigration between 1960 and 1965. Roughly three-fourths of its population was working class, mainly from Andalusia.

The structural problem of administering this rapidly changing industrial society through a centrally regulated state led to the intensification of the worker's and regional nationalist movements, and a united democratic opposition (Maravall 1973). With economic recovery, growing social problems, and continued repression, Catalan aspirations for political autonomy increased. A cultural movement of Catalan intellectuals promoted the public use of the language in literature and drama, and gave birth to the *Nova Cançó* movement of Catalan protest songs. A communist and socialist worker's movement organized toward free unions in illegal shop floor Workers' Commissions. Workers faced price inflation relative to wages, changes in tasks and wages with specialization and new industries, and the lack of free unions to negotiate them (Maravall 1973). The bourgeoisie opposed the regulation of trade and investment and the appropriation of banking capital for state development projects outside the region. Cities such as Terrassa had strong grassroots opposition movements. Terrassa has a reputation going back to the Spanish Civil War of being a well-organized and militant "red" city, with strong working class unions and neighborhood associations, and progressive middle class Catalanist cultural and political organizations.

A regional coalition, the Catalan Assembly, was formed in 1971 to represent all sectors of the opposition, including left and center political parties, unions, local assemblies (including the Democratic Assembly of Terrassa), and neighborhood, professional, social, and church associations in a common program for democracy and regional autonomy. It was the mechanism for an alliance between the movements of the Catalan middle class and the workers. The Assembly coordinated issue campaigns, demonstrations, and other activities through its common program for amnesty, liberty, and autonomy. Its success served as a model for other coalitions across Spain.

Through this process, Catalonia became defined as a geographic region with a historically distinct language and culture, a prosperous industrial economy, and a political tradition of democratic negotiation and contract and free expression, which had been subjugated by a decadent and repressive Castilian state. This conception included native Catalans and immigrant Andalusians—the bourgeoisie and workers—as having common economic and political interests against the state. The Catalan language was used to define the cultural boundary between the region and the rest of the state. While language divided the native middle class and the immigrant workers with class-based ethnic tension, it was seen as something that could be learned, so that the immigrants could be assimilated into the region's historical culture.

In 1975, economic and political conflicts converged. There was a conjuncture of the world economic crisis of 1973–1974 and the political crisis with the death of General Francisco Franco in November 1975. Inflation was around 25 percent, unemployment was high, and Franco's death opened a moment for change. In Terrassa, for example, not only was the boom in wool textiles crashing, but it was in permanent crisis because of competition from synthetics and Third World textiles development. There were waves of coordinated strikes and demonstrations against the government. Terrassa's opposition coalition led to early local recognition and support for the unions, Communist Party rallies, official use of Catalan in the city council, and commemoration of the Catalan national day within the year after Franco's death.

Over the ten years following Franco's death, Spain as a whole went through a process of democratic transformation and continued political and economic crisis. Because of the strength of the opposition movement and the desire of the elite to integrate Spain into the European Community, an official "opening" to political change began in 1976. Municipal elections were held in 1977 and a new democratic constitution that included recognition of regional autonomy was established in 1978. In 1979 a statute of autonomy for Catalonia was approved and a Catalan parliament was elected in 1980. Catalonia, along with all other regions of Spain, is now officially an autonomous community, with increased local control in important areas of regional infrastructure. There is local control in planning, development, and education, but not taxation. Catalans are still

Spanish citizens in affairs of state and civil rights, but regional language, cultural, and other social differences are recognized.

The nature of the Spanish state has changed; but only in 1982 was democracy tested by a true change of government when Socialists won the elections and replaced the government party, which had continued in power since Franco's death.

In Catalonia, the regional government is in the hands of the center-right, Catalan nationalist party, whose main goal has been to reclaim Catalan economic and cultural autonomy. The two most important changes it has pursued are the normalization of the use of Catalan as an official public language, and the shift of government resources to control by the regional government. It has promoted regional economic development, and supported Catalan culture through restoration of historic sites and support for folklore and contemporary artists. This shifts resources to the business and cultural groups that provided the basis for the middle class Catalan movement.

In comparison, Appalachia has not been able to gain greater regional political control through the economic and political changes affecting it. Appalachia is divided by the boundaries of local states whose power is centered outside the region in lowland areas. Regional development has come from urban industrial centers outside, whether through private capital in mining, timber, or textiles, or through government projects such as the Tennessee Valley Authority or the Appalachian Regional Commission. Cultural identity too has been defined by outsiders, whether local color writers, missionaries and settlement schools, or the folk revival movement (Whisnant 1983).

What Appalachia shares with Catalonia is that the form of the modern state and the political role of the region were both determined through civil wars. But where the outcome in Spain was an agricultural-based state that dominated an industrial region, in the southern Appalachians it was an industrial-based state that dominated the agricultural South. Appalachia itself was divided by the conflict by its ties to state governments based on the southern plantation economy, and its origins and economic ties to the Northeast. The consequence was a political suppression of the region. While democratic forms of local government, unions, and other associations developed in the U.S. industrial and agricultural centers of the Northeast and Midwest, the repression of the South under Reconstruction and continued authoritarian forms of local control of rural communities restricted development of indigenous political organizations able to challenge the form of development (Moore 1966). Split between North and South, Appalachia was politically isolated. With a lack of local control and middle class leadership, the grassroots regional development that occurred in Catalonia was not possible. More local forms of family and community resistance were necessary.

CONFRONTING AN ECONOMIC CRISES

The restructuring of the global economy with shifts in the patterns of industrialization and international division of labor since the 1960s has confronted local regions with fundamental change in their modes of production. Initiatives to deal with local problems have had to develop international perspectives. In Catalonia the grassroots mobilization for democracy and increased regional autonomy provided a mechanism to address the economic problems facing the region's declining textile industry. Its coalition strategies provide a useful model for other regions, and point out the important role of politics and national policies in confronting local economic problems such as those faced in Appalachia.

ORIGINS OF THE CRISIS

In the 1950s and 1960s the economy of Catalonia took off on a massive scale as Spain as a whole recovered from the depression and civil war of the 1930s and became an industrial economy for the first time. As an industrial region, Catalonia boomed with production of everyday clothes and cloth for the Spanish market and for Northern Europe. At the peak of the boom from 1970 to 1972, over 76 percent of the active population in Terrassa was in manufacturing, 49 percent in textiles (according to the 1970 census).

Despite some large companies, small-scale production predominated. Most of the factories and shops were very small, with 43 percent having five or fewer workers. Much of the textile machinery was antiquated, bought in the boom when anyone could make money, and clung to through hard work as the sector became backward in decline. It was an industry of small producers tied together by an army of commercial middlemen that got along without an efficient, modern financial system. Its strength was that its small-scale and personal ownership allowed it to respond rapidly to seasonal and fashion changes in a volatile market.

The crisis that occurred in this economy reflects its role as part of one of today's global industries. Along with automobiles, chemicals, steel, and electronics, textiles has been undergoing tremendous change through the rise of manufacturing in newly developing countries and the intensification of international competition. This became critical in the 1970s, and the familiar arguments over what has caused the crises in these global industries include a number of culprits: increased energy costs, "unfair competition" subsidized by foreign governments, the restructuring of the entire industry by market forces, increased control by multinational corporations, and inconsistent government trade policies (Toyne 1984, 1).

In Terrassa the crisis in textiles actually first began to appear during the boom of the 1960s. Synthetics had come to replace wool fibers, and demand was for mixed wool and synthetic cloth. The local industry couldn't adapt because it was too antiquated. When the international economic crisis of 1974 occurred, demand for consumer goods such as new clothes dropped sharply. As oil prices quadrupled and the costs of materials and labor increased, costs soared while demand dropped. The domestic market collapsed, products were left unsold, and many factories closed. While exports to the European community and African countries continued, the condition of the world economy did not permit expansion of exports to make up for the collapse of the domestic market. With the political crisis, investment dropped and few options were available.

The Spanish government had just begun a four-year restructuring of the wool textiles industry in 1975, based on its successful restructuring of the region's cotton industry in the 1960s. Its purpose was to reduce production, get rid of old equipment, reduce the work force, and reorganize the industry through mergers and consolidations. The timing of the plan with the world economic crisis and the political crisis following the death of Franco was unfortunate. Unprofitable enterprises were abandoned, but the capital released did not go into productive reinvestment. The main cost of the plan was absorbed by the workers through higher unemployment. The high unemployment and inflation of 20 percent helped push the successful mass-based movement for democracy, but the economic crisis deepened.

There were 11,105 officially unemployed—out of an active population of 66,256—in Terrassa in 1978. With continued layoffs, this increased to a peak of 17,636 unemployed in the crisis of 1982. With similar conditions across Spain, the post-Franco government collapsed and the Socialists won the elections, promising jobs. In industrial cities such as Terrassa, the situation was so bad that in the ten years after 1975, outmigration roughly balanced natural population growth, and the population of around 165,000 showed essentially no growth. The value of textiles production dropped 85 percent from 1977 to 1985 in constant pesetas, and the metal sector dropped 66 percent. The percentage of the active population employed in manufacturing dropped from 76 at its peak to 57 in 1985.

Through the crisis, the local economy changed internally as well as in its international position. Within manufacturing, the production of cloth for the domestic market declined while yarn for processing elsewhere expanded. The manufacture of textile machinery—a major export in the past—dropped, while electrical equipment increased. Printing and graphics increased. From 1981 to 1984, exports to the European Economic Community—especially to France, Germany, and Italy—increased 151 percent, to 62 percent of total exports, as Spain became more directly integrated into the European economy. Africa and especially Latin America were less important markets because of their own severe economic crises and textiles development.

NATIONAL DEVELOPMENT POLICIES

To create jobs and fund the modernization of the society, the Spanish Socialist government after 1982 promoted a policy of economic restructuring and liberalization of the market similar to that of other industrialized countries, whether under rightists in England or the United States or socialists in France. The Spanish Socialists confronted the inefficiencies of the many state-run enterprises set up under Franco, cutting back the work force to increase productivity, while also promoting technological modernization, regional planning, and investment. They followed initiatives worked out in other European countries through the European Economic Community, even though Spain did not enter the EEC until 1986. The EEC initiatives provided a model and were also the conditions for Spain's entry into the EEC.

In Europe as a whole, rapid change in textiles and other industries had already occurred as a result of adjustments to increased competition following the formation of the European Economic Community. In response, and in the face of the crises of the 1970s a wide range of policy options and strategies were worked out and coordinated through the EEC. Successful adaptations were made to the monetary and oil crises of the 1970s, but because of the changes in global production, the traditional industries of steel, footwear, textiles, and clothing are still in serious trouble in the 1980s. The European work force in textiles, for example, declined 27 percent for 1973–1980, from 3.1 to 2.3 million, due to rationalization and bankruptcies. These workers were not able to find other employment because of the slow growth of the economy (Dolan 1983, 588).

The EEC has worked out restructuring and adjustment initiatives in the four areas of social, regional, investment, and industrial policy. These policies are a product of two opposing views: those of a liberal import policy favoring minimal government aid and free intra-EEC trade, and those of a social policy to mitigate the impacts of industrial adjustment on the workers and society through protective trade barriers and state assistance (Dolan 1983, 615).

It is EEC social policy to retrain workers. Regional policy is aimed at modernizing industry in depressed regions. Investment policy provides loans at less than market rates. Neither EEC regional funds nor investment subsidies can be used for declining industries such as textiles. In regions of declining industries, investors are encouraged to create new employment in other industries. It is European industrial policy aimed at increasing competitiveness that integrates these approaches. Industrial strategies include financial assistance to restructure and convert failing industries; promotion of exports, with production and assembly tasks integrated between specific countries; coordinated collection of industrial statistics; and support for research and development in new technologies (Dolan 1983, 592).

From an international perspective, the Spanish socialist government's strategies in these areas have been largely effective (Organization for Economic Cooperation and Development 1986, 7). It has slowed wage increases, reduced the size of the work force, and increased the flexibility of the labor market by removing the protections of workers put in place under Franco. It has also rationalized social security costs, reduced losses in government-run companies, and liberalized the financial market. In a word, the Socialists are giving business a freer hand than it had under Franco.

One factor pushing Spain in this direction is the long-awaited entry into the European Economic Community that began in 1986. Entry has tremendous implications for the growth of new markets, and its long-term effects are seen as healthy. Spain will be better situated within the international context of the EEC. It will be able to import technology from Germany, export agricultural products to France, and trade with Portugal, Greece, and other countries on equal terms. But the immediate impact is a tremendous adjustment to price increases due to EEC value-added taxes, competition from imports such as fertilizer, plastics, textiles, and steel, and the loss of government export subsidies. Because of these impacts, and specific regulations, there is strong incentive for coordinated strategies to adapt to the changes.

Spanish industrial policy has focused on reconversion or restructuring of traditional industries, the modernization of technology and information services, and promotion of industrial site development and investment in "Zones of Urgent Reindustrialization," or ZUR. A CAD-CAM (computer-assisted design and manufacturing) center in Terrassa will rent out systems for design of machine parts, fabric, and manufacturing processes to industry, and give training courses in area companies. An already existing quality-control laboratory for textiles in the city will get new instrumentation and be networked with two other labs in the region to meet new standards for increased competitiveness and EEC regulations.

The ZURs are central to the government's redevelopment strategies. The six ZURs that existed in Spain in 1986 had received more than $93 million worth of subsidies in their first 18 months of operation, and the Barcelona industrial belt of which Terrassa is a part received the largest amount due to coordinated action by regional and local governments. In its first year it had 56 projects with $143 million worth of investment which created 2,300 new jobs, including such companies as Jumberca, which manufactures textile machinery, Kelsy Hayes, Siliconas Hispania, and Sharp. Sharp will manufacture color televisions, 32 percent of them for export.

The objectives of ZUR projects are to create employment, modernize productive structures, and increase international competitiveness within Europe. Support is available for acquiring and developing land, buildings, and machinery, and for needed research and development and engineering. Benefits include up to 30 percent of investment financing, and the waiver of up to 99 percent of local and import taxes.

The government's social policy includes new forms of labor contracts. To increase entry-level positions for youths who have faced high long-term unemployment, and to facilitate training in new employment areas, the government has created new subsidized apprenticeship contracts. They last for more than three months but less than three years, with wages at the regular level for the job. In Terrassa, 15 to 20 percent of the new contracts registered each month are of this type.

POLICIES OF THE REGIONAL CATALAN GOVERNMENT

Development policies of the regional Catalan government are in the same areas as those at the national level and are aimed at taking advantage of the opportunities they provide. The regional government views the recuperation of the European economy as the main opportunity for the region. Regional industrial strategy therefore focuses on technological modernization and industrial site development to attract new investment. It has been characterized as an attempt to create a "silicon valley." Its technological strategy is to coordinate the initiatives of the various departments of the regional government, and to promote scientific and technical research, the training of technical personnel, and the adoption of new technologies in Catalan industry.

In contrast to Catalonia, Appalachia has been defined as rural and traditional, as if it were outside of the changes going on elsewhere. It is clear, however, that it is also a region undergoing fundamental change in the modern global context. What makes its alternatives different are the national policies pursued in the United States, and the absence of strong grassroots political movements to shape them.

Appalachia's modes of production have also been undergoing profound change. While its base was originally self-sufficient subsistence agriculture, most farming is now a part-time supplement to other work, and serves mainly to allow industry to keep wages and service costs low as people meet many of their needs within their own families. Agriculture shifted to beef and tobacco production in the Central Valley and Piedmont, and tobacco in the mountains. There is specialized poultry production in North Carolina and Georgia and fruit in western North Carolina, southern West Virginia, and western Virginia, all for markets outside the region (Lovingood and Reiman 1986). But it is not agriculture that shapes life in the region today. The two modes of mining and manufacturing dominate the region and determine the source of income and way of life of most people.

In the northwest mountains and plateaus of eastern Kentucky and of West Virginia, mining defines a separate subregion within Appalachia. It is one of poverty, as the mines close, leaving unemployment, a degraded environment, and control of resources by outsiders. There is no manufacturing to provide other sources of income. The poorest areas are on the western periphery of the mining area, which do not even have coal. Along with subsistence agriculture, this is the classic southern Appalachia identified by outsiders; but like other regions of the world, it is one in profound change. Coal production has shifted with modern technology from underground to strip mining; production units are smaller and more temporary as areas are rapidly stripped and abandoned. Coal is exported to Europe through Hampton, Virginia, and its price reflects the international energy market.

The most important mode of production in the region is not even identified with it. Manufacturing provides most of the region's employment and income. The Piedmont to the east, and the Central Valley with its major cities, are urban-centered industrial areas (Lovingood and Reiman 1988). Manufacturing is dispersed throughout the surrounding rural areas in a pattern characteristic of industrial regions. People living in rural areas commute long distances to work in factories throughout the region, and their communities have become growing residential areas that look less suburban because of their landscape. Industry is attracted to Southern Appalachia because of its hard-working labor force, lower wage scales, absence of unions, lower taxes, and available water and energy resources. With good interstate highways and railroads, manufacturing is tied into industrial centers and markets in the Northeast, Midwest, and Southeast. While there is a wide diversity of industries in the region that cushions economic cycles, they tend to be more labor intensive and traditional, such as light assembly or textiles. They are vulnerable to automation and competition from developing regions elsewhere. Like Catalonia, the Southeastern textiles industry has had to readjust to changes in the global economy, and many communities have had local apparel plants close.

While local Appalachian communities have tried creative solutions to their economic problems, the comparison with Catalonia illustrates what is missing and helps explain why local development efforts are often no more than smokestack chasing with local giveaways. In part because the U.S. market itself is so big, national economic policy has not focused on international competition except negatively, using tariffs to limit some foreign competition, and thereby raising the price of goods in the U.S. market. Because of this, policy has not aimed at developing integrated national strategies of retraining, regional redevelopment, investment, and industrial modernization as in Europe and elsewhere. Restructuring was facilitated under the Reagan administration through faster depreciation allowances and tax cuts, reflecting financial rather than production strategies. Less productive economic sectors such as steel were abandoned, and takeovers and mergers were facilitated; but industrial production, employment, and regional redevelopment have not been goals. Even efforts by such regional agencies as the Tennessee Valley Authority and the Appalachian Regional Commission have been limited to the narrow strategy of providing infrastructure such as energy, roads, education, and health care to promote economic development. But with no regional political structures comparable to a regional government nor a grassroots movement to shape and support such efforts, they have not been integrated into a process coming out of the region itself. In the absence of such national policy and political processes, local communities have few options.

COALITION STRATEGIES AT THE COMMUNITY LEVEL

Given these changes in the global economy that determine the position of local regions, and national policies that offer only specific alternatives, local communities have to work out their own best strategies. In the Catalan city of Terrassa, local strategies have aimed at taking advantage of the opportunities available from the national and regional governments. The city began its active policy of re-industrialization and conversion in 1985, following the lines of strategies in Barcelona and Montpelier, France. Local investment and plant site development are promoted using the tax breaks and subsidies for industrial investment available through the ZURs.

The most important aspect of the local strategy is that it is the product of a consensus among local business and government leaders who have broad support. Local leaders have continued the pattern of coalition building that was successful against the dictatorship, except that the main partners are now the Socialist political leaders and technical professionals of the municipal government, with their popular support, and the business community of the Chamber of Commerce.

The municipal government has organized a development council presided over by the Socialist mayor and including representatives of the Chamber of Commerce, realtors, and local savings bank, the local university, and the socialist and communist unions. This is roughly the same broad-based representation as the opposition coalition for democracy under the Franco dictatorship, but the unions are now weak and the communists have lost the power they had when their mass-based movement was the base for the opposition. The council serves as a consulting body for the municipal government to guide municipal policy, coordinate the efforts of local institutions, mediate labor conflicts, and advertise the benefits available for local develop-ment. Its most important function is to identify projects that best fit the local economy by providing more employment and creating secondary support industries.

In its first year of inclusion in the ZUR of Barcelona, local initiatives in Terrassa attracted a commitment of more than $20 million of new investment in 45 companies, creating 370 new jobs in such areas as regulators for energy conservation, electronic compo-nents, and food additives. In the immediate area around Terrassa, there were also important investments by Hewlett Packard, Olivetti, and Sanyo, and creation of a "silicon valley" ZUR technological park. The Hewlett Packard plant that opened in Terrassa in 1985 manufac-tures computer plotters, 98 percent for export to Europe, Africa, and the Middle East.

The easiest strategy to implement has been the rather traditional one of giving benefits to developers to construct industrial plant buildings, so that land can be acquired and sites offered at a lower price. They must meet the requirements of ZUR. The Development Council provides benefits including the waiver of from 75 to 99 per-cent of local value-added taxes on the increased value of land, and of license fees for construction and opening businesses. In the first year and a half, a total of almost $2 million was invested in new sites and plant buildings.

A joint-venture promotion company, PROINTESA, was also created in the fall of 1985 as a private and municipal partnership to stimulate reindustrialization. It includes the municipal government, the chambers of commerce and real estate, and principal business people, but not the unions. Its purpose is to promote industrial investment by advertising, offering developed sites, and helping businesses take advantage of ZUR and other tax and credit benefits. An example is the German AEG electrical motor company's plan to invest $11.4 million in 1986 to modernize and expand its Terrassa plant with ZUR and regional support. It will add 80 new jobs and all electrical motor production will be moved from Germany to Terrassa, with 80 percent targeted for export.

The municipal government also developed a wide range of educational, health, social, and cultural programs to improve the quality of life in the city, and ameliorate the effects of the crisis. The municipal budget increased from 933 million pesetas in 1976 to 5.835 million pesetas in 1985. In constant pesetas it has doubled. In terms of development, its most active agency has been the Urbanism Agency. This agency began in 1982 with a zoning plan designed to overcome the problems of the city's infrastructure from the rapid unplanned growth of the 1960s. There are plans for street paving and lighting, improved drainage and sewage control, new bridges and underground train tracks to improve traffic flow, and parks and green spaces, schools and libraries. Faced with the problem of implementing the plan, the agency then took over the licensing of construction. The present Municipal Agency of Urbanism was created in 1984 to include all the functions of planning, zoning, licensing, and inspection of construction, giving it a strong role in planning, implementation, and enforcement. The agency assists the reindustrialization by providing studies to attract industries, and has helped work out a new land-use policy for pricing industrial sites. With the Hewlett Packard plant, for example, the planning office prepared a study of the economic sectors that supported it in the local economy.

The Chamber of Commerce is the other main force for redevelopment in the city. It is also newly expanded and reorganized with an emphasis on technical assistance and the promotion of trade. Ten years ago it was a small office that had no real role in the local economy. Decisions were made at the Industrial Institute, the association of owners of the local textile industry, which has lost its power. The Chamber is organized into four branches, with commissions on industry, foreign and domestic trade, and urbanism.

The commissions on industry and foreign trade are the most important. The Commission on Industry was created in 1985 to work on the creation of PROINTESA, the Development Council, and ZUR. It facilitates adaptation to rapid changes in the economy, new laws, and entry into the EEC, and actively lobbies the legislature on policy issues. The Commission on Exterior Trade organizes courses on exports, and missions to study potential markets in other countries. It is developing a program to bring together groups of manufacturers to facilitate their joint entry into foreign markets, which will especially help smaller companies. More specialized personnel and information services are developed to stay informed on entry into the EEC. The Chamber is tied into an information center that will connect all the chambers of Spain to Madrid, and eventually Brussels.

These strategies have wide support in the city. Even the most important union in the city—the communist Workers' Commissions, which sits on the Development Council—supports them. From the union's perspective, the strategy of reindustrialization is to promote the introduction of new technology that will strengthen the city's classical economy of textiles and metal. The strategy is to strengthen manufacturing as the economic base, rather than shift to services such as tourism, and to attract industries that fit into the local economy and create jobs instead of some automated potato-chip plant.

The importance of this strategy is that it is based on a broad coalition and gets input and support from all the important economic forces of the city, from business, government, and unions. Because of this, both policies and implementation decisions are deeply informed and are worked out to meet the most needs, with the best fit to the local economy and society. Better choices are made, obvious mistakes avoided, and they are implemented without needless delays and conflicts.

PROBLEMS

Despite all the earnestness and ingenuity of these strategies, however, there are serious problems. The support for industrial site development has fed a boom for developers and contractors, which is monopolized by a few individuals. Prices are therefore high compared to other areas, with less benefit to development. The rapid growth of new programs has built-in inefficiency as inexperienced people become involved in new expensive projects. Taxes have risen at a spiraling rate and have become the main source of criticism against the Socialist government.

At the national level, the Socialist government has been imposing an austerity program after campaigning on job creation. It has held down wages, cut back the labor force, and removed restrictions on employers, in order to promote business. In the process it has been losing political support to continue its redevelopment program. If it is unable to carry out the program over a longer period of time, the benefits of the restructuring—which could be greater productivity, economic growth, and employment—will not be realized.

In terms of the local economy itself however, the main problem is that it is not transformed into a modern high-technology economy, but tends to revert to its older form as an archaic labor-intensive industrial economy. Unemployment continues at 28 percent in the city. Those most affected are in the industrial sectors and the young who can't find their first employment. The main response to the crisis has been the growth of the underground or informal economy (Mattera 1985). This has allowed marginal firms to survive and has provided income to families, but it has transformed the working and social conditions of the city and undercut the process toward modernization.

In 1986, it was estimated that more than ten large textile companies were putting out work—especially clothing—into homes. This is an old pattern of cottage industry in textiles, which continues to be important in apparel assembly around the world. It provides extra pay for families; but its working conditions are unregulated, it doesn't provide benefits, it is untaxed and it is illegal. The cloth is sent out already cut, and goes in stages from home to home. One person sews the collars; another, the sleeves; others, pockets. The most common products manufactured this way are shirts, pants, winter jackets, and sports jackets for children. At a hard rate of work of from 10 to 12 hours a day, a woman can sew from 50 to 100 outfits a week, depending on the article. With this they earned a maximum of from between $100 to $200 a month in 1986. Pay is by the piece, with children's sports jackets, for example, paying 35 cents. Other types of jobs include knitting children's sweaters on a hand loom, or packaging socks in plastic bags. There are also dozens of small illegal shops, where a half-dozen or more women make articles. In this case, all steps in the process are together to eliminate some of the intermediaries and make the process more economical. Small spinning and weaving shops have also appeared. In yarn dyeing, the economy has split into two sectors. Dyeing that is large-scale and highly technological is done above ground, while catching the threads or yarn ends—which is done by hand—is completely submerged. It is shipped out of the factory and done in illegal shops (Peralta 1986, 5–7).

Other common strategies for survival include small family repair shops of unemployed workers from the construction or electrical sectors, who do small jobs such as kitchen renovation, change of electrical installations, and appliance or car repair. Many sales people or representatives go from house to house or shop to shop, working without fixed pay for a commission, each one representing a wide variety of products from different companies, from insurance to school supplies and perfume. Others use their unemployment pay to open small bars, which account for a large portion of the licenses for new businesses in the city.

The labor unions see this growth of the submerged economy and service-oriented microbusinesses as an indication of the extent to which the redevelopment strategies are not dealing with the problems of unemployment. New jobs are not being created; and because of the weakness of the economy and the decline of textiles, the workers have lost the power through their unions to do anything about it. According to the unions, unemployment is not being dealt with because the growth of the submerged economy has not been confronted. It has been facilitated by government policies; and rather than seeing it as a problem, the government cites it as evidence that unemployment isn't really as high as it appears. The reconversion plans pay companies to get rid of old machinery, which they then sell into small black-market companies instead of destroying. The communist Workers' Commissions want to reemerge the economy. Since the production of exports is increasing, the economy is improving. What the Workers' Commissions say is needed is more control over working conditions, taxes, and social security. From their perspective, the re-industrialization plans offer an opportunity to do this by creating incentives for companies to become part of the regular economy again to receive benefits.

As one union official put it, there are three types of work: one, normal with regular hours and pay; another that is submerged, with a minimum of subsistence; and a third, unemployment with no subsistence. With the submerged economy, there are only two options: to convert it into the regular economy, or to eliminate it and create unemployment. The Worker's Commissions want to use the subsidies and technical help such as PROINTESA offers as inducements to stimulate the reemergence of the economy.

From the perspective of Terrassa, Appalachia's family survival strategies of self-reliance in an informal economy of subsistence agriculture, home repairs, and petty commodity production such as crafts should not be viewed as remnants of the past but adaptations to economic vulnerability and the collapse of regional modes of production (Long and Richardson 1978). At the same time, it is clear that Appalachia lacks the kind of grassroots political movement it needs to confront its problems. Because of its historical circumstances, local elites and politicians work behind the scenes to meet the needs of competing interest groups. Often it is government jobs and contracts that are the most accessible local resources and the focus of entrepreneurial activity, rather than economic development. What is missing is the open debate and consensus building that comes from strong coalitions based on grassroots community movements. The best long-term strategies are not considered, and already existing economic activities are not recognized and facilitated, because all sectors of the society do not have a voice. But it is also clear that this is not just a regional problem. It reflects the long history of the form of political and economic development in the United States, the absence of coherent policy at the national level, and the lack of political structures and movements to raise issues and shape policy so that they reflect the best interests of the people and economy as a whole, including Appalachia.

■ 7 ■
Mountain Foragers in Southeast Asia and Appalachia: Cross-cultural Perspectives on the "Mountain Man" Stereotype

Benita J. Howell

When and how did Appalachia become identified as a distinctive region, a "strange land inhabited by peculiar people"? In his massive doctoral dissertation, Cratis Williams (1961) cataloged the ingredients of the mountaineer stereotype as they emerged from 19th-century travel accounts and local color fiction. He found that a consistent image of cultural primitivism, based on "branchwater" Appalachians, persisted well into the twentieth century. Williams argued that this stereotype reflected a real deterioration in living conditions that created a distinct lower class of Appalachians in the decades following the Civil War.

Henry Shapiro (1978) later took up the question of why Appalachia preoccupied affluent urbanites in the latter part of the 19th century, and why so-called branchwater Appalachians in particular fascinated these consumers of local color literature. Shapiro suggested that Appalachia's emergence as a distinctive region followed upon a growing recognition that "the strange land and peculiar people" were out of place in the new industrial culture of modern America. Lifeways that had earlier appealed to a romantic nostalgia for the frontier past now became a challenge to modernization and progress. Appalachia was replete with problems to be solved and deficits to be remedied through home missions work, secular education, community development, or cultural revival.

Both of these accounts explain the emergence of the Appalachian stereotype in the late 19th century by appealing to particular events in American history: the Civil War and its aftermath of devastation in Appalachia; industrial growth and urbanization in the North; and Reconstruction in the South, which was characterized by continuing sectional and sectarian rivalries within religious and philanthropic organizations. But explanations phrased in specific historical terms don't account for the Appalachian stereotype's perplexing resistance to the facts.

Why, for example, was the branchwater mountaineer made the stereotypic representative of the region as a whole, although he was not numerically in the majority, was not particularly visible in the towns and resorts frequented by outsiders, and was not culturally, socially, or economically dominant within the region? Why, toward the end of the 19th century, did many scholars and popular writers assert that Appalachians represented a separate genetic stock from other Americans, whether pure Anglo-Saxon, Highland Scots, Scots-Irish, or English poor white—even though there was ample evidence that the region had received settlers from diverse stocks and sent its share of settlers west to become middle Americans? And why have affluent, educated Appalachians themselves become the primary purveyors of the stereotype, whether in casual comments about "holler folk" or in fiction?

As an anthropologist, I would like to propose that we look beneath the particular events of late 19th-century American history in our attempts to account for the Appalachian "mountain man" stereotype. If we view the Appalachian case in a broader framework of cross-cultural comparison, it appears to be one instance of a more general and fairly widespread phenomenon in which distinctive economic adaptations provide the basis for stereotyping and ethnic labeling. In fact, the Appalachian mountain man stereotype has a close parallel in pervasive distinctions between primitive highlanders and civilized lowlanders that have long organized ethnic relations in Southeast Asia.

This cognitive and symbolic contrast quite possibly has been central to ethnic group relations in Southeast Asia ever since the first millennium A.D., when Hindu commercial states began incorporating mountain foragers and shifting cultivators into trade networks. The object was to obtain forest products for international maritime commerce that linked Southeast Asia with the Mediterranean, the Middle East, and China (see Coedes 1968; Hall 1966; Meilink-Roelofsz 1962; Simkin 1968). Karl Hutterer (1974), interpreting archaeological sites dating from roughly 1000–1600 A.D., found evidence of trade between the coast and interior groups in the Philippines. Chinese records indicate that a large percentage of Philippine trade goods consisted of forest products such as beeswax, abaca, sandalwood, rattan, civet, and animal hides. Presumably, coastal traders did not have access to inland territories and lacked the environmental knowledge to procure these items themselves, so they traded with foragers and swidden farmers of the interior but did not culturally incorporate these peoples into the emerging coastal states. Spanish records indicate that such trading networks definitely were in operation when the Spanish arrived in the Philippines. Hutterer argues that the evolution of lowland societies into commercial states entailed deliberate maintenance of foraging and swidden adaptations among peoples geographically situated to supply the prized forest products. Lowlanders depended on and subsidized the foraging lifestyle, but at the same time labeled it primitive and inferior.

Ethnologists observing interethnic relations in the European colonial period and in contemporary nation-states of South and Southeast Asia have documented continuing symbiotic and often exploitative relations among foragers, peasants, and traders. Thus it appears that long-standing stereotypic contrasts between "civilized" lowlanders and "backward, primitive" highland foragers have become ingrained in South and Southeast Asian folk notions of culture and ethnic identity (e.g., see Lehman 1967). Culture traits that signal "backwardness" bear an uncanny similarity between Asia and Appalachia.

In the Philippines, for example, Negrito peoples known collectively as the Agta carried on a nomadic, foraging lifestyle in which they traded with middlemen or agents from the coast. John Garvan (1963), an Irish-American amateur ethnologist who studied the Agta in the 1910s, noted that Filipinos circulated many erroneous rumors about the Agta. The stereotypic Agta had a monstrous, ape-like appearance (11), was dirty and diseased (12), subject to drunkenness (54), immodest, promiscuous, and incestuous (81), and prone to violence and theft (157–161). Most puzzling to Filipinos was the Agta preference for an independent, nomadic lifestyle. Agta resisted Filipino efforts to engage them in long-term wage work or sharecropping relationships, but they did on occasion appear in farming villages to exchange work for rice, garden produce, or metal implements as well as supplying forest products—lumber, bark cloth, "rattan, honey, beeswax and whatever else might be desired" (79). Garvan described how the Filipino partners in trading relationships took advantage of Agta ignorance of the market value of their products, exercised debt peonage, or sometimes posed as government officials and extorted trade goods from Agta (159–163). In response, Garvan wrote, the Agta "has no need and no desire for any relations with the government. He fears taxes. He fears schools. He fears the police and he fears all kinds of things" (158).

Jean Peterson (1978) has described more recent relationships between Agta foragers and pioneering peasant farmers, whose encroachment into Agta territory has brought many more outsiders into personal contact with Agta and reduced the primary forest available for Agta foraging. These newcomers have continued to establish patron-client trade relationships that use an idiom of friendship but at least potentially leave the Agta open to debt peonage and other forms of exploitation. While Peterson observed a surface cordiality in relations between rural villagers and "their" Agta, the same old stereotypes persisted (64–66). Villagers were disturbed by Agta sexuality, their crude humor, and their children's undisciplined behavior. Stories of Agta violence and savagery continued to arouse fear, particularly among townspeople who had little personal contact with Agta. Negrito origins of the Agta have given Filipinos familiar with American racial prejudice an additional basis for stereotyping. Peterson was told, "These Agta are just like your niggers. They're lazy, thieving, and dirty. It's right in their blood and you can't teach them anything" (79).

Physical difference reinforces but does not account for Agta stereotyping, however. The same stereotypic characterizations have been applied to other highland peoples of South and Southeast Asia who are racially indistinguishable from their lowland neighbors. Lowland Malays, for example, have stereotyped tribal groups of the interior of Borneo and the Celibes as backward, dirty, stupid, and savage (Lasker 1944, 37–40). Yet there is a strong possibility that the lowland Malays have their origins in the very tribes that they denigrate. Using ethnographic and ethnohistoric sources, King (1985) has reconstructed a multilevel system of ethnic stratification based on trade between interior and coastal Borneo. Punan foragers (similar in lifestyle to the Agta, but not Negrito) and Iban Dayak shifting cultivators supplied trade goods to the Maloh. The Maloh were wet-rice cultivators who also served as middlemen in trade with lowland Malays. Maloh were distinguished from Dayak people not by language or race, but by their economy and more hierarchical political organization. The Malay controlled catchment areas upstream, while coastal trade was in turn controlled by Chinese and Buginese from the Celibes. King found that the "Malay" commercial center had in fact been formed as recently as 1815 by Dayak (or Maloh) who converted to Islam (59–62), and he suggested that Punan nomads who settled and planted rice became Dayak (206).

King's findings fit a pattern often reported for Southeast Asia in which contemporary boundaries and distinctions between lowlanders and more primitive highlanders have been demarcated and maintained through the use of discrete ethnic labels. Economic specializations form a framework for different lifestyles which, along with particular cultural behaviors such as religious affiliation, serve as ethnic markers. The use of ethnic labels implies a separate historic origin for each group so labeled; but physical similarities, linguistic affiliations, and historical data such as those reported by King tend to invalidate such claims. Moerman (1965), Lehman (1967), Dentan (1975), and Rousseau (1975) all have shown that tribal identifications are notoriously confusing in Southeast Asia precisely because "tribes" are not genetic and cultural units at all, but reflect an ongoing process of ethnic labeling and manipulation of ethnicity. Cunningham (1987) has recently shown how similar processes of constructing ethnicity have occurred repeatedly in the history of the British Isles.

If the mountain foragers of Southeast Asia do not really constitute separate ethnic groups, what is the basis for their being treated as if they were separate? Both Hutterer and King imply that forager to swidden cultivator, to wet-rice cultivator, to commercial trader represents an evolutionary sequence of development. If this were the case, then contemporary foragers would represent survivals of a truly primitive hunting-and-gathering adaptation—the "contemporary ancestors" of other Southeast Asians. More recent work by Carl Hoffman (1984), however, suggests that it is equally plausible that these groups, like the Appalachian pioneers, went into a mountain forest environment, adapted to its requirements, and in the process shed some cultural baggage and took on the appearance of being more primitive than they actually were.

Hoffman studied a number of different Punan groups in Borneo and concluded that the Punan (the name can be translated as "collectors" or "forest dwellers") do not constitute a homogeneous cultural or linguistic unit. Rather, each Punan group is paired with neighboring swidden farmers who share linguistic and other cultural similarities such as burial customs with their Punan trading partners. Punan appear to constitute a distinct ethnic group only because of behaviors directly associated with their forest collecting. Conventional wisdom once had it that foragers—isolated and enclosed within complex societies—could continue their primitive hunting-and-gathering lifestyle only by resorting to trade with cultivators who supplied them with garden produce, metal tools, and other trade goods. But Hoffman's findings turn this reasoning upside down. Hoffman proposes that, rather than being descendants of aboriginal foragers, the Punan are Dayak who have moved into the primary forest in order to specialize in collecting raw materials to supply the long-distance trading networks. The Punan hunt and gather in order to subsist during their commercial collecting activities in the primary forest, rather than using trade to cushion an inefficient, maladaptive, outdated lifestyle.

In South Asia as well as Southeast Asia, forest foragers have been stereotyped and labeled as distinct "tribes," sometimes incorporated into the bottom levels of the Hindu caste system; sometimes left entirely outside of it. After examining ethnographic data on the Kadar,

Birhor, Chenchu, Vedda, and Nayadi, Richard Fox concluded that social scientists as well as agricultural neighbors erred in viewing these groups as "cultural left-overs or fossils from pre-literate times" (1969, 140). Fox argued that their spatial and sociological isolation from Hindu culture, like their primitiveness, had been exaggerated:

> Far from depending wholly on the forest for their own direct subsistence, the Indian hunters-and-gatherers are highly specialized exploiters of a marginal terrain from which they supply the larger society with desirable, but otherwise unobtainable, forest items such as honey, wax, rope and twine, baskets, and monkey and deer meat. (141)

Fox also explained the often noted social fragmentation of these groups—the mobility of individuals and loose structuring of communities—as an adaptive response to the demands of competitive foraging in which each household tried to maximize its gain (142). Thus, according to Fox, fluid social organization—a trait often denigrated by foragers' lowland neighbors, and interpreted as savage—is actually one more indication that these groups are "professional" rather than true primitives.

Brian Morris (1977, 1982) has provided new ethnographic data on another hill tribe of India, the Hill Pandaram, utilizing ecological and economic rather than evolutionary perspectives to account for their foraging adaptation. Within this framework, Morris focuses on Hill Pandaram contacts with the outside world, rather than assuming them to be isolated. The Forest Department of India has largely taken the place of independent traders in the old commercial system, but Hill Pandaram are still collecting for trade—and not for trade with local villagers alone, but to supply urban markets (1982, 3). As in Southeast Asia, the distinction between country people of the plains and forest people of the mountains has cognitive and symbolic importance. Morris reports that outsiders from the plains feel awe and apprehension in the mountains, that they fear the mountains as an alien environment. These feelings lead to a stereotyping of mountain people (1982, 44). Before Morris met the Hill Pandaram, he learned from villagers that they were

> lacking affectionate ties, sexually promiscuous to such an extent that incestuous relations between close kin were frequent, and lazy and stupid, unable even to discern what their own interests were. Villagers would even say they had no religion or culture. (1982, 2)

Morris later observed:

> They are treated as social inferiors by almost everyone with whom they have dealings....They are commonly said to live like animals and to lack any notions of decent behavior. ...
>
> Welfare and other government officials seem to view the nomad life of collectors as somehow "primitive" and are largely dedicated to making them a sedentary community. Local people in general despise their nomadic, apparently carefree and promiscuous life and their comparatively recent adoption of textile clothing. (1982, 45)

While Morris observed Hill Pandaram behaving with the subservience that villagers expected of them when they visited the villages to trade, they were more independent in the forest and able to preserve a large measure of their independence by limiting their contact with outsiders. Because the Hill Pandaram were living in a government Forest Reserve, their hunting and clearing of swidden patches were technically illegal activities; this fact colored their dealings with forest wardens and commercial traders and meant that their attitudes toward the authorities were similar to those of the Agta.

Without belaboring the point further, it should be obvious that stereotyping and labeling of mountain foragers as distinct "primitive" ethnic groups is a fairly consistent phenomenon throughout South and Southeast Asia. As Bruno Lasker observed:

> Not many years ago [the Moi of Indochina] were reported as wearing few clothes, as not being overclean, as building their houses on stilts or in trees, and as being altogether "savage." The Annamites who now make up the dominant native population of most of Indo-China say of the Moi much the same things that Filipinos say about Ifugaos...coast Malays about the Dyaks [*sic*] of central Borneo, Burmans about Kachins—the same things that Greeks said about the barbarian tribes of Macedonia, Romans about Britons.... Always these more primitive peoples are hunters who if they go in for agriculture at all do only a little of it, afraid to take root in an area from which at any time they may be ousted by superior force. Always the "superior" people call them savages and deny that they have any culture or religion. (Lasker 1944, 23)

Lasker's pointed comparisons with Europe can profitably be extended to Appalachia. Consider the core themes of the Appalachian stereotype cataloged by Williams (1961). While the mountaineer described by travelers before the Civil War resembled the heroic American frontiersman in his self-reliance, love of liberty, and rugged individualism, Williams observed that post-Civil War fiction increasingly emphasized negative traits: lawlessness, violence, ignorance and

disdain for education, suspiciousness of outsiders and outside inter-
ference, sordid living conditions, sexual aberrations (77–123).
Williams concluded that the "backwoods frontiersman" theme in
Appalachian stereotyping was progressively supplanted by two more
negative characterizations: the cultural primitive and the buffoon—
each a savage in his own way and lacking the nobility of the pioneer
frontiersman (160–163).

As appears to be the case for at least some South and Southeast
Asian foragers, Appalachian mountain men left more settled, "civilized" communities to enter the mountains not to farm, but to hunt,
trap, and forage. Williams makes it clear that early travelers consistently commented on encountering hunters who devoted little effort
to farming, readily moved away from populous areas, bartered goods,
and exchanged labor but resisted regular wage work (see Williams'
comments on Toulmin and Michaux at 188–189; Paulding and
Featherstonhaugh, 201–203; and Lanman, 226–229). Lanman observed a vigorous, profitable trade in ginseng in 1848 (see Williams,
229). Both Muir and Lane Allen (see Williams, 264, 292–297) identified hunting as an inducement to settlement of the mountains,
though by the time of their travels they encountered fewer active
commercial hunters than old men who had been hunters in their
youth. Muir and Lane Allen also commented on the commercial importance of ginseng and other medicinal roots, even after the Civil
War. Two more travelers, Buckingham and Olmstead, indicated that
livestock raising was by far the most significant agricultural activity in
the mountains during the 1840s and 1850s (see Williams, 216, 237).
This activity was compatible with other uses of the forest environment
since it was based on the animals ranging freely and consuming acorn
and chestnut mast.

It is generally accepted that the 18th-century "long hunters" who
were the vanguard of white settlement in rugged sections of
Appalachia dealt commercially in hides and pelts; they did not spend
winters roughing it in station camps to put meat on their families'
tables. Family traditions of early settlers verify travelers' observations
that hunting continued to be important—so much so that hunters
actually moved away from settlements in good farming areas in their
pursuit of game. For example, descendants of Jonathan Blevins sometimes express their chagrin that old Jonathan sold valley land in
Wayne County, Kentucky, around 1820 in order to move into the
rugged gorge of the Big South Fork in Scott County, Tennessee; but
they explain that Jonathan felt compelled to seek out more remote
hunting grounds when increasing settlement made game scarce in
Wayne County (personal communication, Oscar Blevins). Having
moved away from settlements in order to hunt and trap rather than to

farm, these men and their families could supplement their income by taking advantage of other commercial activities afforded by their backwoods environment, such as collecting medicinal roots, tanbark, nuts, beeswax, and honey, and raising hogs on forest mast.

In the early 19th century, backwoods hunters and foragers were viewed positively as pioneers opening up the old Southwest and claiming it for settlement. The rugged lifestyle of the pioneer was adventurous and ennobling—a powerful symbol of the American experience. But as Shapiro (1978) suggests, once Appalachian mountaineers were no longer on the physical frontier, their persisting frontier lifestyle required explanation. Just as Hindus, Filipinos, or Malays viewed their foraging specialists as primitives who had failed to make an evolutionary transition into civilization, other Americans viewed Appalachians as "contemporary ancestors" who had failed to modernize, failed to make a transition from subsistence into commercial farming because they had chosen poorly or been pushed into land ill suited to farming.

Even while Asian forest foragers continued to play an important role in supplying essential raw materials to the lowlands, "civilized" Asians misinterpreted the true nature of their economic role in the larger society and the origins of their "primitive" lifestyle. Differences between foragers and farmers were exaggerated and fixed in stereotypic contrasts and characterizations. Thus it should be no surprise that similar stereotypic contrasts and characterizations emerged to explain Appalachian foragers at a time when their economic contributions to the larger society were in fact dwindling in importance. Demand for buckskin decreased and fashions in furs changed; transcontinental railroads made it feasible for huge livestock and meatpacking operations in the West to supply eastern markets; improved technologies and larger-scale factory production resulted in the substitution of synthetic chemicals for tanbark, and new drugs for the old pharmacopoeia. Simultaneously, industrial America made incursions into the mountains. It took only a quarter-century for industrial-scale timbering virtually to eliminate the primary forest. Mining also was destructive of the habitat necessary for commercial hunting and forest collecting. All that remained for commercial foragers was subsistence-level enterprise, and there was less and less land available and suitable for that purpose.

To local color writers who began to develop the "cultural primitive" stereotype of Appalachia in the 1870s and 1880s, their subjects seemed to be clinging to savage lifeways borrowed from the Indians (see Cunningham, 1987, for extended discussion of this point). They seemed unable or unwilling to modernize and too ready to isolate themselves in the mountains. In fact these Appalachians had experienced and were still in the throes of an economic upheaval that rendered their old hunting and foraging specialization useless in the regional and national economy, depriving them of their livelihood. We know that many valley farmers and townspeople recovered from the aftermath of the Civil War and took advantage of new economic opportunities created by industry. It seems plausible that hunters and foragers who did not perceive their situation and adjust quickly became the chronically poor, apathetic, branchwater Appalachians who were stereotyped in increasingly negative terms toward the turn of the century. Given their economic plight, it is hardly surprising that these Appalachians experienced worsening material conditions and cultural disintegration; but unfortunately, these conditions provided an added impetus for stereotyping that blamed the victims of modernization for not modernizing and exaggerated the boundaries separating them from other Americans. Thus, writers of local color fiction took up the task of describing and rationalizing cultural differences and reaffirming the appropriateness of the boundaries between lowlanders and Appalachians (beautiful but uncultured daughters as well as mountain men). Attempts were made to establish historical ethnic origins for these cultural differences in order to set the group further apart as "other" Americans. Appalachians who identified with the wider society—much like Dayak people who became Malay—joined outsiders in their fascination with the primitives who lived upstream.

In his 1979 article, "If There Were No Malays, Who Would the Semai Be?", R. K. Dentan—an anthropologist who studied the Semai of Malaysia—described with perplexity how his quest for them always led him farther into the hinterland. People in the village of Jinteh "chuckled at the word Semai, saying, 'That's what outsiders call us here, but the real Semai live in the mountains.'" Had Dentan been Appalachian, he'd have understood immediately that "Semai" is the Malay equivalent of "hillbilly."

■ 8 ■

Gender Roles as Reflected in Adolescents' Expressed Values and Attitudes: An Eastern Kentucky/ Kenya Comparison

Susan Abbott

Adolescence is the time when human beings move toward consolidation of an identity that reconstitutes their parents' values and ideals, and the values and ideals of their community and historical period, into their own sense of self. Erik Erikson's (1980) work reminds us of the importance of this period in the life cycle. While this chapter does not deal directly with the issue of adolescent self-concept, it does attempt to move in an Eriksonian fashion from information about the patterning of symptoms of bodily and emotional dis-ease to an interpretation that draws not as much on the fundamentals of psychoanalytic theory as on an understanding of historic and contemporary patterns of culture and economic structure. For the purposes of this analysis, identifying the patterning of symptoms provides us with access to the points at which culture, social structure, and the economic arrangements of society contribute to the production of illness for individuals or classes of individuals. This chapter is also explicitly comparative, for I am convinced that it is through comparison of cases that we can best begin the process of identifying those aspects of society and culture that contribute to the well-being or illness of people.

Adolescent mental health—particularly, adolescent depresssion—is understudied in nonpatient populations in the United States and Canada (Ehrenberg et al. 1990a, 1990b, 1991). It is even more scarce to find studies of this kind for adolescents in any part of Sub-Saharan Africa (Mitchell and Abbott 1987). This chapter contributes to this literature through comparative study of two distinct nonclinic adolescent populations embedded in the ongoing life of their home communities and their schools.

The chapter also seeks to understand how local economies affect adolescents as they approach the time when they must leave school and find work where local economic circumstances make it difficult to be successful. In the coalfields of Appalachian Kentucky, structurally based unemployment is high. The de-industrialization of the United States, exemplified by the decline in the steel industry—which began in the 1970s (Weis 1990, 6–11)—coupled with the adoption of new technology for mining and processing coal, has resulted in the permanent loss of large numbers of local jobs for men. Official unemployment figures in the coal-dominated county where these data were collected ranged between 14 percent and 17 percent at the time of the research, while real unemployment was believed to be much higher—some would say, as high as 40 percent. At the same time, service industry jobs paying minimum wage have been increasing and creating local employment opportunities for women. As women increasingly take up work outside the home and men are unable to find any work, gender roles begin to change.

East African economies occupy a different position in the world system from that of Appalachia. They do not possess substantial mineral or fossil energy resources nor are they developed industrial societies. They are developing economies that rely more on export agriculture and tourism. Spared the destructive dictatorship and civil war of Uganda, and the stifling effects of Tanzania's African socialism, Kenya's economy is the most developed of the three countries that composed the old East African Community at the time of independence. Within Kenya, Central Province—which contains Nairobi, the nation's capital—is arguably the country's most developed and most prosperous province. The rural economy of the province is characteristically a mixed one that combines small-holder subsistence and cash crop farming with some wage earning for most families in the former tribal reserves. The traditional lifeways described in the standard ethnographies of the region's inhabitants at the time of British pacification (Routledge and Routledge 1910; Kenyatta 1961; Leakey 1977) no longer exist. World commodity prices, the World Bank, and the International Monetary Fund affect the daily life of the rural Kenyan Kikuyu people, as they also affect all other Kenyans. Unemployment and underemployment are also similar to, or higher than, the levels found in eastern Kentucky. Traditional gender roles are strained and changing under the impact of the new economic arrangements (Mitchell and Abbott 1987).

This chapter, then, presents a comparative analysis of data collected from adolescents in two rural locations: one a coalmining county in eastern Kentucky, the other an ethnically Kikuyu area in Nyeri District of Central Province, Kenya. The specific questions I will address include the following: Are there differences between eastern

Kentucky and Kenyan Kikuyu adolescents' scores on the Health Opinion Survey or HOS (see Table 8.1)? Are there gender differences within and between the two adolescent communities in the kinds of symptoms selected on the HOS? If differences exist, how can we explain those differences? Before we can proceed, we need to contextualize our analysis by comparing the two cultures from which the study participants were drawn.

COMPARISON OF LOCAL CULTURES

On the surface, a comparison of Kenyan secondary students with their counterparts from eastern Kentucky may seem minimally unusual and maximally pointless. The assumption behind this reaction rests on the obvious disparities in the cultures of the two samples. The kinship systems, marriage practices, composition of households, and inheritance practices all differ in substantial ways. The Kentuckians typically grow up in nuclear family households with monogamously married parents. They often live in local rural neighborhoods near kin to whom they are related through a bilateral kinship system that recognizes blood ties equally and similarly through both the mother's and father's side of the family. Each young couple expects to have their own home separate from both sets of parents, although they may locate that house on land belonging to one or the other set of parents. Ideally, inheritance is equally shared among the children, though the one who cares for the elderly parents may get more.

Kenyan Kikuyu, in contrast, grow up in mother/child households where the father, who can marry more than one wife at a time if he wishes, usually occupies his own house on the same homestead. If he has more than one wife, each wife has her own house and kitchen. The Kikuyu are a patrilineal society, which means they count their kin only through the father's side of the family. They recognize the mother's kin as closer than nonkin, but not equivalent to the father's line of descent. In their system, only males can inherit land—the key resource for survival among a farming people. When a young couple marries, the new wife moves from her natal home to her husband's natal home where her husband will provide a new dwelling separate from his mother's but sharing the same yard. Kikuyu sons never leave home.

Further differences can be seen in the division of labor at the household level. In the de-industrializing eastern Kentucky community, women work predominantly as housewives, with only some—lower than the national average—working for wages outside the home; while most rural Kikuyu women work as the primary family farmers who are responsible for feeding themselves and their children and for making a contribution to their husband's food supply. They also raise cash crops for sale. A few pursue additional sources of income through sale of handcrafts, and a very few have wage-paying jobs as shop assistants or waitresses, or work as salaried employees such as teachers or nurses. This is typical of much of Sub-Saharan Africa. Finally, the local and national political systems differ, although both systems have been heavily influenced historically by British institutions.

Similarities exist as well. High underemployment and unemployment rates, production of primary commodities—in the one case, coal, in the other case, coffee, tea, and milk—and shifting gender roles have already been mentioned. Additionally, both local communities support elites whose positions are based on differences in education, occupation, and income; however, the stratification system in eastern Kentucky is an older one. The boundaries between the strata in eastern Kentucky are sharply drawn, and the lifestyles of those differently located in the structure are more divergent than in rural Kenya. The local Kenyan system was still in the process of emerging when these data were collected in 1971–1972. The boundaries were fuzzier, but the direction in which the system was moving was as clear as the growing pile of dressed building stones destined to be assembled into a European-style dwelling by one community resident who worked in Nairobi—a dwelling as dramatically different from those surrounding it as the coal company superintendent's house next to the coalminer's clapboard dwelling. Finally, in both communities Protestant Christianity predominates, although the denominations differ. At the time of the research, the Kenyan community still retained some pre-Christian practices and beliefs.

All the schools from which students were selected to fill out the questionnaire were located in rural areas tied to more populous regional towns or large urban centers that offered certain kinds of shopping, medical care, and government services not available locally. Both rural locations were peripheral to the cores of their respective regions when the original data were collected.[1] And though both areas have some local wage jobs, both have a history of migration to other areas to find wage employment, although the pattern of migration differs between the two communities. In Kenya the usual pattern involves labor migration of males only; their wives and children stay on the rural homestead, where the women farm and run the home place (Abbott 1976; Weisner and Abbott 1977). In eastern Kentucky, migration for wage employment more often involves the relocation of the nuclear family unit (Schwarzweller, Brown, and Manglam 1971).

One last point of comparison should be drawn. One sample of students is a highly selected group who have survived an intense national examination system to earn a place in secondary school in a system where, at the time these data were collected, only 7 to 10 percent of rural primary school children completing the last year of primary school achieved a seat in a government secondary school. These youth are buoyed by the expectation that they will do much better in the emerging cash economy and urban society of Kenya than their less fortunate peers. The other group is composed of students living amid a depressed rural industrial economy fallen victim to the usual boom/bust cycles of the coal industry and its recent technological changes, and a shifting international division of labor, that have together permanently changed the employment picture of the region. *All* the youth in the study are affected by the international economy, but they live in contrasting local structures and occupy different places in those structures.

METHODOLOGY

The two samples were selected in a similar manner. In the Kenyan study (Abbott and Arcury 1977), six secondary schools in the vicinity of my ongoing 1971–1972 community study participated. Three of the schools were girls' secondary schools, two were boys' secondary schools, and one was a co-educational secondary school. Sex-segregated secondary schools were the norm at the time in Kenya. The author supervised the administration of the questionnaire in each classroom. In all, 176 students completed the questionnaire, as can be seen in Table 8.2. The mean age of the sample was 17.7 years, with a range of 14 to 25 years.

The eastern Kentucky sample (N = 152) was drawn from the three high schools under the jurisdiction of the local county school board. The questionnaire was given to all high school juniors in class on the day in which it was administered. Three seniors also filled out the questionnaire in one of the high schools. In one high school, the author herself oversaw the administration of the questionnaire. In the other two high schools, teachers administered it after receiving instructions from their respective school principals.[2] The purpose of the questionnaire and the manner in which it was to be administered were explained to the principal by the author. The mean age of the Kentucky sample was 16.6 years, and ranged between 16 and 19 years (see Note 2).

The first part of the questionnaire was derived from Robert Edgerton's "Culture and Ecology Interview Schedule" (1971), which was designed for use in a comparative study of personality, values, and behavioral styles of adults from four different East African cultures. For this adolescent research, it was used in both settings with only minor modifications. The questionnaire was administered in English in both settings. (Instruction in Kenyan secondary schools is carried out in English.) Codes were developed based on the students' responses to the 82 questions included in the questionnaire. The questionnaires were then coded. A variety of descriptive statistics were used to analyze the responses.

The Health Opinion Survey composed the second part of the questionnaire. The HOS is a standard 20-question self-report of symptoms suitable for comparing groups (Macmillan 1957), and it has been used in cross-cultural studies to meet the need for a brief, inoffensive test that could be utilized on a community-wide basis (Abbott and Klein 1979; Mitchell and Abbott 1987). The HOS is not used to diagnose disorder. As Abbott and Klein (1979) and, more recently, Murphy (1986) point out, however, it is composed of items frequently found to be symptomatic of either depression or anxiety, or common to both syndromes. It has a possible score range of 20 to 60. Table 8.1 lists the HOS questions arranged by symptom type—a classification of the HOS items that is fully described in Abbott and Klein (1979). This study presents two kinds of analysis of the HOS responses: gender differences in global scores, and gender differences in the selection of individual items.

COMPARISON OF THE TWO SAMPLES

Space limitations preclude a full discussion of similarities and differences between the two samples, however Table 8.2 provides pertinent information. I will limit myself to highlighting three aspects of the table.

First, the Kentucky sample is predominantly working class, although it includes some children of middle class businessmen, managers, and professionals. The mean years of education of the students' fathers is 11.6 years with a range of 0 to 21 years, while their mothers have slightly more education. The adult men and women in the Kikuyu community study have far less education. The men's mean is 2.3 years, but their range is similar to the Kentuckians—0–22 years—while the women had a mean of 1 year of education and a more restricted range of 0 to 6 years. Approximately 50 percent of adult men and women had no formal schooling.

Second, the Kentucky students' educational and occupational aspirations are like U.S. youth as a whole in that they all aspire to at

Table 8.1
The Health Opinion Survey with Beck's Categories

Beck's Categories*	HOS Items—Tentative Groups
	Anxiety Symptoms
	2. Do your hands tremble enough to bother you? ** Often (3) Sometimes (2) Never (1)
	3. Are you ever troubled by your hands or feet sweating so that they feel damp and clammy?
	4. Have you ever been troubled by your heart beating hard?
	8. Are you ever bothered by nightmares (dreams that frighten and upset you)?
	9. Have you ever been bothered by shortness of breath when you were not exerting yourself?
	Depression Symptoms
Somatic	1. Do you have any physical or health problems at the present time? Yes (3) No (1)
Somatic	7. How often are you bothered by having an upset stomach?
Somatic	10. Do you feel that you are bothered by all sorts (different kinds) of ailments in different parts of your body?
Work Retardation	13. Has ill health affected the amount of work (housework) you do?
Work Retardation	18. For the most part do you feel healthy enough to carry out the things you would like to do? *** Often (1) Sometimes (2) Never (3)
Sadness	19. Do you feel in good spirits? ***
Pessimism	20. Do you sometimes wonder if anything is worthwhile anymore?
	Symptoms Possible in Either Condition
Insomnia	5. Do you tend to feel tired in the mornings?
Insomnia	6. Do you have trouble getting to sleep and staying asleep?
Anorexia	12. Do you ever have loss of appetite?
Somatic	14. Do you feel weak all over?
Somatic	15. Do you ever have spells of dizziness?
Weight Loss	16. Do you tend to lose weight when you worry?
	Indeterminate Items
	11. Do you smoke (or snuff)?

Note: Scoring is indicated for each item.
  * (Beck 1977).
  ** Scoring for items 2 through 17 and 20 is the same.
  *** Scoring for these items is reversed.

Appalachia in an International Context

Table 8.2
Demographics of Eastern Kentucky and Rural Kenyan High School Students
Compared

	Eastern Kentucky	Rural Kenya
1. Sex		
Male	58	85
Female	94	91
2. Age in Years		
Mean	16.6	17.7
Range	16–19	14–25
S.D.	1.17	1.58
3. Number of Siblings		
Mean	2.46	6.2
Mode	2.0	6.0
Range	0–17	0–14
S.D.	2.06	2.26
4. Grade in School	Juniors (11 yrs)	Form 3 (10 yrs)*
	Seniors	Form 4 (11 yrs)
5. State of Birth		
Kentucky-Appalachian	73.2%	Central Province
Other Kentucky	5.3%	
Non-Kentucky	24.3%	
6. Years Resident in County		
Mean	13.8	No information
Mode	16.0	
Range	1–19	
S.D.	5.3	
7. Father's Education in Years		
Mean	11.6	2.3**
Mode	12.0	0.0
Range	0–21	0–22
S.D.	4.08	(50% have no education)
8. Mother's Education in Years		
Mean	11.9	1.0***
Mode	12.0	0.0
Range	13–23	0–6
S.D.	3.58	(50% have no education)
9. Status of Parents' Marriage		
Intact	80.8%	No information
Divorced/Separated	14.7%	
One or Both Deceased	4.5%	
10. Students' Educational Aspirations		
High School Only	34.9%	No information
More than H.S.	13.8%	
Four-year College	40.1%	
Don't Know	11.2%	
No Information	2.8%	

Table 8.2, continued

	Eastern Kentucky	Rural Kenya
11. Job Aspirations		
Housewife	2.7%	No information
Blue Collar/Pink Collar	32.4%	
Technical	8.8%	
Low Level Prof./Business	20.3%	
Professional	8.8%	
Don't Know	27.0%	
12. Health Opinion Survey Scores		
a) Group Scores		
Mean	33.0	32.4
Range (20–60 possible)	22–52	21–55
S.D.	5.97	5.01
b) Females		
Mean	34.5	32.2
Mode	34.0	33.0
Range	22–52	21–55
S.D.	6.45	5.605
c) Males		
Mean	31.5	32.5
Mode	26.0	31.0
Range	22–48	22–45
S.D.	5.50	4.351

* Kenya follows the British model of school structure.

** This figure represents the educational attainment of all married men in a rural community near the schools from which the students were drawn for the study. The men ranged in age from 30 to 70, and they are not necessarily the fathers of the students sampled for the study. Most Kenyan secondary schools are boarding schools, and entrance is gained through performance on a national competitive examination. Students may or may not be assigned to a school near their home community.

*** This figure represents the educational attainment of all married women between the ages of 30 and 70 in the same community as the married men described above. These adult women are not necessarily the mothers' of these students.

Source: Authors' data.

least a high school education, but they differ from the U.S. norm in that fewer aspire to a four-year college education. Nationally, about 66 percent of working class youth aspire to four years of college, while only 40 percent of these Kentucky students say they want a college education (Crowley and Shapiro 1982a, 395). Further, although the occupational aspirations of the Kentucky students accurately reflect the occupational structure of the United States as a whole, they are lower than the stated aspirations of American working class youth of the same age, who aspire to high-status technical and professional occupations in much higher proportions. Based on national survey data, about 50 percent of American adolescents say they want such occupations, compared to 37.9 percent of this sample.

Third, a very low percentage of the girls said they wanted to be housewives as their primary occupation: only 2.7 percent. This contrasts sharply with the dominant picture of working class girls' aspirations and what has been characterized as their marginalized wage-labor identity (Douvan and Adelsen 1966; McRobbie 1978; Crowley and Shapiro 1982b, 35–37; Gaskell 1984; Valli 1986). It is congruent, however, with Weis's (1990, 54–79) recent findings among working-class high school girls of similar age in a Northeast U.S. "rustbelt" city. These points will be taken up again after we explore the two groups of students' responses to the Health Opinion Survey.

RESPONSES TO THE MENTAL HEALTH MEASURE

The analysis of the two groups' responses to the HOS yielded interesting contrasts and some similarities. Although the total scores on the HOS for both groups are similar (see Table 8.2), gender differences exist. The eastern Kentucky females have the highest mean scores (34.5), while the boys have the lowest (31.5). The Kikuyu means, which are close together, fit between these extremes. Next, the total scores on the HOS were grouped into low, middle, and high categories based on the score distributions for each sample. HOS score-by-sex-of-respondent contingency tables were created for both samples. Chi^2s were computed for each. The Kentucky sample produced a Chi^2 of 10.5505 with two degrees of freedom which was significant at the $p < .005$ level, while the Kenyans did not produce a significant result ($Chi^2 = 1.7374$, sig. = .4195).

Following the analytic strategy used by Abbott and Klein (1979), Table 8.3 presents the results of the final individual-items analysis of the HOS. Here we can see the content of the students' responses. The Chi^2 tests were computed by comparing males and females within each cultural group. Not only are the eastern Kentucky girls the most symptomatic overall, but they select as many anxiety symptoms as they select depression symptoms. The Kenyan Kikuyu girls, who are also more symptomatic than their male counterparts, do not select anxiety items to the same extent; their symptoms are predominantly depression symptoms, with a few symptoms common to both forms of distress. Males in both populations are relatively free of the symptoms included on this instrument, with the Kentucky boys the least symptomatic of all.[3]

The answer to the first two questions posed at the beginning of this comparison is yes. There *are* differences between eastern Kentucky and Kenyan adolescents' responses to the HOS. And gender *is* a factor in patterning the adolescents' responses in both populations.

Table 8.3
Comparison, by Sex, of Eastern Kentucky and Kenyan High School Students on HOS Items, Using Chi^2

HOS Items	Females		Males	
	Eastern Kentucky	Kenya	Eastern Kentucky	Kenya
Anxiety Items				
2. Hands shake	—	—	—	—
3. Hands/feet sweat	6.837 p<.03	—	—	—
4. Heart pounds	6.924 p<.03	—	—	—
8. Nightmares	21.14 p<.0000	—	—	—
9. Cold sweats	—	—	—	3.655 p<.0011
17. Short breath	—	—	—	—
Depression Items				
1. Phys. problem	5.152 p<.023	—	—	—
7. Upset stomach	17.3484 p<.0002	19.234 p<.0001	—	—
10. All sorts ailments	—	—	—	—
13. Work affected	—	8.683 p<.013	—	—
18. Health to work	—	—	—	—
19. Good spirits	—	—	—	—
20. Anything worthwhile	8.7597 p<.0125	20.391 p<.0001	—	—
Both				
5. Morning tiredness	—	—	—	14.601 p<.0007
6. Disturb. sleep	9.7684 p<.0076	6.973 p<.0306	—	—
12. Loss appetite	13.3096 p<.0013	5.891 p<.05	—	—
14. Feel weak	7.3305 p<.0256	—	—	—
15. Dizziness	—	—	—	—
16. Lose weight/worry	31.0657 p<.00001	—	—	—
Indeterminate				
11. Smoke/chew tobacco	—	—	32.0619 p<.00001	—

Source: Authors' data applied to Table 8.1.

ADOLESCENT GENDER IDEALS

The students' responses to some of the open-ended questions on the questionnaire reveal their construction of gender ideals. Only the answers to the questions with gender content are analyzed here, and I am relying on an earlier analysis of some of these data, which was reported in Abbott and Arcury (1977).

Among the questions the students were asked was this: "Would people in your community prefer to have sons or daughters?" To a striking degree, the eastern Kentucky girls and boys both believed that sons were preferred in their community (see Table 8.4). Sixty-two percent gave that response. Slightly more than 27 percent said that people had no preference or that they wanted both; and finally, only 6.3 percent believed that daughters were preferred. The Kenyans reversed the positions of "sons" and "both": 52.7 percent believed that both were preferred, while 38.9 percent felt sons were preferred. Similar to the Kentuckians, only 8.4 percent saw daughters as preferred. It is notable that youth who have grown up in a patrilineal kinship system with its explicit male bias are more likely to say that people value both daughters and sons than youth who have grown up in a bilateral kinship system that treats females and males similarly when counting kin and officially counts the sexes equal when deciding on inheritance. How are we to understand this?

The students were next asked to justify the gender preference they identified. The Kentuckians said that sons were preferred because, first and foremost, "they can work." Next, they are "less worry." Third, "they continue the family line." Fourth, "they are a companion for the father." Fifth, "they can be athletes." And finally, they just "like

Table 8.4
Preferred Sex of Child: Eastern Kentucky and Kenyan High School Students' Beliefs

| | Eastern Kentucky | | Kenya | |
	%	N	%	N
Son	62.0	(49)	38.9	(65)
Both	27.9	(22)	52.7	(88)
Daughter	6.3	(5)	8.4	(14)
Unsure	3.8	(3)	0.0	(0)
Total	100.0	(79)	100.0	(167)

Note: This is the question as it appeared on the questionnaire: "Would people in your community prefer to have sons or daughters?"
Source: Author's data.

boys." When the Kenyan Kikuyu said sons were preferred, they mentioned such things as "they care for the parents while the daughters leave," they continue the family line and can inherit, they are more "profitable," and, finally, they can become local leaders. On the other hand, when the Kikuyu were describing the reasons for why both were desirable (which was their dominant response), they would say "they are both profitable," "they are both useful," and "they are both equal." Those Kentuckians who gave the "both" response usually followed it with something like "they don't care what they have as long as they're happy and healthy. People love them both equally." When it came to daughters, the Kikuyu pointed out that daughters bring in bridewealth to the family when they marry, that they help with the house and farm work, that they are useful for reproduction, and that they give their earnings to their parents. The few Kentuckians who felt daughters were preferred said that the daughter could be a companion for the mother, or that they just liked girls, and one believed that girls were less difficult to deal with than boys.

Table 8.5
The Desirability of Traits for Males and Females: Eastern Kentucky and Kenyan High School Student Comparisons on Four Questions

| | Eastern Kentucky | | | | Kenya | | | |
| | Males | | Females | | Males | | Females | |
	SR*	IND**	SR	IND	SR	IND	SR	IND
Question								
1. Kind of man people respect	69.4 (12)	30.6 (11)	80.9 (34)	19.1 (8)	41.8 (33)	58.2 (46)	46.6 (41)	53.4 (47)
2. Kind of woman people respect	70.3 (26)	29.7 (11)	87.8 (36)	12.2 (5)	78.1 (57)	21.9 (16)	72.6 (61)	27.4 (23)
3. Kind of man woman wants to marry	71.8 (23)	28.2 (9)	85.7 (36)	14.3 (6)	8.2 (6)	91.8 (67)	9.6 (8)	90.4 (75)
4. Kind of woman man wants to marry	65.7 (23)	34.3 (12)	92.7 (38)	7.3 (3)	45.0 (36)	55.0 (44)	70.2 (59)	29.8 (25)

*SR = Social relational skills, traits, behavioral predispositions like being of good moral character; being a good mother or father; attaining married status; attaining elder status; being obedient to authority; being loving, caring, sensitive; being respectful; being stable; being sociable; having a good temperament; being wise. The Kentucky sample was more likely to mention loving, caring, and sensitivity as desirable traits.

**IND = Individual achievement, high status, or traits that are likely to contribute to achievement and status. This includes items such as a high level of education, wealth, or a high position in society as well as traits like physical attractiveness, leadership qualities, intelligence, and so forth.

Source: Author's data.

Other questions also help us understand these students'
perceptions of gender roles (see Table 8.5). "What kind of man
(woman) do people around here respect?" and "What kind of man
(woman) does a woman (man) want to marry?" produced some
important insights. The responses were combined for analysis into
two major categories. One included all responses that reflected an
emphasis on individual achievement of status and/or wealth, including traits likely to contribute to achievement—such as high levels of
education, leadership qualities, intelligence, and so forth. The other
category brought together all responses that reflected deference to
authority, emphasis on fulfilling traditional role expectations such as
being a good mother or father, exhibiting moral rectitude, and other
personal qualities such as being a loving and caring person.

Comparing the responses to the two questions phrased for men
produced a dramatic contrast. When describing the kind of man
people respect, the eastern Kentuckians—both males (69.4 percent
and females (80.9 percent)—place greater emphasis on moral aspects
of a person's behavior, attitudes toward authority, and qualities of the
person such as having a good temperament, being loving and caring,
wise, and sociable, than the Kenyan Kikuyu for whom individual
achievement and attaining wealth are given higher priority (males
58.2 percent, females 53.4 percent). This difference is particularly
striking in their responses to the question about the kind of man a
woman wants to marry: over 90 percent of the Kenyans gave responses in this category, and both the boys and girls agreed. The
Kenyans are more willing to recognize other values when thinking
about the kind of man people respect, but the majority still opt for
achievement and wealth.

Turning our attention now to the students' perceptions of
qualities desired in a woman, the eastern Kentuckians repeat their
pattern of response for the qualities desired in men (in the case of a
woman's qualities, males 70.3 percent, females 87.8 percent). The
Kenyan Kikuyu responses have shifted now, and a mixed picture
emerges. The Kikuyu students' beliefs about the kind of woman that is
respected are similar to the Kentuckians' views in this matter: people
respect women who demonstrate qualities of moral rectitude, are good
mothers, are sociable, and have good temperaments (males 78.1 percent, females 72.6 percent), much more than they respect women
who are rich or have achieved high levels of education or other kinds
of high status (males 21.9 percent, females 27.4 percent).

There is another interesting aspect to the responses. The Kenyan
Kikuyu girls and the eastern Kentucky boys are more than twice as
likely (27.4 percent and 29.7 percent vs. 12.2 percent) to believe that
women of achievement and wealth are respected than eastern

Kentucky girls (12.2 percent). The pattern becomes even more pronounced when the students are asked to typify the kind of woman a man wants to marry. The Kentucky boys are four and a half times more likely to say a man wants an achieving, high-status wife than the Kentucky girls are (34.3 percent vs 7.3 percent), the Kenyan girls say so about four times more often (29.8 percent) than the Kentucky girls, and the Kenyan boys who are the most interested in an achieving, high-status wife, say so about seven and a half times more frequently (55 percent) than the girls in Kentucky. Within both sample groups, however, the girls are similar in that they are both less likely to believe that a man would want an achieving wife than are their male peers. It appears that in both cases there is higher cross-sex agreement regarding gender ideals for males than there is for females; this discrepancy is a probable source of conflict for girls in both cultures, and the eastern Kentucky girls are more discrepant in their beliefs from their male peers than the Kikuyu girls are from Kikuyu boys.

One final point should be made. The gross lumping of responses into two categories obscured an important difference in the kinds of answers supplied by the two groups of students. While the Kentuckians' most common responses could be classified as representing some aspect of moral rectitude, they also put heavy emphasis on love, loving, knowing your prospective spouse loves you and that you love him or her. The Kenyans put an emphasis on knowing your duties and role expectations as a married person and on having an ability to work hard. The ability to work hard was particularly important for women. Further, to the question of what kind of woman a man wants to marry, being physically attractive was most commonly a response by the Kentucky girls. It was mentioned by only one of the Kentucky boys, but several girls mentioned it as a primary attribute.

DISCUSSION

The perceived preference patterns for offspring, in combination with gender ideals, as reflected in the students' responses to this study's questions are reflective of cultural patterns and social and economic structures of the two communities. Even though Kenyan Kikuyu culture explicitly privileges males in many ways, it is a culture in which women have real power based in their economic roles as the family farmers, in their role in reproduction (which is highly and explicitly valued), and in the emotional hold they have over their sons, who in the past never left home. They are an example of a social and cultural arrangement that Peggy Sanday (1981) calls "mythical male dominance."

These young Kenyans have mothers at home who are proud of their physical strength and ability to do hard physical labor in their gardens, who produce much of the food the family eats through their own labor with help from their children, who haul firewood and water on their backs for the family (see note 1), who tend coffee trees and milk cows.

Kenyan Kikuyu mothers often see their own interests as different from their husbands' interests in marriages that are sometimes comfortable and sometimes not, where husbands and wives do not sleep together and often do not eat together. Many of the Kenyan students have fathers who live most of the time where they have a wage-paying job, so that they grow up seeing him only every few months for a brief visit—a situation their mothers more often than not find congenial since it gives them maximum independence in running the farm and rearing the children.

Although most of the Kenyan students' families see themselves as Christian, they all know the earlier Kikuyu origin myth that tells a story about a time when women ruled and men were weak. It explains how the women were able to stop the men who had risen in successful rebellion against the women, from achieving total symbolic supremacy over the women. The men had hoped to forcefully change the feminine names of the ten Kikuyu clans to masculine names. The women threatened to kill all their children and to refuse to have others if the men changed the clan names. An uneasy truce was achieved, for the women held the ultimate trump card: the men's patrilines could not continue without the cooperation of nonrelated women, and the women knew it. It should not surprise us, then, to see many Kenyan Kikuyu adolescents believing that boys and girls are equally valued. Both adult women and men are expected to make important economic contributions to the family, and this expectation has not changed despite other changes in the culture, society, and economy.

The eastern Kentucky adolescents, on the other hand, are growing up in a different kind of culture. The dominant conservative Christianity of the area constantly reemphasizes the role of the man to be the proper head of the family as prescribed in the Bible when God said to woman, "I will greatly multiply your pain in childbearing; in pain shall you bring forth children, yet your desire shall be for your husband, and he shall rule over you" (Genesis 3:16). Farming of any kind—a subsistence mode that gave a sense of self-esteem and accomplishment (and also much hard work) to earlier generations of eastern Kentucky women as they pridefully counted their jars of canned produce from their kitchen gardens and covered their children at night with quilts skillfully stitched by their own hands—is gone.

Many people do not even put in kitchen gardens each year; many people—especially those living in the remnants of the old coal camps—do not have the ground to garden even if they wanted to. Some have forgotten how.

The distinctly masculine ethos of the coal industry is pervasive. The local economy—dominated by coal, and lean on jobs of any kind—has retarded the movement of women into wage-earning jobs. At the time of this study, approximately 60 percent of American women with children under 14 were working outside the home for wages. Only 40 percent of the mothers of the students in this study had any kind of wage-paying job; and most of those with jobs were in low-paying traditional women's jobs as secretaries or as restaurant or low-level health workers.

It is clear that the students in Kentucky still believed that a married woman's role was limited to housekeeping and child-rearing and supporting her husband, based on their responses to other items in the questionnaire, while they saw supporting the family as the primary attribute of the role of husband-father; and it was the male economic role that ranked highest among the reasons given by the eastern Kentucky students to explain their preference for sons over daughters. Within this context it is interesting to note again that very few of the Kentucky girls said they aspired to futures in which they would be exclusively housewives.

Prior to the impact of the Western world on Kikuyu culture—before the modern nation of Kenya was formed by the British—women and men were reared into a set of predominantly ascribed roles, although there was apparently some room for men to achieve some distinction based on their own initiative as warriors and later as elders. Some pursued wealth as traders with great success enabling them to marry more wives than other men, father more children than other men, and—through strategic marriages of these offspring—achieve more influence and standing than other men. That world is gone now and the old virtues no longer hold. The contemporary Kenyan world places a premium on achieved status based on individual competitiveness. Sharon Mitchell and I pointed out in an earlier analysis of the Kikuyu data (Mitchell and Abbott 1987) that the Kikuyu boys seem to be adapting more readily to these new demands than the girls. We also pointed out that there was evidence to suggest the girls were under greater pressure, particularly in rural areas, to continue conforming to the traditional role expectations of Kikuyu women, even if they completed secondary school. The Kenyan data suggest that the girls, in comparison with the boys, are suffering more conflict between the expectations and attitudes of a community that expects conformity to the traditional female role and their training in the individualizing, competitive values and attitudes of the new order represented by achievement in school and attainment of a job after school. H. B. M. Murphy (1982) has suggested that the shift from a social system based primarily on ascribed status to one based on achieved status rooted in individual competitiveness leads to increased depression in the transitional groups. Apparently, this is happening among the transitional adolescent Kikuyu in our study, and it is impacting the girls more than the boys for reasons described above. There is greater effort made by local rural communities to try to keep girls conforming with traditional roles.

It is possible that something similar is going on with the eastern Kentucky girls as well, although they present a somewhat different symptom pattern consisting in as many anxiety symptoms as depression symptoms, and as a group they are overall more symptomatic than the Kikuyu girls. The eastern Kentucky region is under increasing economic pressure to change a way of life that has been patterned on the labor demands of the coal industry. Thirty percent of the adolescents in the study have fathers directly employed in some aspect of coalmining, and the industry affects every other business in the county one way or another.

This order of things seems to have been in place now for about 70 years (Arcury 1988), so it is about three generations deep. As the grandparents of these adolescents took up mining, they established a division of labor that required a full-time housekeeper who ran the home and reared the children and maintained the coalminer who was in the mines 12 hours a day, six and sometimes seven days a week. There were few or no jobs for women outside the home, and there certainly was no role for a woman in the mines. At the same time, women lost their role as farm wife when they moved into the coal camps. The result was a more constricted life for many women. Now their role is changing again. The coal industry is changing its labor demands; it needs fewer and fewer workers to maintain the same levels of productivity. The whole region is struggling to diversify and find alternatives. The county that is home to the students in this study has yet to attract significant alternatives except in the service sector. There are more jobs for women than there used to be, although they are predominantly minimum-wage jobs.

Within this context, I suggest that the Kentucky girls' distress is a response to their perception that girls are not as valued as boys, and to their desire to move out of the traditional role for women in a context with few local examples to follow and a local social structure, economy, and set of cultural values that are not particularly encouraging. Recall that only 2.7 percent of these eastern Kentucky girls said they wanted a future as a housewife (see Table 8.2). This is a strong indicator that they are imagining a life different from that of the majority of their mothers. At the same time the girls hold conflicting values and attitudes related to ideal men, women, and spouses. They, also represent a transitional generation in Murphy's (1982) sense, then, and we would expect the relatively high levels of depressive symptoms we found in this population.

Both groups of girls, in eastern Kentucky and in Kenya, were clearly more symptomatic than their respective male classmates. We can understand this in terms of Murphy's (1982) ideas about transitional generations and the pressure put on girls in both local settings to continue to conform to traditional gender roles more so than males.[4] But why should the eastern Kentucky girls be so much more symptomatic than the Kenyan girls? I believe that the Kentucky girls are worse off because their traditional role ties them to a support role in the household, not to a role in economic production like the traditional role for Kenyan Kikuyu women. These eastern Kentucky girls are two to three generations removed from the farm wife roles of their grandmothers and great-grandmothers—roles that gave them a central place in the economic survival of their families. Kenyan girls have the traditional model of a mother who is responsible for feeding her family; she is the one who must provide food through her own efforts, whether that be through her gardening, or through her purchase of foodstuffs from money she earns in the market by selling things she has grown, or—for the few—through the wages she has earned from a job she holds. For her, there is no expectation that she will marry and be supported by her husband. It is reasonable to speculate that the Kenyan girls therefore, have a greater sense of self-efficacy than the Kentucky girls.

According to the self-efficacy theory of depression (Bandura 1986; Kanfer and Zeiss 1983; Ehrenberg et al. 1991), feelings of futility and despondency may arise when people feel they can have little effect in changing the circumstances of their lives that they wish to change. In the case of our study, these eastern Kentucky students are about to begin their final year of high school and are rapidly approaching the time when they will have to act if they hope to realize a different life from what their mothers have had. The limited opportunities their local community can provide means they must find a way to leave to get additional schooling or training of some kind. This will require a disruption of family ties, possible active resistance from family members who do not really want the daughters to change the pattern of their lives, and the need to locate financial support for further training—to name only the most obvious obstacles. A lowered sense of self-efficacy to bring about the desired change may contribute to the high level of depression and anxiety symptoms these girls reported.

A final point should be raised regarding the boys in these samples. Why are they so free of symptoms? One would think that the high rates of unemployment and underemployment they see around them would raise doubts about their futures, as well, possibly leading to decreased self-efficacy and increased symptoms of mental health problems. One explanation is that they are also distressed by their future occupational prospects and by the changes in their traditional gender roles, but that the Health Opinion Survey is not an adequate measure of their distress because it is expressed in a different constellation of symptoms. Some have suggested that American males mask depression in a constellation of "acting out" behaviors, including frequent abuse of alcohol and drugs (Ehrenberg et al. 1990a, 1990b).[5] Perhaps Kenyan Kikuyu males do, too. It is also possible that they are simply less stressed than the girls because they are currently experiencing less pressure to change their roles and they feel more valued than the girls because of the primacy given them in both Appalachian and Kenyan Kikuyu culture.

Another point should be made about the Kenyans. Earlier in the chapter it was pointed out that they are a highly selected population: they are among the 7 percent or so of rural youth who get sufficiently high scores on a national examination to gain a place in a government secondary school. This means that they know they have a better than average chance of obtaining a position of some kind when they successfully complete secondary school, as well as the hope of doing well enough on the next round of national examinations to go eventually to higher secondary school and then to a university. Among their rural peers, they are the most successful at school.

The eastern Kentuckians are a cross-section of their local community in a way the Kenyans are not. They represent a broader range of academic ability in a society that requires all to attend school until 16 years of age, and that strongly encourages its youth to stay until 18 when they receive a diploma. The earlier argument based on self-efficacy theory might lead one to expect the Kenyan boys to have been the least symptomatic, given their relatively privileged position in Kenyan society at the time—not the eastern Kentuckians, who clearly do not occupy such a position while facing the decay of highly paid industrial employment represented by unionized coalmining. But this is not the case. Culture may be operating here in the interaction between gender roles and the formation of illness. It may be that it is more acceptable for Kenyan males to admit to certain symptoms than it is for eastern Kentucky males.

CONCLUSION

In conclusion, this comparison has highlighted the ways in which changing gender roles in the face of widespread economic and social change interrelate with symptoms of depression and anxiety in two nonclinical samples of adolescents—one from Kenya in East Africa, and the other from Appalachian Kentucky in the United States—thus contributing to a scarce, but important, literature. Girls in both samples were more symptomatic than their respective male classmates, while the Appalachian girls were the most symptomatic of all. This finding should be followed up with additional research using more sensitive measures of the full range of adolescent emotional distress. Such research would permit a test of the suggestion that the boys have similar levels of distress but express it differently. Focused interviews carried out with a second sample of girls and boys in the Appalachian location would permit exploration of the interpretation that these are transitional generations particularly prone to depression. Any such interviewing should be done in conjunction with interviewing their mothers and fathers, so that generational changes could be documented. In the Kenyan case, the most profitable new research would be a return visit to the original schools, using the same questionnaires but with the addition of a more comprehensive measure of emotional well-being. Because 20 years have passed since the original data collection, contemporary responses could be compared to the responses reported here. This would provide a rich basis for measuring the extent of change in reports of stress in relationship to change in gender roles.

NOTES

Funding for the Kikuyu field research was provided by the Carnegie Corporation through the Child Development Research Unit, Harvard University and the University of Nairobi, John W. M. and Beatrice B. Whiting, Directors. These data were collected between August 1971 and December 1972. The eastern Kentucky field research was funded through an Appalachian Studies Fellowship-Mellon Foundation funding awarded through Berea College, and through two grants from the University of Kentucky Research Committee. The data were collected between February and August 1987. Data analysis was funded by the University of Kentucky. I want to thank the students and school authorities in both research locations for their cooperation and help in making this chapter possible, though I cannot mention them by name because of the need to protect their privacy. I also want to thank Becky Eller for assistance with codebook construction and data coding, and Helen Crawford for her help in manuscript preparation. An earlier version of this paper appeared under the title "Symptoms of Anxiety and Depression among Eastern Kentucky Adolescents: Insights from Comparative Fieldwork" (Abbott 1989).

1. A recent return visit to the same community where these data were originally collected confirmed my predictions about the emergence of growing distinctions in the lives of local residents. The number of stone houses in the community has grown substantially: 20 percent of the community's homesteads now have at least one stone house, while others now have houses constructed of dressed lumber with concrete floors and metal roofs. Development projects have brought paved roads, piped water, increased rural electrification, and phones for a few houses. It is now possible to live in the research community and commute via public transportation to work in the provincial capital 20 miles away. The more elaborate and expensive homes are primarily built by those who have obtained good paying jobs in the urban areas such as Nairobi. These persons are reinvesting in the rural area by building houses for themselves and/or their parents. Typically they intend to retire to their land in the countryside.

2. Sixty-six percent of the questionnaires from one of the three high schools were unusable. It was clear from the students' responses that they refused to cooperate in filling out the questionnaire, and more boys did so than girls. I can only speculate on the reasons. It seems to have been given on the last days before dismissal for summer vacation; probably, the teachers did not frame the task in a way that was convincing enough to students whose only interest was in leaving as soon as possible. There were no difficulties of this kind in the other two schools: in one (the one I directly supervised), 100 percent of the questionnaires were usable; in the other, they were 95 percent usable. Because of the problem with the students' attitude toward the task in the first school, the analysis of the values questions for this paper is limited to the subset of questionnaires from the two schools where no difficulties were encountered, although the demographic data and the HOS analyses are based on the total set of usable quentionnaires.

3. A detailed analysis of the Kikuyu students' HOS responses is available in Mitchell and Abbott (1987). It should be noted here that this instrument may not be tapping the kinds of distress more typical of males—for example, excessive consumption of alcohol and other drugs. There has also been a recent suggestion made by Keefe et al. (1993) that Appalachians tend to report higher levels of somatic symptoms and a greater incidence of depression. The researchers are still analyzing their data. We must keep these cautions in mind as possible limitations on our results.

4. A recent review of the sociology literature on families and adolescents for the decade of the 1980s conducted by Gecas and Seff (1990), reports that more pressure is exerted on girls than on boys in American families in general to conform to traditional (housewife) roles—particularly pressure exerted by fathers. (See page 946 of their review for a discussion of this literature.)

5. Ehrenberg et al. (1990b) report that, in their study of Canadian adolescents, more males than females are depressed in early adolescence but that the pattern shifts to one in which more females than males in mid-to-late adolescence are mildly depressed. In late adolescence the proportions of clinically depressed adolescents is the same for both males and females. The researchers also report that their findings are consistent with other studies done in the United States and Great Britain. About one-third of their sample adolescents were mildly to clinically depressed.

■ 9 ■

From the Mountains to the Maquiladoras: A Case Study of Capital Flight and Its Impact on Workers

John Gaventa

In recent years the U.S. economy has lost hundreds of thousands of jobs in manufacturing. According to a study by the Office of Technology Assessment, in the years between 1979 and 1985, 11.5 million workers lost their jobs as companies decided to shut down or relocate manufacturing plants, increase productivity, or shrink output. These plant closings and layoffs have prompted warnings of the "deindustrialization of America," and have caused major disruptions in workers' lives, ranging from long-term and short-term unemployment, underemployment, foreclosures, and associated family stress.[1]

Until recently, the South was often thought to be exempt from these trends. For decades, in fact, de-industrialization of the "frostbelt" North meant the growth of the "sunbelt" South. The South was on the receiving end of capital mobility, as runaway shops from the North came south in search of a "favorable business climate"—meaning low-wage labor, cheap resources, and community subsidies. But by the early 1980s, the trend began changing, and the industries that had once moved to the South also began to close or relocate overseas. As Southern economic historian James Cobb writes,

> Industries fleeing the South are purchasing one-way tickets to Taiwan and other exotic destinations just as readily as they used to depart Akron, Ohio for Opelika, Alabama.[2]

An example of the impact of de-industrialization may be seen in Tennessee. At one level, economic development in the state has been successful. The South has lured dozens of factories within its borders and has received national attention for its recruitment of mega-manufacturing plants such as Saturn. But like other Southern states overly preoccupied with industrial recruitment, Tennessee has failed to keep many of its traditional manufacturing plants. Between 1980 and 1985, the state saw, 2,844 of its manufacturing plants closed down; 605 of them employed more than 50 workers each. Between April 1986 and the end of 1987, some 10,000 workers lost jobs as 60 plants—each with 50 or more workers—closed or made permanent layoffs. These layoffs were in all sectors of the manufacturing economy: textiles, apparel, paper, chemicals, furniture, machinery, and transportation.[3]

Despite the trends, plant closings in the South have received little public attention. The region has heralded its success in recruiting industries from the North; closings are a threat to the sunbelt image. Moreover, where closings have occurred, they have often been more invisible—in smaller, more rural industries, with less unionized and less powerful workers—than have closings in the auto plants or steel industries of the urbanized North.

Until now, few studies have described the process of capital flight or analyzed its impact on the workers and communities affected. Why are plants leaving, and where are they going? Do workers in the sunbelt experience problems of dislocation similar to those of other regions? The following case study provides a classic story of the movement of capital from the North to the South, and then to the Third World, in constant search of cheaper labor and a more favorable business climate.

THE MOVE TO THE APPALACHIAN SOUTH

The Jim Robbins Seat Belt Company was originally based in Michigan and first considered Knoxville, Tennessee, as a plant site in the early 1960s. The mood of the time encouraged industrial growth and expansion. Demand for seat belts was also growing, and the company moved rapidly to meet it.

Early one morning in November 1965, Robbins's chief executive officer telephoned the industrial development executive of the Knoxville Chamber of Commerce about possible sites for a new plant. That same afternoon, corporate officials arrived in Knoxville in an executive jet piloted by the company's owner, Jim Robbins. A lease on an abandoned Du Pont facility was signed. The following Monday, the company began hiring about 50 workers. Within two weeks employment was up to 100, with two shifts daily producing 50,000 belts a week—all under contract with Ford and General Motors.

By 1967, local employment had risen to 1,200 people, and production was up to 60,000 assembled seat belts a day—enough to meet 60 percent of Ford's requirements and a large percentage of GM's. Local papers heralded the operation as the largest seat-belt manufacturing company in the world, producing more than 19 million belts a year.

The company heads cited Knoxville's favorable business atmosphere and the attitude of the workers as playing a big part in their decision to locate in the city. In 1967 the company president, Bill Johnson, praised Knoxville's "progressive local government," which was "interested in the requirements of industrial development." The city government had helped the company acquire land, cut through red tape for installation of utilities, and in general displayed a "cooperative spirit." "The workforce has a progressive attitude and a desire to work which is essential for industrial growth," Johnson said. "They're good workers and they're intelligent too. Your labor force here trains very quickly." Moreover, he stated bluntly, "The future of our expansion in Knoxville depends on the business atmosphere."[4]

The business atmosphere was also affected, of course, by wage differentials between Michigan and Tennessee. In 1972, according to the U.S. Census of Manufacturers, the average wage for production workers in the industry was $2.58 an hour in Knoxville, about half the $5.04 an hour that similar workers received in the Detroit area. And the company did what it could to ensure that the favorable "business atmosphere" continued. By 1973, only eight years after the location of the initial plant, the Jim Robbins Seat Belt Company had become the largest manufacturing contributor to the local chamber of commerce. One company official led a chamber of commerce project to produce a film that would document local industry's impact on the area's economy. The company made donations to the United Way, to a local black college, to the YMCA.

By 1979 the company employed almost 3,000 workers and ranked—with two other textile firms, Levi Strauss and Standard Knitting Mills—among the city's largest industrial employers.[5]

THE BUBBLE BURSTS: FROM TENNESSEE TO ALABAMA

The atmosphere of industrial growth began to change very quickly in the 1980s. In an eight-month period during late 1979 and early 1980, the company laid off 1,500 employees. This was followed by a further series of layoffs, bringing employment down to between 300 and 400 workers by 1983.

At first, in 1981, company officials publicly attributed the layoffs to the deepening effects of recession on the automotive industry. By 1983, as the country climbed out of the recession, the company blamed the slump in new U.S. car sales and increased imports.

However, at the same time the company was saying it could not afford to reinvest in Knoxville, it was investing handsomely in a new facility in Greenville, Alabama—a rural, nonunion area anxious to acquire new industry. Between 1980 and 1985 the company carried out three expansions there, and increased its Alabama workforce threefold, from 300 in 1980 to 960 in 1985.

In Alabama, the company echoed the story that Knoxville officials had heard 15 years before. The company needed room to expand. Greenville offered a "large and motivated workforce, most easily trainable and many already seasoned in industrial sewing, thanks to the area's history of textile and carpet production." Moreover, the strong work ethic of the local labor force was complemented by the "upbeat, cooperative ready-to-serve attitude of local officials and business leaders."[6]

As Knoxville had 15 years earlier, Greenville responded quickly. The mayor's office, the industrial development board, and local banks provided revenue-bond financing for the purchase of the first building in 1980, and another in 1982. The Alabama Development Office helped the company by providing a training program in sewing and assembly, and by handling all employee recruiting and pre-screening.[7]

As in the move to Tennessee, differences in wages were also a factor. Butler County, where Greenville is located, is more rural than Knoxville, with fewer unions and fewer industrial competitors. In 1982, wages for manufacturing workers in Butler County were approximately 60 percent of those for similar workers in Knoxville.[8]

ECONOMIC BLACKMAIL

Rather than reinvest in equipment and retraining in Knoxville, then, the company moved to a new area that offered cheaper, non-union labor and favorable state subsidies. Moreover, as the company increased its facilities in Alabama, it used the threat of further layoffs and movement of capital to exact concessions from the Knoxville workforce. By the 1980s "the company increasingly used job black-mail against us, playing the Knoxville workers off against the Alabama employees," said one local union official.

In 1983 the company offered to bring some of the jobs back to Knoxville, but only if workers there would reduce job classifications and accept pay cuts. Desperate for jobs, the union members accepted the offer, returning to work for wages lower than those rejected three years before. "We're hoping it will be a start of a major turnaround," the union official said at the time. "It's definitely a trend going in the right direction."[9]

The optimism did not last long. Not long after a few jobs returned to Knoxville from Alabama, they were transferred again—this time to new plants in Mexico. In August 1985, more than 200 workers were laid off, leaving employment at slightly above 200 in an area that only six years before had been declared the seat-belt capital of the world.

FROM THE MOUNTAINS TO THE MAQUILADORA ZONE

For its new seat-belt facility, the company chose the town of Aqua Prieta, one of the smaller and newer *maquiladora* border towns. Freely translated, the word *maquilar* means "to assemble." The *maquiladoras* are companies located along the Mexican border that assemble products with Mexican labor for re-export back to the United States or to other countries.[10] The *maquiladora* zone is now growing at a phenomenal rate, as hundreds of U.S. plants move across the border for lower wage labor.

Located in the state of Sonora, directly across the border from Douglas, Arizona, the town of Agua Prieta is typical.[11] In recent years more than 20 manufacturing plants have located in the town, almost all of them sewing, electronic, automotive part, or other labor-intensive operations from the United States. With factory work abundant, the population has more than tripled in ten years, from 18,000 in the mid-1970s to more than 60,000 people by the mid 1980s. Growth has outstripped services and infrastructure. Plants sprawl in unfinished industrial parks. Mexican workers—attracted from miles around—find housing and services in short supply.

The new seat-belt plant opened on January 1, 1986. According to sources in the plant, the company employs about 500 people and is growing. There, in repetitive, noisy assembly-line work, the workers cut the webbing and assemble the seatbelts for shipment back to Greenville for U.S. distribution.

The wages are minuscule compared to those in the United States. Workers in this plant, as in others along the Mexican border, work $9^1/_2$-hour days for about $3.50 a day, or 37 cents an hour—one-sixteenth of the wages that workers were receiving for comparable work in Knoxville in the mid-80s.

Although the wages seem low to the U.S. visitor, the jobs are welcomed by local workers, on the whole. Bumper stickers on cars parked near the plant claim in Spanish, "I love Bendix." (By then, the seat-belt company was the Bendix division of a large conglomerate.) Local merchants are glad of the revenues. Even the local union, which is tied into the official national union, does little to question the arrangement. In short, the business climate is very, very favorable. As one U.S. resident along the border told me, "If you think economic boosterism is big in your part of the world, you haven't seen anything until you come here."

It may be more intense, but this pro-business climate arises out of a very familiar development policy: recruit industry from the North. In Mexico, the *maquiladora* zone has emerged as the official solution to regional underdevelopment. But to large multinational businesses like the seat-belt company, it is simply one more area in the world economy that, desperate for development at any price, will provide cheaper labor and a more favorable business climate.

THE GROWTH OF THE MULTINATIONAL:
MERGERS AND CONGLOMERATION

As the U.S. seat-belt company moved from the North to the urban South, then to the rural nonunion South, then to Mexico, it also was becoming integrated into a larger multinational corporate empire. When the company came to Knoxville in 1965, it was a private venture owned by Jim Robbins, a self-made Michigan millionaire with holdings ranging from banana and cotton plantations in Venezuela to seat-belt and plastics factories in the Detroit area. Shortly after the move to Knoxville, Robbins was killed while flying his private jet near his buffalo and pheasant ranch in Platte, South Dakota. A year later the firm was bought by the Allied Chemical Corporation, a vast chemical and manufacturing firm. In 1982, Allied took over the Bendix Corporation; and in 1983, the seat-belt operation became the Bendix Safety Restraints Division.

In 1985, Allied merged with the Signal Corporation to form Allied Signal, now one of the largest manufacturing holding firms in the world. As workers in Knoxville were being laid off as a result of the movement of their jobs to Mexico, top officials of Allied and Signal were receiving at least $50 million in cash, stock giveaways, options, and other benefits in what the *Wall Street Journal* marked as one of the largest windfalls for corporate executives in merger history.[12]

THE IMPACT ON WORKERS

With a climate of competition between workers and communities in different locations for scarce jobs, large corporations can use the threat—and the reality—of massive plant closings and layoffs as a tool for "economic blackmail" and bargaining for labor concessions. Allied used the movement of jobs to Alabama as a tool to exact concessions from workers in Knoxville. Even when the concessions were made, the company still laid off workers in Tennessee in order to gain yet cheaper labor and more favorable conditions in Mexico.

Conventional economists might argue, of course, that such industrial location and relocation are a natural process of economic development and that such movement of capital ultimately serves to produce jobs and economic growth for workers and communities. However, Allied Signal workers have not fared well in this process of economic transition. Interviews with 170 of the workers laid off in 1985 show the following evidence of long-term distress:

■ Some 15 months after being laid off, 44 percent of the workers were still unemployed.

■ Of those workers who had been able to find new jobs, less than half (47 percent) had been able to get full-time work; 53 percent were working at part-time jobs.

■ Of the workers who had been able to find new jobs, average wages had dropped from $5.76 an hour to $3.70 an hour.

■ While they worked at Allied, none of the workers earned less than $5 an hour. For those who had obtained new jobs, 91 percent were earning less than $5 an hour and three-quarters were now making less than $4 an hour.

■ The jobs the workers lost were union jobs. For 91 percent of them, there was no union at their new jobs.

■ Ninety-five percent of the workers lost their health insurance when they were laid off. Only 48 percent were now covered under a new plan.

■ The impact of the layoffs was especially severe on older workers, women, and families with only one primary earner in the household.

Workers in Knoxville suffered this decline in wages and quality of life despite the fact that, overall, Knoxville enjoys a growth economy. Its loss of manufacturing jobs has been far outpaced by a gain of jobs in the nonmanufacturing sectors—especially services and wholesale and retail trade. However, seatbelt workers have fallen through the cracks of economic transition. When those laid-off workers have gotten new jobs, the largest percentage have been in the service sector, where they have lower wages, fewer hours, and no union representation.

The Allied case is representative. National studies have also found that the increasing number of service jobs may be accompanied by a declining standard of living for many workers.[13] In fact, the seat-belt workers seem to have fared worse than dislocated workers nationally. Only 47 percent were able to obtain new full-time jobs, compared to 60 percent nationally. Some 15 months after being laid off, almost 60 percent of the workers reported an average household income of less than $10,400 a year (the poverty line for a family of four in the mid-1980s).

To survive such poverty, most of the workers (93 percent) drew unemployment compensation after the layoff, and about half did so for the full 26-week period for which they were eligible. Once their unemployment benefits ran out, these workers were faced with major problems of survival. Remarkably few used food stamps—only 18 percent of the total. Most people turned to more informal means of survival, made possible in part by the somewhat rural culture of the area: 22 percent reported that they gardened or farmed, 22 percent did odd jobs, and 21 percent borrowed money, often from friends and relatives.

But for many workers, this informal system did not provide protection against severe hardship. For instance, almost a quarter of the workers faced large medical expenses while laid off. One woman, age 37, had three teenagers, all of whom had medical emergencies: one son broke his arm; the other two were involved in car and motorcycle accidents. Facing a debt of $18,000, she had to declare bankruptcy. For her—a woman who had worked all her life, starting at 15—such a decision could only come with a high psychological cost.

Another woman was facing $16,000 in medical bills. She was relatively lucky: her husband had a job as a government meat inspector. But even so, she was working two jobs to try to pay off her debts—by day at a photography shop for $4.50 an hour, by night at a pizza parlor for minimum wage.

Loss of income also had an impact on housing. More than a third of the workers interviewed had a mortgage on their homes, and almost a quarter faced monthly rent payments. No cases of actual foreclosure were reported, but some had to sell their homes and rent apartments or move in with relatives.

And they were not alone. Many workers with large medical bills or housing costs have gone into debt, used up their savings, worked extra jobs, or depended on relatives' help to meet their expenses. Many cut back on basic needs for themselves and their children— clothing, food, transportation, and electricity. Others have dipped into savings that were intended to provide their security in the future. The uncertainties of unemployment or of working minimum-wage jobs take their toll in countless other ways as well. Almost half (48 percent) of the laid-off workers reported psychological problems such as stress and depression.

LACK OF JOB TRAINING

It is precisely this type of economic "skidding" that job-training programs are designed to ameliorate. Theoretically, the laid-off Allied workers were eligible for retraining benefits under Title III of the Job Training and Partnership Act of 1982 (designed for displaced workers) and under the Trade Adjustment Assistance Act, or TAA, designed for workers losing their jobs because of imports. In fact, both programs failed to meet the retraining needs. Even though at least 236 of the workers laid off in 1985 were found to be eligible for retraining programs, almost two years later only two had actually enrolled in the retraining, under TAA sponsorship. One state department of labor official described the problem this way: "We don't have programs for 200 people who are refugees from the garment industry....If we got 10 of these folks into job training programs, we'd be lucky." The government attitude toward these workers was described more bluntly by another federal official: "Their skill level is such that you can't do anything with them."[14]

TOWARD NEW STRATEGIES

In sum, then, capital mobility and economic transition have created severe hardship for workers in Knoxville, Tennessee, with problems ranging from unemployment to mental stress, from loss of income to loss of health benefits and housing. This case supports the thesis that problems related to plant closings and worker dislocation occur even as new service jobs are being created, and they happen in the South as well as the North.

These problems present new challenges for economic development policy. Traditionally the South has concentrated on industrial recruitment as its strategy for economic development, yet trends show that industries—once recruited—are leaving and that new industries are less likely to come. The jobs that are being created are not necessarily bringing increased economic well-being for working people; many workers are trapped in a spiral of low-wage and part-time underemployment or even unemployment. Programs designed to help train workers for the better jobs in the "new economy" are failing to assist those most in need of them. As James Cobb points out, "There is a grim irony in the fact that the South, having worked so diligently to create a business climate attractive to footloose industries, should now find its economic future threatened by an increase in industrial mobility."[15]

But so far, Tennessee, like most Southern states, has paid little attention to countering de-industrialization. Policies and programs on job dislocation must be added to those that concentrate on job creation. Community stability must become as important as capital mobility.

The labor movement must also confront de-industrialization trends, or it will see many of its hard-won gains eroded. The situation calls for new strategies on the part of labor: continue to represent workers in existing jobs (made increasingly difficult by the climate of economic blackmail and concession bargaining), fight to save the manufacturing jobs at risk, and organize new service-sector jobs to obtain improved wages and benefits.

In other parts of the country, workers have met these challenges by joining with community coalition groups and policymakers to support legislation that would require early warnings of plant closings; taking over ailing plants and running them as worker-owned or community-owned enterprises; getting more involved in the economic development process by participating in local industrial boards, state development agencies, and economic development initiatives; establishing coalitions with workers and communities in other parts of the country and in other countries to counter economic blackmail.[16]

If the case of the seat-belt workers is indicative of broader trends—and I believe it is—then policymakers, labor unions, and community groups throughout the South must explore new strategies to counter the effects of capital flight and worker dislocation. We must learn to measure development potential not only by the business climate, but also by the climate for workers and communities.

NOTES

This chapter is based on a longer report by John Gaventa, "From the Mountains to the Maquiladoras: A Case Study of Capital Flight and Its Impact on Workers," written in 1988 and available from the Highlander Research and Education Center, 1959 Highlander Way, New Market, TN 37820. This chapter was also published in John Gaventa, Barbara Ellen Smith, and Alex Willingham, *Communities in Economc Crisis: Appalachia and the South* (Philadelphia: Temple University Press, 1990). Special thanks to Mark Pitt and Doug Gamble of the Georgia-Tennessee-Alabama Joint Board of the Amalgamated Clothing and Textile Workers Union for assistance provided, and to ACTWU Local 1742 for its cooperation.

1. For effects of layoffs, see Bluestone and Harrison, *The Deindustrialization of America: Plant Closings, Community Abandonment and the Dismantling of Basic Industry* (New York: Basic Books 1982), and Robert B. Reich, "The Hollow Corporation," *Business Week*, March 3, 1986.

2. Cobb (1986, 98).

3. See Fox et al. (1987); additional data from the Tennessee Department of Economic Security.

4. *Knoxville News Sentinel*, November 29, 1967, for text of speech by Bill Johnson, "The Decision To Locate in Knoxville and Resulting Success," November 29, 1967.

5. In the summer of 1988, both Levi's and Standard announced that they were closing down their Knoxville operations.

6. *Nation's Business*, May 1985, 40J.

7. Ibid.

8. Based on U.S. Department of Commerce, Bureau of the Census, Census of Manufacturers, 1982. Data on wages of textile and apparel workers in Butler County were not available.

9. Quoted in *Knoxville News Sentinel*, November 23, 1983. Information about Knoxville worker concessions derived from interviews with local union officials and from a comparison of "Agreements between Allied Corporation...and Amalgamated Clothing and Textile Workers Union," December 1, 1980, with agreements dated March 15, 1982, and December 1, 1985.

10. In Mexico, the companies are exempt from certain laws, such as those governing foreign investment, and do not have to pay import duties on materials to be assembled for export. The process is also encouraged by the U.S. Tariff Code, Sections 806.30 and 807.00, which reduce tariff duties on imports assembled abroad using components in the United States.

11. Observations about Agua Prieta are based on personal visit and interviews, September 24–26, 1987.

12. *The Wall Street Journal*, August 12, 1985.

13. See, for example, "Great American Job Machine," in Bluestone and Harrison.

14. Correspondence, U.S. Department of Labor and Senator Albert Gore, April 24, 1987; and Senator Gore to Mark Pitt, ACTWU, May 13, 1987. Quotations are from telephone interviews with the author.

15. Cobb (1986).

16. See, for example, Gilda Haas, *Plant Closures: Myths, Realities, and Responses* (Boston: South End Press, 1985).

▪ 10 ▪

From the Apennines to the Appalachians: Regional Development in Italy and the U.S.

Phillip J. Obermiller

In the John Sayles film *Matewan*, Italian immigrants join with black migrants from Alabama and native West Virginian miners in a coal strike. It is clear that the differences in the three groups' languages and cultures do not diminish their common interests as miners. In a particularly telling episode, a black miner shows his Italian counterpart how to protect against rooffalls after learning that the Italian had worked as a shoemaker before arriving in the West Virginia coalfield. The presence of Italian workers in Appalachia is not just a cinematic device; it is well documented that Italian labor helped to build the region's railroads, dig its coal, and organize its unions (Eller 1982; Portelli 1984; Wolfe 1975).

Parallels between the social structure, the culture, and even the topography of Appalachia and southern Italy (or the Mezzogiorno, as it is commonly known) have been noted by authors such as Alessandro Portelli (1984) and Margaret Ripley Wolfe (1975). Given the extent of the Italian-Appalachian connection, however, it is remarkable that this relationship has not been examined more closely.

In this chapter we explore the similarities between Appalachia and the Mezzogiorno, with particular attention to the social and economic conditions arising from their positions as poor regions within wealthy industrialized nations. We then examine the implementation of development plans intended to reduce the social and economic disparities affecting each region: the Cassa per il Mezzogiorno in Italy and the Appalachian Regional Commission in the United States.

Our purpose here is to compare planning efforts and outcomes in regions with similar conditions. A cross-national and historical perspective can be helpful to students of Appalachia in evaluating endeavors in planning economic development as well as proposed strategies for change in the Appalachian region.

SOME OBVIOUS DISTINCTIONS

At first glance Appalachia and the Mezzogiorno have little in common. The Mezzogiorno is on a peninsula washed by the Adriatic, Ionian, and Tyrrhenian seas. Appalachia's "coastal waters" are limited to two northern Appalachian counties (Erie in Pennsylvania and Chautauqua in New York) that lie on Lake Erie's southern shore. The predominant religion in the Mezzogiorno is Roman Catholicism; in Appalachia the residents typically belong to Protestant denominations or sects. The languages of the two areas have different roots: the English of Appalachia comes from Celtic and Germanic sources, while the Italian dialects of the Mezzogiorno have their origin in Latin.

Although native people with ancient cultures still live in Appalachia, much of the region's history belongs to people born since the onset of the Industrial Revolution. Even the region's contact with British and French colonialism was relatively brief and tangential. Appalachia has little experience with political ideals other than those of republicanism and democracy. In short, Appalachia can be seen through the lens of world history as a region truly belonging to the modern era (cf. Eller 1982).

By contrast, the Mezzogiorno has experienced the development of Western civilization for more than two thousand years. Because of its central location, southern Italy has been conquered and colonized by virtually every major power in the Mediterranean basin. Perhaps in part as a result of its oppressive political history, key elements of the medieval feudal system survived in the Mezzogiorno until the late nineteenth century. Well into the twentieth century, inhabitants of the region still were being characterized as peasants. Indeed, most of the social change in the region has been realized only in this century (cf. Lopreato 1967).

SOME IMPORTANT SIMILARITIES

Despite the differences in their historical backgrounds, Appalachia and the Mezzogiorno have many commonalities. The topography of both regions is quite similar; nearly 85 percent of the land area of the Mezzogiorno is occupied by mountains and hills. Both are subject to the natural disasters associated with mountain areas: floods, landslides, and sheet erosion. Climatic conditions, including comfortable summers and bleak winters, are similar in both regions.

Appalachia and the Mezzogiorno have populations of over 20 million each. Major metropolitan areas are few and scattered in both regions; villages interspersed with small towns of between 2,000 and 8,000 residents are the norm. As is typical of mountain areas, communication and transportation between towns tends to be linear—from smaller to larger—rather than clustered by locality. This situation promotes a social isolation and a dependency on hierarchical trade patterns that inhibit cooperation among adjoining communities in both regions.

Federal government policies are of remote interest in these towns and villages, and agents of federal programs are often viewed as incompetent or untrustworthy. Local politics have a much more direct impact on the lives of villagers and townspeople, consequently generating more involvement and more concern than federal, state, or provincial issues.

Because both regions act as barriers across natural transportation routes from east to west on their respective continents, commerce tends to flow around them. The industrial base in each region is small; primary industries such as agriculture or mineral extraction are historically important forms of production. More recently, the service sectors of both regional economies have begun to grow (Bethemont and Pelletier 1983; Kublawi 1986).

A one-way flow of capital out of each region can be traced to similar patterns of absentee land ownership. Despite attempts at reform, two-thirds of the Mezzogiorno remains in the hands of absentee landlords; a smaller but still significant proportion of Appalachian land is controlled by nonresidents (Appalachian Land Ownership Task Force 1883; Franklin 1961). Both regions are backwaters in the highly developed economies of their respective countries.

These economic disparities translate directly into grating hardships for many people in Appalachia and the Mezzogiorno. Per capita income in each region is a fraction of that of their respective countries; rates of unemployment, poverty, and illiteracy are much higher (Bethemont and Pelletier 1983; Tickmyer and Tickmyer 1987). Regional mortality rates and disease incidence characteristically are higher than national averages. Although commentators such as Banfield (1958) and Weller (1965) attribute these conditions to the cultural characteristics of the people of the Mezzogiorno and Appalachia, the poverty of the two regions results more from structural conditions than from cultural traits.

The regions also show strong cultural parallels. Family and religion are still key institutions in both areas. Strong kinship ties, an abiding sense of individual pride, an attachment to place, and a commonsense realism that is often labeled "fatalism" are also common to both groups (Peabody 1970). A compelling similarity is found even in the aberrations in the two regions that result when social customs collide with oppressive economic or political circumstances—for example, the clear kinship patterns in gang formation or in some criminal activities.

Another obvious similarity between the Mezzogiorno and Appalachia is their history of migration. The Mezzogiorno has been a major donor area for migration streams to northern Europe, Australia, North and South America, and more recently to the industrialized areas of northern Italy (King 1986; Rogers 1970). The Appalachian migration occurred later and was less geographically diverse, but was similar to the Italian experience in that the flow was from rural to urban areas and depended heavily on extended family ties for its success. Out-migration depopulated entire towns in both regions, and return migration contributes considerably to the momentum of social change (King, Strachan and Mortimer 1986).

Despite their historical differences, in modern times the regions display striking structural similarities. Just as Appalachia has become part of the "other America," the Mezzogiorno forms one of the "two Italies." For both, the flow of labor and capital has been outward, generally from an impoverished rural south to a prosperous industrialized north (Holland 1971). Recognition of these regional economic discrepancies has led to the development of federal planning strategies meant to correct the inequities. In Italy the organization responsible for the development of the Mezzogiorno is the Cassa per il Mezzogiorno (or, Fund for the South). Appalachian development in the United States is the responsibility of the Appalachian Regional Commission.

THE CASSA PER IL MEZZOGIORNO

Formal development in the Italian south began at the end of World War II and can be examined in four distinct stages. From 1945 until 1950 the Mezzogiorno participated in the general postwar reconstruction assisted by the U.S. Marshall Plan conducted throughout Italy. The years between 1950 and 1957 formed a period of preindustrial preparation in the Mezzogiorno, with major efforts at land reform, land reclamation, and general infrastructure building. Between 1957 and 1964 the focus was on industrialization; growth pole theory was used to locate publicly owned industries in the south. Since 1964 more attention has been paid to the development of subregions and the integration of regional planning into a larger national plan (King 1975).

In 1945 the Mezzogiorno was suffering from the despoliation of war and from the ravages of war planning. The Fascist planners had upset early land reforms and designated the region "the granary of the new Italian empire" by encouraging agriculture and prohibiting industrial development in the south of Italy (Holland 1971, 71). By 1948 an independent research institute, the SVIMEZ had been organized to document conditions in the region and to provide the data that would provide a basis for development planning.

The Cassa was instituted in 1950 with the initial mandate to implement a new land reform program. Secondary attention was given to improvements in regional agriculture and infrastructure. Within four years, the Cassa's mandate was extended to include offering industrial credit through special credit institutes, and its program of infrastructural improvements was expanded to include grants of up to 50 percent of the cost of improvements undertaken by local communities and organizations. Late in this period Italian planners—obviously influenced by the French concept of growth poles—began discussing the need to invest in "propulsive sectors" within the Mezzogiorno.

By 1957 the Cassa had changed its focus from land reform and improvements in agriculture to industrial development. The new policy called for the south to receive a 40 percent share of the total investment in state-owned industries, and a 60 percent share of the total public plant investment. At the same time, specific "growth areas" were defined: areas of intensive growth were designated around large urban areas in the region, and smaller "nuclei of industrialization" were dispersed across the region.

Despite modest successes since 1950, the Cassa has not achieved its goals. In his study of the villagers of Franza, Joseph Lopreato provides a striking illustration of the Cassa's shortcomings:

> The community had to rely on a number of unheated, unequipped, and poorly built private houses as classrooms for the several sections of the five local grades.
>
> A few years ago, under the auspices of the Cassa per il Mezzogiorno, a new school was planned and construction started. But for various unfathomable reasons, adequate funds were not forthcoming, and the initiated building has been serving since as a public latrine. (Lopreato 1967, 138)

Many of the Cassa's land reform policies were poorly executed or simply ill conceived. Large landholdings were broken up and made available to small farmers without regard to the actual productive potential of the individual parcels; as a result, some farmers were left with marginal or unproductive land. None received the technical assistance necessary to increase productivity or to develop cooperative marketing mechanisms for their produce.

One farm-improvement project of the Cassa included the relocation of farming families from the villages to houses constructed for them on their new landholdings. From the planners' viewpoint, this marvelously efficient idea eliminated the farmers' tiresome, time-wasting daily trek to and from their distant fields. From the viewpoint the farm families, however, the imposed isolation deprived them of the gregarious social interaction of village life, which was a key source of stimulation and entertainment in a workday otherwise filled with drudgery. Many of the sturdy new houses built by the Cassa were soon abandoned for the familiar, dilapidated, and more convivial quarters back in the village.

Creating the infrastructure for industrialization proved to be a necessary but insufficient basis for the development of new industries in southern Italy. The Cassa's planners relied too heavily on the assumption that once they had created the opportunity for private industries to locate in the south through industrial credits, low cost loans, and improved roads, sewers, and water and energy supplies, the natural mechanisms of the market would attract those industries to the region. This reliance on spontaneous growth through natural market mechanisms brought disappointing results (Holland 1971).

Moreover, the policy of relocating or building new state-owned industries in the Mezzogiorno also failed since these industries were less capital intensive, and offered basic services and commodities (e.g., construction, hydroelectric power) that required few workers. In the case of both public and private industrial growth in the south, the skilled, highly paid jobs often were filled from the trained and experienced labor pool of the north; local workers were left to compete for whatever "trickle-down" benefits remained.

The Cassa's growth pole policy yielded similarly discouraging results. Forty-two growth and nucleus areas had been designated by 1970, using a process that was influenced more strongly by political considerations than by the potential for development. The selection of some of the smaller, more rural nuclei was more a gratuitous effort to give the impression of fairness than a serious attempt at industrial development (King 1975). Indeed, a 1970 report issued by SVIMEZ criticized the policy of encouraging "industrial nuclei" as one of building "cathedrals in the desert" (Holland 1971, 78).

After spending $14 billion over a 20-year period (1950-1970), the Cassa—whose charter was extended in 1980—had not achieved its goal of eliminating regional economic disparities between northern and southern Italy (King 1975). Nor had it done much better at achieving its particular objectives of instituting land reform, improving agriculture, building an infrastructure, and developing an industrial base in southern Italy.

THE APPALACHIAN REGIONAL COMMISSION

The Civil War was fought across much of what was to become known as Appalachia, just as World War II despoiled the Mezzogiorno some 80 years later. Nonetheless, the work of Reconstruction did not affect the Appalachian mountains to the same extent that the Marshall Plan aided recovery in southern Italy. After the Civil War, however, the Appalachian region did experience a degree of industrialization, primarily through the opening of new coalmines and railroads.

Compared with Italy, the United States is an extremely young nation, and concerns about land reform were not great in a country that saw itself until recently as a nation of unsettled frontiers. Consequently Appalachia did not experience the efforts at land reform that swept through the Mezzogiorno in the postwar era.

Against this historical backdrop, planning for regional economic development in Appalachia skipped the stages of industrialization and land reform. With the passage of the Appalachian Regional Development Act in 1965 and the concomitant founding of the Appalachian Regional Commission, or ARC, the focus immediately became improvement of the region's "basic facilities," particularly in transportation. Highway improvement and road-building projects have consumed more than half of the ARC's budget each year from 1965 through 1990.

Like the Cassa, the ARC promoted subregional development, working through 69 multicounty jurisdictions called local development districts, or LDDs. In its early stages the commission also espoused the growth pole principle of development—a form of economic triage in which areas that held the most promise for progress would receive the most resources through the ARC, while the neediest counties would receive little or no development assistance. This strategy was replaced later by the "worst first" model in which those counties with the most desperate needs received the most help.

The most innovative development in regional planning in the United States as compared with Italy was the ARC's relation with local (i.e., LDD), state, and federal jurisdictions. Instead of the top-down planning design used by the Cassa, the ARC is governed by a consortium of governors from each of the 13 Appalachian states. It acts as an intermediary among the jurisdictions it serves. For example, the commission cooperates with LDDs to attract funds from other federal agencies for water management, sewage treatment, health care, and human services facilities. In the late 1960s, however, the ARC adopted a policy of "induced urbanization" in central Appalachia—a scheme to move poor people to urban centers where human services could be consolidated and delivered efficiently. This plan was implemented despite the federal Office of Economic Opportunity's simultaneous efforts in Appalachia to provide assistance "in place," that is, to people living in their home places.

The scope of the ARC has never been as great as that of the Cassa, and its accomplishments are equally modest. The infrastructural improvements made by the ARC have not caused the industrial base in Appalachia to increase significantly. The limited extent of the ARC's benefit to many Appalachian people is summarized most clearly by Michael Bradshaw in his analysis of the commission's first 25 years:

> The great paradox of Appalachian development since 1960 is that although relatively greater sums of money have been invested in central Appalachia, this part of the region has shown the lowest ability to increase its economic and social indicators relative to the rest of the United States. (Bradshaw 1992, 142)

After a quarter-century of operation and with budgets ranging from $50 million to nearly $400 million a year, the Appalachian Regional Commission has not substantially changed the living standards of the poorest Appalachian counties. It has achieved the greatest success in the peripheral areas of the region closest to other developing areas. The commission's accomplishments in economic development tend to correlate closely with growth in the overall national economy, rather than showing any direct relationship to the implementation of its policies.

CONCLUSION

In view of the similarities between the Mezzogiorno and Appalachia, an examination of development planning and implementation in each region is instructive. Regional disparities remain significant in both Italy and the United States, despite the efforts of the Cassa per il Mezzogiorno and the Appalachian Regional Commission. The standard tenets of regional planning—such as the development of growth poles—have not worked in either case. Although the ARC was not involved in land reform or strategies for industrialization, its concentration on infrastructure development produced no better outcomes than did similar efforts in southern Italy. Moreover, the ARC's efforts to coordinate among federal, state, and local jurisdictions did not bring results significantly better than those of the Cassa's hierarchical methods.

Social and economic discrepancies among regions in developed nations such as the United States and Italy have not been amenable to bureaucratic and highly rationalized development efforts. New models, however, are evolving among the residents of the Mezzogiorno and Appalachia; grassroots development strategies are flourishing across the mountains of both regions. These local efforts offer the greatest hope for regional development in the coming decade.

▪ 11 ▪

Poor Regions, Poor Theory: Toward Improved Understanding of Regional Inequality

Peter R. Sinclair

With special reference to Canada, I am going to discuss how social scientists explain regional inequality and development. Why do people in some parts of the country live better than those in other parts? What influenced the particular form that the uneven development of Canadian capitalism has followed—centralization in Montreal and later in southern Ontario, but retarded growth in the Atlantic provinces and western Canada? Why has the problem of inequality endured for so long? Why can't the disadvantaged regions catch up faster? These are the questions of regional inequality—old questions for sociologists, economists, geographers and historians. But we need fresh answers because our concepts are often woolly and our theories sport blinkers that obscure competing evidence. They fail to explain why particular regions are poor.

In thinking about issues of regional inequality, I have come to realize more clearly that the complexity and variation in social life make it impossible to expect a single *general* theory to explain individual cases. I have long been uncomfortable with the view that good explanation derives from general theory. So much theoretical work seems forced into a realm of hazy abstraction in order to protect the goal of generalization; yet the answer is not to abandon theory for endless description of the "facts." We need general concepts to describe the world and even to frame our questions. And we need theory, if by theory we understand a claim to have identified what brings about the situation that has puzzled us. Thus I hope this analysis can be a step toward better theory.

By regional inequality or disparity I mean the unequal spatial distribution of goods and services. Ultimately, this is a question about differences in the quality of life that people can expect according to where they live. Regional inequalities are not merely differences to be explained and about which no value position need be taken; the differences that we are discussing make some regions inferior when compared with other regions with respect to such key aspects of life as health and educational facilities, employment opportunities, incomes and tax burdens. I shall not retreat from the value position implied by this statement into the more neutral language of regional differences that Ralph Matthews (1983), a distinguished sociological commentator on regional questions, prefers. Indeed, this would be impossible since the selection of some differences as worthy of analysis must be based on an implicit frame of evaluation.

Another preliminary problem is the definition of regional boundaries. A case can be made for using people's own perceptions of region as the basis for the construction of boundaries (Matthews 1983). But without a gigantic research program to collect new data in line with these units, it is unlikely that we could then proceed very far or fast. Moreover, there is no popular consensus as to what a particular region's boundaries should be. Instead, I shall follow the convention of adopting Canada's provincial political structure as the basis for presenting information, and occasionally I shall aggregate provincial data to refer to the Atlantic region or the prairies. I agree with Gidengil (1989) that provinces are heterogeneous in many respects, but the range of available data on smaller units (e.g., the subprovincial regions that she adopts) is too limited in time and subject for my purpose.

The first part of the chapter reviews the extent or scale of Canadian regional inequality in both its economic and social dimensions. Then I look at how sociologists in Canada have borrowed development theory from students of the Third World. Next, I try to assess its explanatory value when applied to the problem of underdevelopment in Atlantic Canada. Finally, some suggestions are made on how best to pursue a more adequate explanation, namely, the examination of historically contingent combinations of internal and external factors that recognize human agency and necessarily limit the scope of generalization.

SOME DIMENSIONS OF REGIONAL INEQUALITY

Economic Inequality

It need hardly be said that material conditions are central to how people experience their lives. That is why we pay so much attention to various economic indicators of inequality among regions or provinces. My focus here is on the period 1961–1988, but it is worth

Table 11.1
Canadian Per Capita Personal Income—by Province, 1961–1987

	1961	1966	1971	1976	1981	1987
Newfoundland	54.5	59.9	63.6	67.9	65.7	68.6
Prince Edward Island	55.0	60.1	62.6	70.6	69.7	72.6
Nova Scotia	72.8	74.8	77.9	76.7	74.7	81.2
New Brunswick	63.6	68.9	73.5	74.4	70.7	76.1
Quebec	84.4	89.2	88.8	94.2	94.1	95.4
Ontario	110.8	116.4	117.0	110.1	105.9	111.7
Manitoba	88.3	91.9	93.9	89.6	91.0	92.4
Saskatchewan	66.4	93.1	80.4	94.8	94.9	87.7
Alberta	93.6	100.1	99.6	101.2	114.2	100.5
British Columbia	107.5	111.6	108.2	109.0	111.8	98.2
Canada (MEAN)	$1,174	$2,303	$3,425	$6,877	$12,046	$18,079

Note: Decimal figures represent per capita personal income as a percentage of the national average; Canada = 100.
Sources: Calculated from *Statistics Canada* (1988b, Table 38) and *Canadian Economic Observer*, February 1989.

remembering that the pattern of regional economic inequality has changed only moderately since as far back as 1926 (Phillips 1982).

To judge the extent to which regional inequality has been reduced requires careful attention to several different indicators (see Table 11.1 and Figure 11.1). Personal income per capita gives a rough indication of typical material living standards. The relative position of the Atlantic provinces and Quebec improved by about ten points between 1961 and 1987 (almost all change coming *before* 1976), but they remained below the national average and a long way behind Ontario. Ontario has maintained a dominant position, except that it was replaced at the top by Alberta for 1981. Manitoba and Saskatchewan never attained the national average from 1961–1981 (although they had done so at times prior to 1961). British Columbia's relatively prosperous days were ended, it seemed, by 1987. When the data are graphed as in Figure 11.1, it is evident that the only dramatic change is the recent fall of British Columbia.

If earned income[1] is examined, the position of the Atlantic provinces is considerably worse and the improvement over the period is only about half of what we observed for personal income (see Table 11.2). This implies that much of the progression in personal incomes has depended on welfare state transfer payments rather than on the development of regional productive capacity, as Wien (1988, 18)

Figure 11.1
Per Capita Personal Income, as Percent of National Average, 1961–1987

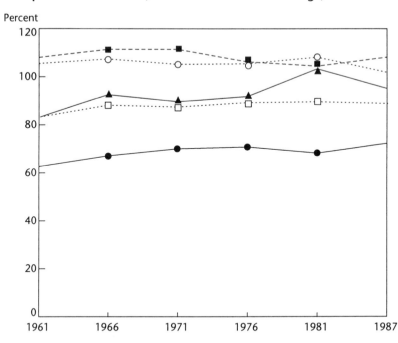

Percent

— ● — Atlantic   ··□·· Quebec   – ■ – Ontario   — ▲ — Prairies   ··○·· B.C.

Table 11.2
Canadian Per Capita Earned Income—by Province, 1961–1987

	1961	1966	1971	1976	1981	1987
Newfoundland	56.0	55.5	57.5	58.8	58.5	59.5
Prince Edward Island	52.6	50.5	53.3	61.9	62.5	64.6
Nova Scotia	68.8	65.9	70.2	68.9	68.0	74.6
New Brunswick	62.8	63.5	69.0	68.2	65.0	69.3
Quebec	90.3	90.4	88.5	92.5	93.4	94.2
Ontario	120.9	118.1	119.3	113.0	108.3	116.8
Manitoba	93.4	90.3	93.7	89.3	89.0	90.8
Saskatchewan	68.4	94.8	78.8	95.0	90.2	78.6
Alberta	101.6	100.0	99.7	103.5	116.9	99.0
British Columbia	113.4	110.3	107.7	109.0	111.5	95.5

Note: Decimal figures represent per capita earned income as a percentage of the national average; Canada = 100.
Source: Calculated from *Statistics Canada*, 1988b.

Table 11.3
Selected Canadian Economic Indicators, 1988

	Gross Domestic Product	GDP as % of Canadian Mean	Participation Rate	Unemployment Rate
Canada	$23,156	100.0	66.7	7.8
Newfoundland	$13,477	58.2	62.9	16.4
Prince Edward Island	$13,517	58.4	64.0	13.0
Nova Scotia	$16,150	69.7	60.8	10.2
New Brunswick	$15,967	69.0	58.8	12.0
Quebec	$21,716	93.8	64.0	9.4
Ontario	$26,325	113.7	69.6	5.0
Manitoba	$19,968	86.2	66.7	7.8
Saskatchewan	$18,079	78.1	66.4	7.5
Alberta	$26,421	114.1	72.0	8.0
British Columbia	$22,464	97.0	65.7	10.3

Source: Canadian Economic Observer, September 1989.

points out. Decades of federal-provincial development agreements have had little impact.

The gross domestic product (GDP) measures the value of goods and services produced in a given territory. It is vital to understand that, during the period that personal incomes were improving in all of Atlantic Canada relative to Canada as a whole, the GDP was falling further behind. For the period 1962–1981, the average rate of growth of GDP was lower in the Atlantic provinces than in all of Canada (*Statistics Canada* 1988b, xxi).

Let me summarize the situation at the beginning of the 1990s. The basic pattern with respect to incomes was that the East was poor, while only Ontarians were significantly above average. The Atlantic provinces were faring particularly badly on income criteria. Moreover, the disparity was much greater if we take GDP as our measure (see Table 11.3). For 1988, the highest GDP per capita was actually in Alberta—a situation that reflected the value of its resources, although a relatively large share of that value appeared to be lost to the people, in that Alberta was well behind Ontario in per capita income. GDP in Newfoundland and Prince Edward Island was only *half* what it was in Ontario and Alberta. Associated with relatively low per capita income and GDP we would expect high rates of unemployment and a smaller labor force. For the eastern provinces these expectations were confirmed for 1988, but Manitoba and Saskatchewan had average rates of labor force participation with average or below-average unemployment, while British Columbia was more like Atlantic Canada with respect to unemployment (see Table 11.3).

Table 11.4
Levels of Schooling in Canadian Population 15 Years and Older, 1951–1986
(in Percentages)

| | Education Levels | | | | | |
| | Less than Grade 9 | | | University Graduates | | |
	1951	1971	1986	1951	1971	1986
Canada	51.9	32.3	17.7	1.9	4.8	9.6
Newfoundland	68.7	44.4	26.9	0.5	2.1	5.6
Prince Edward Island	53.1	36.9	20.1	0.8	3.2	7.4
Nova Scotia	48.6	31.5	17.6	1.3	4.1	8.7
New Brunswick	60.3	41.2	24.4	0.9	3.4	7.3
Quebec	61.2	40.9	24.3	1.9	4.6	8.6
Ontario	46.9	28.2	15.0	2.6	5.3	10.8
Manitoba	51.2	32.1	18.5	1.3	4.6	8.9
Saskatchewan	55.7	35.6	19.6	1.0	3.5	7.4
Alberta	45.9	23.8	11.1	1.3	5.5	10.8
British Columbia	39.1	22.8	11.7	2.2	5.0	9.5

Source: *Statistics Canada* (1989, Table 1).

Table 11.5
Levels of Schooling by Province, 1951–1986, as a Percentage of the
Canadian Average for Persons 15 Years and Older

| | Less than Grade 9 % of National Average | | | University Graduates % of National Average | | |
	1951	1971	1986	1951	1971	1986
Newfoundland	132.4	137.5	152.0	26.3	43.8	58.3
Prince Edward Island	102.3	114.2	113.6	42.1	66.7	77.1
Nova Scotia	93.6	97.5	99.4	68.4	85.4	90.6
New Brunswick	116.2	127.6	137.9	47.4	70.8	76.0
Quebec	117.9	126.6	137.3	100.0	95.8	89.6
Ontario	90.4	87.3	84.7	136.8	110.4	112.5
Manitoba	98.7	99.4	104.5	68.4	95.8	92.7
Saskatchewan	107.3	110.2	110.7	52.6	72.9	77.1
Alberta	88.4	73.7	62.7	68.4	114.6	112.5
British Columbia	75.3	70.6	66.1	115.8	104.2	99.0

Source: *Statistics Canada* (1989, Table 1).

Education and Health

Some basic information on economic dimensions of inequality has been presented, but the problem of inequality does not end in our personal and collective wallets. I shall now look at health only briefly (because my data are rather old) and in more detail at education. If we consider the distribution of physicians across provinces in 1984, once again the Atlantic provinces—with the exception of Nova Scotia— were deficient, but so were Saskatchewan and Alberta. Prince Edward Islanders were in the worst position, with one physician for every 803 persons. In this respect, Quebecers fared best, with 476 people per physician (*Canada Year Book 1985*, 114). Per capita health expenditures in the provinces clustered reasonably close to the Canadian mean, although Alberta was spending 30 percent more than Newfoundland in 1982 (*Canada Health Manpower Inventory 1984–85*, 212).

Turning to schooling, we find that the education levels of the Canadian people vary more dramatically by province (see Tables 11.4 and 11.5 and Figure 11.2). These differences are important if we value

Figure 11.2
Per Capita Personal Income, as Percent of National Average

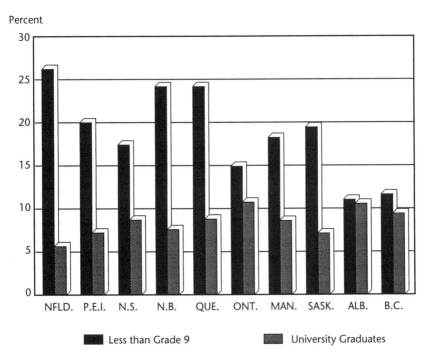

knowledge and informed critical thinking. Education is of obvious practical relevance because the educational level of the people of a region indicates the extent to which they are capable of participating fully in an industrialized society in which many occupations require technical knowledge and in which literacy is a basic necessity. It is often assumed that functional illiteracy occurs among people with less than a grade nine level of education. Even as recently as 1986, about one in six Canadian adults failed to meet this criterion, while the provinces varied from a low of 11.1 percent in Alberta to a high of 26.9 percent in Newfoundland (see Table 11.4). East of Ontario, only Nova Scotia was close to the Canadian average. Indeed, only Alberta, British Columbia, and Ontario were below that average. Moreover, while the improvement everywhere has been tremendous when 1951 figures are compared with those for 1986, the provinces that were characterized by a high percentage of people with less than grade nine education in 1951 were *worse off* relative to the other provinces by 1986 (see Table 11.5). In this sense, inequalities have increased.

If we look at university education, we find that the percentage of the population with a university degree has grown everywhere, with Alberta and Ontario the most successful by 1986. The provinces that were below average in 1951 had all improved their positions both absolutely and relatively over this time period, suggesting greater attention to higher education than to the secondary schools. It is noteworthy that Quebec, in third place in 1951, fell to sixth place by 1986, despite its much publicized quiet revolution.

The poor showing of the Atlantic provinces is not evidently a matter of lack of interest or attention to education in recent years. Newfoundland, for example—with the worst educational record in Canada—actually spent more than all other provinces in 1984 when we look at expenditures on education as a percentage of total personal income or in terms of dollars per member of the labor force (Statistics Canada 1987, 246–247). Nova Scotia and New Brunswick were also above the national averages in these expenditures. What may be happening is that the best educated people leave in disproportionately large numbers for work opportunities in Ontario and elsewhere. Most years since 1956, Newfoundland and the other Atlantic provinces have been net population losers through interprovincial migration (House et al 1989, 9–11) and migrants are typically better educated than those who stay put. Another possibility—one that applies to Newfoundland—is that funds may be used inefficiently; for example, they may be used to support the denominational school system.

EXPLANATIONS

We have seen that economic and social inequality continues to characterize Canadian provinces and regions. The problem is how to account for this state of affairs. There is no shortage of attempts to provide an answer in the social science literature, but I cannot enter into a full review of all positions that have been brought forward to explain regional inequalities.[2] Instead, I shall focus on the two theoretical models that have been most prominent, both in sociological writing (if we allow a broad conception of sociology) and implicitly in state policy. These two models may be labeled the *regional deficiency* and the *system problems approaches*.[3] In evaluating these models I shall give special attention to how they have been applied to Atlantic Canada,[4] which is clearly the most marginal or disadvantaged region in Canada.

REGIONAL DEFICIENCIES

What I call the regional deficiency approach is not really a single model, but a group of theories that have in common the identification of some deficiency, within an underdeveloped or poor region, that would explain its condition. It includes the staples theory and the more orthodox economic or geographical interpretations.

Staples Theory

One type of deficiency is essentially environmental in that development or underdevelopment is considered to follow from the availability of natural resources and how they are utilized. The Canadian staples school, stemming from the seminal work of Harold Innis, identifies the key to regional development as the presence of a valued staple resource, the extraction of which should stimulate other economic activity. Failure to develop a region then reflects the lack of valued resources, or inappropriate state policies to promote development, or the absence of appropriate entrepreneurial actions with respect to those resources and their potential linkages to other economic activities. Here the geographical and economic factors mix with cultural values that are thought to promote or discourage economic activity.

The staples approach to Atlantic Canada is best illustrated in Saunders' (1984) economic history of the Maritimes. Of particular interest is his account of the failure of the Maritime provinces to sustain economic growth at a rate similar to central Canada after the initial flurry of post-Confederation investment. Saunders argues that geographical factors forced industry in the Maritimes into a more dispersed pattern of smaller firms than elsewhere in Canada. Many plants (textiles, boots and shoes, light iron and steel) then closed due to central Canadian competition: central Canadian industries were nearer to the largest markets, they were larger units of production, they could acquire cheaper raw materials and power, and they had access to better or cheaper transportation facilities. In the early 20th century, the population of the Maritimes was too small and scattered to attract the new industries based on mass production of consumer goods and the region was more distant from the emerging markets in western Canada (Saunders 1984, 84–85).

I have no wish to deny that natural resources and location are important, but they cannot be made to carry all the burden of explanation. If areas like western Norway or Iceland—with modest resource endowments and relatively isolated—can experience significant periods of prosperity, we should not assume that geography is the exclusive or fundamental determinant of Atlantic Canada's condition. In various ways, the other theories to be considered provide alternatives to geographical determinism.

Cultural Theory

A second type of regional deficiency is primarily cultural. Some commentators do not accept that the Atlantic provinces have been poor primarily because of their resource endowment and location. They point, at least in part, to cultural values: Atlantic Canadians are poor because they lack entrepreneurship; they are not interested in investing in productive industry and accumulating capital. For example, George's (1970) economic analysis failed to identify any significant cost disadvantage that could explain retarded economic development in the region, and so he concluded that the answer must lie in the low level of entrepreneurship of the people. Acheson (1972) refers to lack of self-confidence among the region's businesspeople, and Alexander (1974, 18) alludes to the "weakness in entrepreneurship" in Newfoundland.[5] His reference is to the culture of the business elite, but others point more widely to mass culture. Clark's (1978) study of rural New Brunswick puts particular emphasis on a cultural syndrome of low ambition, low achievement, and migration in what amounts to an Atlantic Canadian version of the "culture of poverty" thesis fashionable 20 years ago in explaining the persistent poverty of blacks in the United States.

Such references to cultural deficiencies are really Canadian versions of modernization theory, which focused in the 1950s and 1960s on the difference between the developed industrial core of North America and Western Europe in contrast with the backward, newly formed, Third World nations. A developed society was characterized as having a complex institutional structure with an industrial economic base and a modern set of values that stressed individual acquisition and achievement. What held the Third World back was said to be a traditional and inappropriate culture that failed to stimulate work, saving, and investment. Thus the solution was education in modern values and the transfer of the institutions and technologies of industrial capitalism.

Modernization theory was also the implicit base of two influential critiques of Newfoundland development policy in the 1960s. Ottar Brox (1972) and Cato Wadel (1969) pointed to the co-existence of traditional and modern economic sectors—often in conflict with each other, as the root of the poverty problem—and they supported smaller scale, locally controlled development that built on traditional patterns.

State Policy

I shall now look briefly at how these theories underpin Canadian state policy. Although there have been many program changes and much debate about appropriate strategies, deficiency theories have been influential in state policy for since the early 1960s. Perhaps the primary reason is that deficiency theories focus on internal regional problems and point to development strategies that do not require a radical reconstruction of the social order. It may be thought that inappropriate values can be corrected eventually by appropriate education, which means more public investment in schooling and even the transfer of funds from the central government to the provinces in order to achieve this objective. Nevertheless, educational levels still lag behind in Atlantic Canada; and whether the type of education received is appropriate, especially in the rural areas, has now been questioned (see, for example, the wide-ranging recommendations of the Newfoundland Royal Commission on Employment and Unemployment [Newfoundland and Labrador 1986]).

Insofar as underdevelopment is thought to be related to the dispersal of the population in small scattered communities, the answer has been to promote migration to "growth poles" as in the federal-provincial program of the 1960s to relocate the people of Newfoundland's outports. Unfortunately, the growth centers didn't grow and the program itself was often criticized for pressuring people to move to places that offered them no real opportunities (e.g., Matthews 1983, 118–136). Where the problem has been identified as poor location relative to investment and market centers, the answer has been to pour state funds into various regional development programs that provide incentives to corporate investors to establish plants in the disadvantaged regions. Equalization payments from the federal government allow the poorer provincial governments to maintain their services and programs. Indeed, about half the revenue of the governments of Prince Edward Island and Newfoundland come from Ottawa. And transfer payments make up a relatively large share of the incomes of individuals in the Atlantic region. Although incomes and employment might have been less without any such help, the results are still discouraging, which suggests that the problem is more fundamental.

Paradoxically, the involvement of the state in the programs described, as well as in the system of transfer payments to individuals, has been criticized by neo-classical economists such as Courchene (1986) for creating another deficiency that holds down economic growth. The problem is market failure. It is argued that the state artificially supplements living standards when it introduces minimum wage laws and makes transfer payments, thereby discouraging people from accepting low paid jobs or from migrating to other areas. The welfare state system prevents the market from equalizing investment and labor opportunities across the country. Apart from moral objections, the key point to be made against the market failure position is that the poor regions were poor before the state intervention. The market did not bring about adjustments, but left socially distressed regions that could not be ignored forever by the state (see also Sager 1987, 135).

SYSTEM PROBLEMS: DEPENDENCY AND UNDERDEVELOPMENT

In the 1970s and 1980s, there was a growing dissatisfaction among sociologists with the various theories and reforms outlined above. Instead, a more radical group of theories emerged that points to fundamental problems in the structure of Canadian society, and even in the international system of which it is part, as explanations for regional inequality. Two main lines of influence may be identified in this new political economy of regionalism: one stemming from Canadian staples theory and another from Latin American dependency theory.

Staples theory, the first major source of influence, is not simply a geographical deficiency approach. Depending on how it is developed, staples theory can have radical implications. Insofar as the development of a staples economy requires external markets, this means that a region's economic growth depends fundamentally on external demand over which it has no control. It may also be critically influenced by external state policies. Thus, having acknowledged the importance of geographical and environmental factors, several authors have then complained that the Canadian federal government did not maintain a transportation policy that would have permitted more profitable production in the Maritimes. Early in the 20th century, preferential rates for the Maritimes were abolished in response to pressure from central Canadian interests (Acheson 1977; Forbes 1977). Underdevelopment arose and persisted because of the power of external, other Canadian business to influence state policy. If the remedy is thought to lie in getting a fairer deal in Confederation, there are no truly radical implications; but Clow (1984) points to the nature of Canadian federalism, in which most influence lies in the central regions, as a structural feature of Canadian society that has systematically impeded development of the Maritimes. In such ways, staples theory can influence more radical approaches.

The second major source of influence has been theories of underdevelopment in Third World countries. Modernization theory was subjected to a devastating assault from several variants of dependency theory, particularly from scholars whose focus was on Latin America. Rather than accept the conclusion that the causes of underdevelopment were cultural and internal, the *dependentistas* looked at underdevelopment as a function of the way that the Third World was linked to the First World. Third World countries were kept poor because more powerful, metropolitan countries extracted their economic surplus, while similar relationships existed within the Third World societies themselves as the metropolitan core exploited the peripheries. The closer the ties, the worse the exploitation and underdevelopment. Societies were underdeveloped because they were dependent. The only hope for Third World development was to break the chain and escape from capitalist bondage. Of course, this is a simplification of A.G. Frank's (1967) famous metaphor of the *metropolis-satellite chain*.

Frank and his followers operated at a high level of generality and conveniently ignored that capitalist development (in the sense of economic growth) did occur in many peripheral regions. Recognizing, however, that some economic development did take place in Latin America, Cardoso (1972, 1973) introduced the influential concept of *associated dependent development*. Third World economies were said to be dependent upon their links with more powerful economies—a dependency that conditioned what was possible for them. Yet they could grow in ways dictated by the inflow of foreign investment through multinational corporations. As Evans (1979, 31) put it in his study of Brazil, dependent development "implies both the accumulation of capital and some degree of independence on the periphery."

Dependency Theory in Canada

Sociological theories that were developed to analyze Third World underdevelopment have been imported, as it were, to cope with the problem of regional inequality in Canada. Davis (1971), referring to Canada as a whole, and Archibald (1971), looking only at the Atlantic provinces, applied the metropolis-satellite model. Like Frank, they failed to deal adequately with social relations within the regions; and in Archibald's case, information on the industrial development of the Maritimes that runs counter to the theory is ignored (i.e., locally financed industrialization after 1880).

Probably the most influential Canadian dependency theorist has been Wallace Clement. Clement (1978) approaches regional inequality as a problem in class relations and capitalist underdevelopment. He opens his analysis with a summary of dependency theory (looking at the work of Frank, Galtung, and Sunkel), which he finds a useful guide to the Canadian situation. He emphasizes, however, that areas do not exploit other areas; rather the capitalist class—resident primarily in the golden triangle of central Canada—undertakes this exploitation. Clement then presents information on the regional distribution of the economic elite as an illustration of the unevenness of economic development. In dependency terms, he sees this unevenness as a result of the extraction of surplus from the underdeveloped region (1978, 99). Yet, as Sager (1987, 120) points out, this critical assertion is not documented. Clement would have to show that the industrialization of eastern and western Canada had been prevented or arrested by the actions of central Canadian capitalists. Without specification and demonstration of the mechanism of underdevelopment, we are left simply with the unexplained indicators of regional inequality.[6]

Another prominent exponent of dependency theory is Ralph Matthews. Matthews expressed strong support for Cardoso, whose "theories seem particularly relevant to an analysis of regionalism in Canadian society because they depict the Canadian situation so accurately" (1983, 74). He went on to describe the "hinterland" regions as "most assuredly *dependent developed* in that their economic growth is highly constrained and determined by decisions made outside the regions in the economic centers of this and other countries" (74). What is lacking here is any detailed analysis to demonstrate how a region can be developing and dependent at the same time, and where the source of growth may lie. What would have happened to the poor regions in the absence of external capital and the decisions of the federal state? Would they really have become independent, autonomous regions on a par with central Canada? Are the characteristics of the region itself really irrelevant?

Post-dependency: The General Criticism

Dependency theory has been heavily attacked in the general development literature. Although dependency theory was advocated by various writers who thought of themselves as applying Marxist principles to Third World problems, the theory received much of its most trenchant criticism from within Marxism.

Laclau's (1971) biting critique attacked dependency theory because it looked upon capitalism and feudalism in terms of exchange or markets, whereas the core of economic life in Marxist theory is the system of production—in particular, the relations of production. From this starting point, Warren (1973; 1980) went on to argue that the insertion of capitalism into the Third World context had promoted local accumulation rather than resulted in underdevelopment. His controversial argument is diametrically opposed to dependency theory. Warren claimed that there had been a major increase in the capitalist development of the Third World since 1945, that colonialism encouraged progressive social change, that the obstacles to development lie in the internal contradictions of Third World countries, and that ties of subordination were waning with the rise of indigenous capitalism. Almost echoing modernization theorists, Warren argued that the problem for most places has been too little capitalism.

Another response to dependency theory's emphasis on exchange has been to point out that there is confusion between the concept of capitalist mode of production and the concept of participation in a world system dominated by capitalism. A mode of production may exist in a subordinate relationship to capitalism, yet not be capitalist itself. Thus, Laclau (1971) challenged Frank's view of Latin America on the grounds that Frank failed to see that feudalism had survived there, albeit dominated by capitalism. This criticism led to an analysis of the interconnection or articulation of modes of production in ways particularly influenced by French economic anthropology.[7] The basic point was that noncapitalist relations of production survive in many forms and locations because they are advantageous to capital. For example, a noncapitalist, subsistence mode of production contributes to the reproduction of labor and thus allows wage rates in the capitalist sector to fall below the real value of labor. In a sense, capitalist production is subsidized. At the same time, capital controls the situation and ensures that the noncapitalist mode remains underdeveloped.

Bernstein (1977) and Wolf (1982) are among an important group of theorists who see the interconnection as a *process of incorporation* within capitalism.[8] This is a more dynamic perspective than the articulation theory. The natural or peasant subsistence production becomes transformed into commodity production, and peasants become increasingly dependent on markets to the point where the household cannot reproduce itself except within the capitalist framework. The results are exploitation and impoverishment that is based on social relations internal to the region or society.

In summary, what emerged in the 1970s was a renewed emphasis on capitalism as a mode of production that dominated but did not eliminate pre-capitalist modes of production in underdeveloped or dependent regions. The development of capitalism and the class relations at the structural core of capitalism were now viewed as the underlying source of underdevelopment in general, including regional inequality in Canada. Relations within regions and not simply between regions, were treated as important.

Post-dependency Theory in Canada

I shall now summarize the main Canadian writing in the neo-Marxist tradition, which has drawn upon this general literature in attempting to explain regional inequality.

In 1978, Clement had already stressed class relations in his regional study, but within the context of dependency theory. In the same volume, Cuneo (1978) approached regional inequality from a more orthodox Marxist position, with no reference to the debates mentioned above. Differences in the socio-economic characteristics of Canada's regions, and population flows between regions, were explained as regional dimensions of the class composition and inherent dynamic tendencies of Canadian capitalism. In effect, some regions were poor because capitalism had not concentrated in them (cf. Warren 173; 1980, as discussed above). The fact that concentration and centralization of capital is part of the dynamic of capitalism is not in dispute—but why in central Canada? Cuneo (1978, 128) is one of the few radical scholars to attempt an answer. He believes that the concentration is a matter of geographical proximity to centers of U.S. capitalism, but the point is not elaborated and it is hard to accept that location alone is the driving force of investment decisions.

Veltmeyer (1979; 1980), working on Atlantic Canada, also criticized dependency theory for its focus on exchange relations between regions rather than on the more fundamental social relations of production. He proposed that Atlantic Canada was underdeveloped because Canadian capital—concentrated historically in central Canada—required and created a source of cheap labor that might be called upon when necessary—Marx's concept of the *industrial reserve army*.

This theory has an initially seductive plausibility that does not stand up to closer scrutiny. Corporate capitalism could certainly benefit from earlier historical patterns that left so many Atlantic Canadians economically stranded, determined to survive independently as long as possible, yet susceptible in the last analysis to the lure of wages in the capitalist labor market. That is, many members of small producer households have migrated permanently or worked for wages for limited periods in order to supplement their farm or fishing incomes and to support other family members who stayed in full-time primary production. The labor power of such people is usually unskilled and cheap, and easily replaceable and discardable from the perspective of corporate or state employers. It is worth noting here that the labor reserve is only advantageous to capital insofar as the particular labor force in question is not required to absorb what it produces. That is, the labor of the Maritimes could best be used by central Canadian industry or by export-oriented Maritime industry.

As Bickerton (1982, 193–194) has pointed out, Veltmeyer's thesis ignores *internal* factors that contributed to the relative decline of Maritime industry and the continued poverty of the region's primary producers. Nor is it clear, once again, why core and periphery are located as they are (Sager 1987, 128). Why the Atlantic provinces should be the home of the industrial reserve army remains mysterious. Furthermore, the form of explanation is an untestable Marxist functionalism: poor people exist in the Maritimes because they have to in order to maintain Canadian capitalism. But Canadian capitalism does not *have* to be maintained; and even if it did, it would not have to depend on labor from the Maritimes.

We have seen that, by the 1970s, Marxists in general began to discuss the articulation of modes of production in quite sophisticated ways. In Canada, too, students of particular regions and regional industries searched for explanations within a similar framework. Both Sacouman (1977) and Veltmeyer (1979) followed this approach implicitly in portraying subsistence and independent commodity production[9] as part of the dynamic of capitalism, which creates cheap, surplus labor. Soon Sacouman (1979) was referring to primary producers in both the Prairies and the Maritimes as engaged in a *domestic mode of production* (involving some combination of subsistence and commodity production) that was maintained to the advantage of capitalism and that took different forms in different regions. It was a short step from this point to his attempt to synthesize explicitly the dependency and modes of production approaches:

> The central argument is that uneven underdevelopment in the rural Maritimes has occurred largely through partial/blocked transformation of the domestic mode of production. Semi-proletarianization of household members of the producer unit has helped give them less than subsistence for their labor. (Sacouman 1980, 234)

This semi-proletarianization refers to a condition in farming and fishing wherein producers legally own property and work it with household labor, but their incomes are "more and more directly determined by capitalist dominance" (237). Although this work does advance our knowledge of the organization of production in the Maritimes, it suffers from a reliance on functional explanation for the structures of regional inequality. Also, Sacouman relies on aggregate statistics and does not really demonstrate survival strategies at the level of the household.

The problems with neo-Marxist theories of regional inequality, and of Atlantic Canada's situation in particular, are indicative of the malaise in the development literature on which they draw so heavily. In much of that literature, it appears as if the structures of underdevelopment never change and are basically the same everywhere. That is, every case—at whatever period—and in whatever location—is explained with reference to the same general model. It is noteworthy, for example, that Frank can produce no policy to cope with underdevelopment other than to appeal for a general socialist revolution. To do more would demand attention to particular circumstances. Thus, I agree with Mouzelis (1988, 28) that underdevelopment and dependency theories are too general to explain the widely different trajectories through which various Third World societies have moved.[10] The general models do not clearly spell out the causal mechanisms that lead to one pattern rather than another. Furthermore, the historical evidence is often missing or at variance with the claims of theorists, as Eric Sager (1987) has recently shown with respect to most Marxist discussions about the Maritimes.

THE WAY FORWARD?
SOME NOTES TOWARD A SOCIOLOGICAL ACCOUNT

I think that our understanding can be improved by abandoning the quest for a single general theory of development and regional inequality. Mouzelis (1988) is on the right track when he advocates a middle range approach that would specify a set of development paths each of which would include one or more societies or regions. And to explain these patterns, we will need to look for causal forces both external to and also within the region in question. The sociological task here is to avoid a totally idiographic approach by carefully searching out what regions have in common, without forcing into a single box those cases that differ radically in other important respects. In this final section, I shall set out what appears the most promising framework within which to seek out these patterns.

The problem of regional economic inequality is essentially a question of why capital, and thus employment and incomes, should be located in some places rather than others. Recently, Wood (1989, 133–135) has reminded us that capitalist development involves pressures both toward centralization and toward dispersal of capital. Centralization is encouraged by the attractions of labor supply, the size and proximity of markets, and the easy availability of capital, goods, and services, all of which help to raise profits. But centralization may also result in high rents, more organized workers, and higher wages, all of which serve to depress profits and promote relocation. Thus there is no substitute for concrete social historical analysis of the constellation of forces that influence the development of a particular region. Following Marx, Wood specifies three sets of factors that influence the location of capital:

1. *Forces of production*, including natural resources (land), technology, and labor power. Whether scarcity in nature imposes an excessive burden on capital or stimulates innovation and productive development is left open.

2. *Social, historical, political, cultural and other factors* that permit or discourage the establishment of capitalist relations of production and influence the concrete substance of any such relations. Clearly, the characteristics of the forces of production at any historical moment are shaped by prior experience that has generated a particular level of technical development, that affects the conditions under which labor can be united with capital, and that even affects the degree to which nature can support further exploitation. It is in

unravelling this complex social element in development that sociologists can expect to make their most valuable contribution to the general problem.

3. *Proximity to markets*, which is complicated by the cost and speed of the transportation system. This third category is primarily a question of the constraints on profit levels imposed by the conditions of marketing. Location is important not simply with reference to productive capacities, but also in relation to markets (Wood 1989, 133–135).

The development of a region is determined theoretically by the *historically contingent combination* of these factors. Deficiencies in one of these areas may be compensated by special advantages in others. These factors seem to me to have the advantage of requiring that we connect social life with nature and technology. I want to emphasize that the social factors should be considered with the recognition that social and cultural life is *constructed* by people who face immediate constraints and are influenced by the past. That is, social life is influenced by context, but cannot simply be "read" from the context.

Writing about the fisheries of northwest Newfoundland (Sinclair 1985), I have shown how simplistic, unilinear, and structural theories cannot account for the process of change that has actually taken place as real people respond to their environments and the actions of others. A similar general perspective is found in the work of Long (1984; 1988; Long and Roberts 1984), who advocates a type of analysis that will uncover "processes in which ordinary people—peasants, workers, entrepreneurs, bureaucrats, and others—actively engage in shaping the outcomes of processes of development" (Long 1984, 169). Long would have us look at the interplay of local and external forces, the latter always filtered through local or internal regional structures (171). In particular, the interaction of different sectors of production may be captured in the concept of

> a 'regionalized system of production' that is made up of a system of linkages that develop over time between a dominant sector and its economic and social hinterland....This system...is continuously being re-molded by the struggles that go on between particular individuals and social groups, and it is also affected by the ways in which powerful outside forces impinge upon it. (Long 1984, 175–176)

This perspective is more voluntaristic than Wood's, but it is compatible with his (and Marx's) commitment to examine particular regional histories, cultures, and struggles.

We should be aware that metropolitan structures have not simply been imposed upon a passive population; that is the important message in Brym and Sacouman's (1979) early work on social movements in Atlantic Canada. Students of the region know that people get by through complex economic strategies centered on the household, involving various state programs as well as formal and informal economic activities, and occasionally resorting to collective resistance. If most residents simply would leave—as some neo-classical economists wish—regional disparities might disappear, but at great social cost. Disparities remain because, in part, people with low incomes and inferior educational qualifications find ways to evade the pressures to relocate themselves. As House (1986) implies, we should not assume with so many neo-Marxists that such people are backward and thus bad judges of what is best for them. This is not to justify regional disparity, for such indicators as unemployment rates or per capita income reflect real problems for people who prefer to remain where they are rather than follow the signs to Toronto. We need to understand them and their decisions better and learn how to counteract regional inequality without forcing people to migrate. Poor regions are ill served by poor theory. We can at least try to do better.

NOTES

1. Earned income here includes wages, salaries, and benefits; net farm income; and net income from unincorporated business. The latter category includes most self-employed persons, but it also includes rental income, which makes the use of the term earned income slightly inaccurate.

2. But see Matthews (1983, 37–55) for a more extensive analysis.

3. I have collapsed Wien's (1988) three categories by treating the staples approach as essentially a variant of regional deficiency.

4. For an earlier overview, see Barrett (1980); and for a more recent impressive analysis, see Sager (1987).

5. Alexander (1977) also referred to the fragmentation of the upper class in Newfoundland as a significant factor in its relative underdevelopment.

6. An interesting empirical case study broadly grounded in dependency theory is House's (1980; 1981) analysis of coastal Labrador.

7. For an early review of the debate over the articulation of modes of production, see Foster-Carter (1978). A critical appreciation of the French anthropologists whose work was influential among neo-Marxist critics is provided by Clammer (1975). An excellent example of research particularly pertinent to regional issues is that of Norman Long and his colleagues on highland Peru (Long 1975; Long and Roberts 1984).

8. For a summary, see Vandergeest (1988) and Long and van der Ploug (1988).

9. That is, production of goods for the market using almost exclusively the labor of members of the household, who also own the means of production.

10. I have made the same point with reference to theories that predict either the disappearance or timeless survival of domestic commodity production (Sinclair 1985).

References

Abbott, Susan. 1976. "Full-time Farmers and Weekend Wives: An Analysis of Altering Conjugal Roles." *Journal of Marriage and the Family* 38:165–174.

———. 1980. "Power among the Kikuyu: Domestic and Extra-domestic Resources and Strategies." In *Anthropological Papers in Honor of Earl H. Swanson, Jr.,* edited by Lucille Harten, Claude Warren, and Donald Tuohy. Pocatello: Idaho State University Museum.

———. 1989. "Symptoms of Anxiety and Depression among Eastern Kentucky Adolescents: Insights from Comparative Fieldwork." In *Health in Appalachia: Proceedings of the 1988 Conference on Appalachia.* Lexington: Appalachian Center, University of Kentucky.

Abbott, Susan, and Thomas Arcury. 1977. "Continuity with Tradition: Male and Female in Kikuyu Culture." *Youth and Society* 8:329–358.

Abbott, Susan, and Ruben Klein. 1979. "Depression and Anxiety among Rural Kikuyu in Kenya." *Ethos* 7:161–188.

Acheson, T. W. 1972. "The National Policy and the Industrialization of the Maritimes, 1880–1910." *Acadiensis* 1:3–28.

———. 1977. "The Maritimes and 'Empire Canada'." In *Canada and the Burden of Unity,* edited by D. J. Bercuson. Toronto: Macmillan.

AFSCME (American Federation of State, County, and Municipal Employees). 1984. *The States, the People and the Reagan Cuts: An Analysis of Social Spending Cuts.* Washington, DC: AFSCME.

"Agriculture in Newfoundland." n.d. Government of Newfoundland and Labrador, Department of Rural, Agricultural and Northern Development, Agriculture Canada.

Alexander, David. 1974. "Development and Dependence in Newfoundland." *Acadiensis* 4:3–31.

———. 1977. *The Decay of Trade*. St. John's, NS: Institute of Social and Economic Research.

———. 1983. *Atlantic Canada and Confederation: Essays in Canadian Political Economy*. Toronto: University of Toronto Press.

Appalachian Alliance. 1978. *A Protest from the Colonies*. New Market, TN.

———. 1982. *Appalachia in the Eighties*. New Market, TN.

Appalachian Land Ownership Task Force. 1983. *Who Owns Appalachia? Land Ownership and Its Impact*. Lexington: University Press of Kentucky.

Appalachian Regional Commission (ARC). 1979. *Appalachia—A Reference Book*, 2nd ed. Washington: GPO.

———. 1979a. "ARC Sponsors Conference on Raising a New Generation in Appalachia." *Appalachia* (January/February):1–56.

———. 1981. *Appalachia—A Reference Book: Supplement to the Second Edition*. Washington: GPO.

———. 1983. "Report on the State of the Region's Economy, No. 002. Washington: GPO.

———. 1983a. *Job Skills for the Future*. Conference Proceedings, Jackson, Mississippi. Washington: GPO.

———. 1983b. *Job Skills for the Future. Workshop Reports I, II, III, and IV*. Conference Proceedings, Jackson, Mississippi. Washington: GPO.

———. 1985. "A Region of Contradictions." *Appalachia* 18 (3): Special issue on "Twenty Years of Progress."

———. 1985a. *State of the Appalachian Economy: 1980–1985*. Washington: GPO.

Archibald, Bruce. 1971. "Atlantic Regional Underdevelopment and Socialism." In *Essays on the Left*, edited by Laurier LaPierre. Toronto: McClelland and Stewart.

Arcury, Thomas A. 1988. "Agricultural Diversity and Change in Industrializing Appalachia: An Ecological Analysis of Eastern Kentucky, 1880 to 1910," *CDC Development Paper #23*, Center for Developmental Change, University of Kentucky.

Arnold, S. J., and D. J. Tigert. 1974. "Canadians and Americans, A Comparative Analysis." *International Journal of Comparative Sociology* 15 (March–June).

Arnott, D. 1978. "East Kentucky: The Politics of Dependency and Underdevelopment." Ph.D. dissertation, Duke University.

Balsom, D. 1985. "The Three-Wales Model." In *The National Question Again*, edited by J. Osmond. Llandysul, Wales: Gomer Press.

Bandura, A. 1986. *The Social Foundations of Thought and Action*. Englewood, NJ: Prentice Hall.

Banfield, Edward C. 1958. *The Moral Basis of a Backward Society*. Glencoe, IL: Free Press.

Baratz, Morton S. 1955. *The Union and the Coal Industry*. New Haven: Yale University Press.

Barrett, L. G. 1980. "Perspectives on Dependency and Underdevelopment in the Atlantic Region." *Canadian Review of Sociology and Anthropology* 17:273–286.

Beacham, A. 1964. *Depopulation in Mid–Wales*. Cardiff, Wales: HMSO.

Beaver, Patricia D. 1986. *Rural Community in the Appalachian South*. Lexington: University Press of Kentucky.

Beck, Aaron T. 1977. *Depression: Causes and Treatments*. Philadelphia: University of Pennsylvania Press.

Bellah, Robert N., et al. 1985. *Habits of the Heart: Individualism and Commitment in American Life*. Berkeley and Los Angeles: University of California Press.

Benyon, Huw, and Peter McMylor. 1985. "Decisive Power: The New Tory State against the Miners." In *Digging Deeper: Issues in the Miners' Strike*, edited by Benyon. London: Verso.

Berger, Peter L., and Richard Neuhaus. 1977. *To Empower People: The Role of Mediating Structures in Public Policy*. Washington: American Enterprise Institute for Public Policy Research.

Bernstein, Henry. 1977. "Notes on Capital and Peasantry." *Journal of African Political Economy* 10:60–73.

Bethemont, Jacques and Jean Pelletier. 1983. *Italy: A Geographical Introduction*. London: Longman.

Bible, The. 1962. Revised Standard Version. New York: New American Library.

Bickerton, James. 1982. "Underdevelopment and Social Movements in Atlantic Canada." *Studies in Political Economy* 9:191–202.

Billings, Dwight B., Jr. 1979. *Planters and the Making of the "New South": Class, Politics and Development in North Carolina, 1865–1900*. Chapel Hill: University of North Carolina Press.

Bingham, E. 1983. "The ARC—Some Questions Relative to Its Past and Possible Future." In *The Appalachian Experience: Proceedings of the Sixth Annual Appalachian Studies Conference*, edited by M. Buxton. Boone, NC: Appalachian Consortium.

Bluestone, Barry, and Bennett Harrison. 1982. *The De-industrialization of America: Plant Closings, Community Abandonment, and the Dismantling of Basic Industry*. New York: Basic Books.

———. 1986, December. *The Great American Job Machine: The Proliferation of Low-wage Employment in the U.S. Economy*. Study prepared for the U.S. Congress, Joint Economic Committee. Washington: GPO.

Booth, David. 1975. "Andre Gunder Frank: An Introduction and Appreciation." In *Beyond the Sociology of Development*, edited by I. Oxall, T. Barrett, and D. Booth. London: Routledge.

Boyte, Harry C. 1980. *The Backyard Revolution: Understanding the New Citizen Movement*. Philadelphia: Temple University Press.

Bradshaw, Michael. 1992. *The Appalachian Regional Comission: Twenty-five Years of Government Policy*. Lexington: University Press of Kentucky.

Brown, James. 1972. "A Look at the 1970 Census." In *Appalachia in the Sixties: A Decade of Reawakening*, edited by David Walls and John Stephenson. Lexington: University of Kentucky Press.

Brox, Ottar. 1972. *Newfoundland Fishermen in the Age of Industry*. St. John's: Institute of Social and Economic Research.

Brym, Robert J., ed. 1986. *Regionalism in Canada*. Toronto: Irwin.

Brym, Robert J., and R. James Sacouman, eds. 1979. *Underdevelopment and Social Movements in Atlantic Canada*. Toronto: New Hogtown Press.

Bulmer, M. 1975. "Sociological Models of Mining Communities." *Sociological Review* 23 (February):61–92.

Buttel, Frederick H., and Howard Newby, eds. 1980. *The Rural Sociology of the Advanced Societies: Critical Perspectives*. Montclair, NJ: Allanheld and Osmun.

Buxton, M. 1975. *The Appalachian Experience*. Boone, NC: Appalachian Consortium.

Campbell, J. C. 1921. *The Southern Highlander and His Homeland*. Lexington: University of Kentucky Press.

Carawan, Guy, and Candie Carawan. 1986. *Voices from the Mountains*. Urbana: University of Illinois Press.

Cardoso, Fernando. 1972. "Dependency and Development in Latin America." *New Left Review* 74 (14):83–95.

———. 1973. "Associated-Dependent Development: Theoretical and Practical Implications." In *Authoritarian Brazil*, edited by A. Stepan. New Haven: Yale University Press.

Carr, R. 1966. *Spain 1808–1939*. Oxford: Clarendon Press.

Castells, M. 1983. *The City and the Grassroots*. London: Edward Arnold.

Catholic Bishops of Appalachia. 1975. *This Land Is Home to Me*. A Pastoral Letter on Powerlessness in Appalachia.

Caudill, Harry M. 1976. *Darkness at Dawn*. Lexington: University Press of Kentucky.

———. 1982. An interview, "Appalachia's Progressive Destruction." *Roanoke Times and World News*, April 4, F 6.

Chenery, Hollis B. 1962. "Development Policies for Southern Italy." *Quarterly Journal of Economics* 76:515–547.

Christenson, C. L. 1962. *Economic Redevelopment in Bituminous Coal.* Cambridge: Harvard University

Clammer, John. 1975. "Economic Anthropology and the Sociology of Development: 'Liberal' Anthropology and Its French Critics." In *Beyond the Sociology of Development,* edited by I. Oxall, T. Barrett, and D. Booth. London: Routledge.

Clark, S. D. 1978. *The New Urban Poor.* Toronto: McGraw-Hill.

Clavel, P. 1983. *Opposition Planning in Wales and Appalachia.* Cardiff: University of Wales Press.

Clement, Wallace. 1978. "A Political Economy of Regionalism in Canada." In *Modernization and the Canadian State,* edited by Daniel Glenday, Hubert Guindon, and Allan Torowetz. Toronto: Macmillan.

Clow, Michael. 1984. "Politics and Uneven Capitalist Development." *Studies in Political Economy* 14:117–140.

"Coal: Saver of a Region." 1981. *Roanoke Times and World News.* June 28, 29, July 1, 2, 4, Section A.

Cobb, James C. 1986. "The Southern Business Climate: A Historical Perspective." *Forum for Applied Research and Public Policy* 1:2 (Summer).

Coedes, G. 1968. *The Indianized States of Southeast Asia.* Honolulu: East-West Center Press.

Commission on Religion in Appalachia (CORA). 1982. "Assessment and Plan-ning for the 80s." Knoxville. Mimeo.

Concerned Citizens of Martin County (CCMC). 1980. *Beauty...The Town That Refused To Be Moved.*

Cooke, P. N. 1981. "Local Class Structure in Wales." *Papers in Planning Research 31.* University of Wales Institute of Science and Technology, Cardiff.

———. 1982. "Class Relations and Uneven Development in Wales." In *Diversity and Decomposition in the Labour Market,* edited by Graham Day. Aldershot, Hampshire, England: Gower.

Courchene, Thomas. 1986. "Avenues of Adjustment: The Transfer System and Regional Disparities." In *The Canadian Economy: A Regional Perspective,* edited by Roger Savoie. Toronto: Methuen.

Couto, Richard A. 1983. "Metaphysical Pathos of Peripheral Economics: TVA and Regional Development in Appalachia." Paper presented at the annual meeting of the British Sociological Association, Cardiff, Wales.

———. 1984. *Appalachia—An American Tomorrow.* Nashville: Vanderbilt University Press.

———. 1984. *Appalachia—An American Tomorrow: A Report on the Economic and Social Trends in the Appalachian Region.* Knoxville: Commission on Religion in Appalachia.

——. 1984. "Vein Dreams: Rural Health in a Troubled Economy." *Health PAC* 15 (2):17–19.

——. 1986. "Women and Poverty in Appalachia," *Forum for Applied Research and Public Policy*, 1 (3):101–10.

——. 1987. "Changing Technologies and Consequences for Labor in Coal Mining." In *Workers, Managers and Technological Change*, edited by Daniel B. Cornfield. New York: Plenum Publishing.

——. 1994. *An American Challenge: Economic Trends and Social Issues in Appalachia*. Dubuque, IA: Kendall/Hunt.

Cox, Gary. 1982. "Current and Projected Socio-economic Conditions of the Levia Fork of the Big Sandy River Basin of Kentucky and Virginia." Appalachian Development Center, Morehead (KY) State University.

Craig, Gerald M.. 1982. "A Historical Perspective: the Evolution of a Nation." In *Understanding Canada: A Multidisciplinary Introduction to Canadian Studies*, edited by William Metcalf. New York: New York University Press.

Craypo, Charles. 1979. "The Impact on Labor of Changing Corporate Structure and Technology." *Labor Studies Journal*, 3 (3).

Creighton, Ragu L., and James E. Vitale. 1979. "Future Transportation Issues Facing the Appalachian Region." In *Appalachia into the 80s*, ARC Proceedings. Washington: GPO.

Crowley, Joan E. and David Shapiro. 1982a. "Aspirations and Expectations of Youth in the United States. Part I. Education and Fertility." *Youth and Society* 13:391–422.

——. 1982b. "Aspirations and Expectations of Youth in the United States. Part II. Employment Activity." *Youth and Society* 13:33–58.

Cuneo, Carl J. 1978. "A Class Perspective on Regionalism." In *Modernization and the Canadian State*, edited by Daniel Glenday, Hubert Guindon, and Allan Torowetz. Toronto: Macmillan.

Cunningham, Rodger. 1987. *Apples on the Flood: The Southern Mountain Experience*. Knoxville: University of Tennessee Press.

Daley, Nelda, and Sue Ella Kobak. 1990. "The Paradox of the 'Familiar Outsider'." *Appalachian Journal* 18:3 (Spring):248–261.

David, John Peter. 1972. "Earnings, Health, Safety and Welfare of Bituminous Coal Miners Since the Encouragement of Mechanization by the United Mine Workers of America." Ph.D. dissertation, University of West Virginia.

——. 1984. *Charleston Gazette* (West Virginia), September 12.

Davis, Arthur, K. 1971. "Canadian Society and History as Hinterland versus Metropolis." In *Canadian Society: Pluralism, Change, and Conflict*, edited by Richard J. Ossenberg. Scarborough: Prentice Hall of Canada.

Davis, Kingsley, and W. E. Moore. 1945. "Some Principles of

Stratification." *American Sociological Review* 10 (2).

Day, Graham. 1979. "Underdeveloped Wales." *Planet* 33/34:102–110.

——. 1980. "Wales, the Regional Problem and Development." In *Poverty and Social Inequality in Wales*, edited by Gareth Rees and Teresa L. Rees. London: Croom Helm.

Day, Graham, and R. Suggett. 1985. "Conceptions of Wales and Welshness: Aspects of Nationalism in Nineteenth Century Wales." In *Political Action and Social Identity*, edited by Gareth Rees, et al. London: Macmillan.

Dentan, R. K. 1975. "If There Were No Malays, Who Would the Semai Be?" In *Pluralism in Malaya: Myth or Reality*, edited by Judith Nagata. Leiden: Brill.

DeYoung, Alan J., et al. 1982. *Educational Performance in Central Appalachia: Statistical Profile of Appalachian and Non-Appalachian School Districts*. Lexington: The Appalachian Center, University of Kentucky.

Dolan, Michael. 1983. "European Restructuring and Import Policies for a Textile Industry in Crises." *International Organization* 37: 583–615.

Douvan, Elizabeth, and Joseph Adelson. 1966. *The Adolescent Experience*. New York: John Wiley and Sons.

Dubofsky, Melvyn, and Warren Van Tine. 1977. *John L. Lewis: A Biography*. New York: Quadrangle.

DuBois, Tom. 1983. "Steel: Past the Crossroads." *Labor Research Review* Winter:5–25.

Duncan, C. L., and Ann R. Tickmyer. 1983. "Comparisons of the Quality of Life in the Coal and Manufacturing Counties of Eastern Kentucky." *Appalachian Journal*, 10 (3):228–243.

Edgerton, Robert. 1971. *The Individual in Cultural Adaptation: A Study of Four East African Peoples*. Berkeley and Los Angeles: University of California Press.

Ehrenberg, Marion F., David N. Fox, and Raymond F. Koopman. 1990a. "The Millon Adolescent Personality Inventory Profiles of Depressed Adolescents." *Adolescence* 25:415–423.

——. 1990b. "The Prevalence of Depression in High School Students." *Adolescence* 25: =905–912.

——. 1991. "The Relationship between Self-efficacy and Depression in Adolescents." *Adolescence*. 102:361–374.

Eller, Ronald. 1982. *Miners, Millhands, and Mountaineers: The Industrialization of the Appalachian South, 1880–1930*. Knoxville: University of Tennessee Press.

Emmett, I. 1983. "Is Social Reality Merely a Social Construct?" *University of Manchester Occasional Paper in Sociology 10*.

Erikson, Erik. 1980 (1959). *Identity and the Life Cycle*. New York: W. W. Norton.

Evans, Peter. 1979. *Dependent Development: The Alliance of Multinational, State, and Local Capital in Brazil*. Princeton: Princeton University Press.

"Farm Production." n.d. Government of Newfoundland and Labrador, Department of Rural, Agricultural and Northern Development, Agriculture Canada.

"Farm Women through the Eyes of Their City Sisters." 1985. *Manitoba Co-operator*. April 11.

Finley, Joseph E. 1972. *The Corrupt Kingdom: The Rise and Fall of the United Mine Workers*. New York: Simon and Schuster.

Fisk, Malcolm. 1980. "Poverty and Housing in Wales: An Account of Current Problems." In *Poverty and Social Inequality in Wales*, edited by Gareth Rees and Teresa L. Rees. London: Croom Helm.

Forbes, Ernest. 1977. "Misguided Symmetry: The Destruction of Regional Transportation Policy for the Maritimes." In *Canada and the Burden of Unity*, edited by D. J. Bercuson. Toronto: Macmillan.

Ford, Thomas R., ed. 1962. *The Southern Appalachian Region: A Survey*. Lexington: University of Kentucky Press.

Ford, Thomas R., Thomas A. Arcury, and Julia D. Porter. 1981. *Changes in the Structure of Central Appalachian Mountain Families and Household, 1958–1976*. Lexington: Center for Developmental Change, University of Kentucky.

Foster, Brian L. 1974. "Ethnicity and Commerce." *American Ethnologist* 1:437–48.

Foster-Carter, Aiden. 1978. "The Modes of Production Controversy." *New Left Review* 107:47–77.

Fox, Richard G. 1969. "Professional Primitives: Hunters and Gatherers of Nuclear South Asia." *Man in India* 49 (2):139–160.

Fox, William, et al. 1987. *Entries and Exits of Firms in the Tennessee Economy*. Knoxville: Center for Business and Economic Research.

Francis, H., D. Smith, and W. G. Frost. 1980. *The Fed: The South Wales Miners Federation*. London: Lawrence and Wishart.

Frank, Andre Gunder. 1967. *Capitalism and Underdevelopment in Latin America*. New York: Monthly Review Press.

Franklin, S. H. 1961. "Social Structure and Land Reform in Southern Italy." *Sociological Review* 9:323–349.

Fried, Robert C. 1968. "Administrative Pluralism and Italian Regional Planning." *Public Administration* 46:375–392.

Friedmann, Harriet, and Jack Wayne. 1977. "Dependency Theory: A Critique." *Canadian Journal of Sociology* 2:399–416.

Frost, W. G. 1899. "Our Contemporary Ancestors in the Southern Mountains." *Atlantic Monthly* 83:311–319.

Garvan, John M. 1963. *The Negritos of the Philippines*, edited by Hermann Nochegger. Vienna: University of Vienna Institute of Ethnology.

Gaskell, Jane. 1984. "Gender and Course Choice." *Journal of Education* 166:89–102.

Gaventa, John. 1980. *Power and Powerlessness: Quiescence and Rebellion in an Appalachian Valley*. Champaign: University of Illinois Press.

———. 1988. "From the Mountains to the Maquiladoras: A Case Study of Capital Flight and Its Impact on Workers." Highland Research and Education Center, New Market, TN.

Gaventa, John, Barbara Ellen Smith, and Alex Willingham. 1990. *Communities in Economc Crisis: Appalachia and the South*. Philadelphia: Temple University Press.

Gecas, Viktor, and Monica A. Seff. 1990. "Families and Adolescents: A Review of the 1980s." *Journal of Marriage and the Family* 52: 941–958.

George, Roy E. 1970. *A Leader and a Laggard: Manufacturing Industry in Nova Scotia, Quebec, and Ontario*. Toronto: University of Toronto Press.

Gidengil, Elisabeth. 1989. "Diversity within Unity: On Analyzing Regional Dependency." *Studies in Political Economy* 29:91–122.

Gish, Pat. November 30, 1983. "1983 Is a Lot Like 1968." *The Mountain Eagle* (Whitesburg, KY), B11.

Haas, Gilda. 1985. *Plant Closures: Myths, Realities, and Responses*. Boston: South End Press.

Hall, D. G. E. 1966. *A History of Southeast Asia*. New York: St. Martin's Press.

Hall, Tony. 1981. *King Coal: Miners, Coal, and Britain's Industrial Future*. Harmondsworth, Middlesex, England: Penguin Books.

———. 1986. *Nuclear Politics: The History of Nuclear Power in Britain*. Harmondsworth, Middlesex, England: Penguin Books.

Hall, V. Aileen. 1983. *Poverty and Women in West Virginia*. Charleston, WV: Women and Employment, Inc.

Hechter, Michael. 1975. *Internal Colonialism: The Celtic Fringe in British National Development*. London: Routledge and Kegan Paul.

———. 1984. "Internal Colonialism Revisited." In *New Nationalisms of the Developed West*, edited by E. Tyryiakin and R. Roguwski, Boston: Allen and Unwin.

Hechter, M., and W. Brustein. 1980. "Regional Modes of Production and Patterns of State Formation in Western Europe." *American Journal of Sociology* 85:1061–1094.

Himmelfarb, Alexander, and C. James Richardson. 1979. *People, Power, and Process: Sociology for Canadians*. Toronto: McGraw-Hill Ryerson.

Hoffman, Carl L. 1984. "Punan Foragers in the Trading Networks of Southeast Asia," In *Past and Present in Hunter Gatherer Studies*, edited by Carmel Schrire. New York: Academic Press.

Hoffman, E. D. 1979. *Fighting Mountaineers*. Boston: Houghton Mifflin.

Holland, Stuart K. 1971. "Regional Underdevelopment in a Developed Economy." *Regional Studies* 5:71–90.

——. 1976. *Capital versus the Regions*. London: Macmillan.

Horowitz, Gad. 1966. "Conservatism, Liberalism, and Socialism in Canada." *Canadian Journal of Economic and Political Science* May.

House, J. D. 1980. "Coastal Labrador: Incorporation, Exploitation, and Underdevelopment." *Journal of Canadian Studies* 15:98–113.

——. 1981. "Big Oil and Small Communities in Coastal Labrador: The Local Dynamics of Dependency." *Canadian Review of Sociology and Anthropology* 18:433–452.

House, J. D. 1986. "The Mouse that Roars: New Directions in Canadian Political Economy. The Case of Newfoundland." In *Regionalism in Canada*, edited by Robert J. Brym. Toronto: Irwin.

House, J. D., with Sheila M. White and Paul Ripley. 1989. *Going Away...And Coming Back: Economic Life and Migration in Small Canadian Communities*, Report No. 2. St. John's, NS: Institute of Social and Economic Research.

Howells, K. 1985 "Stopping Out: The Birth of a New Kind of Politics." In *Digging Deeper: Issues in the Miners Strike*, edited by Huw Benyon. London: Verso.

HRB-Singer, Inc. 1975. *Overview of Subsistence Potential in Pennsylvania Coal Fields*. Washington: Appalachian Regional Commission.

Hutterer, Karl L. 1974. "The Evolution of Philippine Lowland Societies." *Mankind*. 9 (4):287–299.

Jencks, Christopher. 1972. *Inequality: A Reassessment of Family and Schooling in America*. New York: Harper & Row.

——. 1979. *Who Gets Ahead? The Determinants of Economic Success in America*. New York: Basic Books.

Joint Economic Committee, U.S. Congress. November 28, 1985. "Family Income in America."

——. May 9, 1986. "Working Mothers Are Preserving Family Living Standards."

Jones, L. 1975. "Appalachian Values." Berea: Berea College Appalachian Center.

Kanfer, K., and A. M. Zeiss. 1983. "Depression, Interpersonal Standard Setting, and Judgments of Self-efficacy." *Journal of Abnormal Psychology* 92:319–329.

Keefe, Susan E., Janice L. Hastings, and Sherry F. Thomas. 1993. "Psychological Testing in Rural Appalachia." Paper presented at

Annual Meeting of the American Anthropological Association, Washington, D.C.

Kentucky Fair Tax Coalition (KFTC). 1982. *Struggling for Tax Justice in the Mountains: The Story of the Kentucky Fair Tax Coalition.*

Kenyatta, Jomo. 1961 (1938). *Facing Mt. Kenya.* London: Secker and Warburg.

King, Russell. 1971. "Italy." In *Regional Development in Western Europe,* edited by Hugh D. Clout. London: John Wiley & Sons.

——, ed. 1986. *Return Migration and Regional Economic Problems.* London: Croom Helm.

King, Russell, Alan Strachan, and Jill Mortimer. 1986. "Gastarbiter Go Home: Return Migration and Economic Change in the Italian Mezzogiorno." In *Return Migration and Regional Economic Problems,* edited by Russell King. London: Croom Helm.

King, V. T. 1985. *The Maloh of West Kalimantan: An Ethnographic Study of Social Inequality and Social Change Among an Indonesian Borneo People.* Dordrecht, Holland: Foris Publications.

Kreiger, Joel. 1983. *Undermining Capitalism: State Ownership and the Dialectic Control of the British Coal Industry.* Princeton: Princeton University Press.

Kresl, Peter Karl. 1982. "An Economic Perspective: Canada in the International Perspective." In *Understanding Canada: A Multidisciplinary Introduction to Canadian Studies,* edited by William Metcalf. New York: New York University Press.

Laclau, Ernesto. 1971. "Feudalism and Capitalism in Latin America." *New Left Review* 67:19–38.

Laclau, Ernesto, and C. Mouffe. 1985. *Hegemony and Socialist Strategy: Towards a Radical Democratic Politics.* London: Verso.

Lasker, Bruno. 1944. *Peoples of Southeast Asia.* New York: Knopf.

Leakey, Louis S. B. 1977. *The Kikuyu.* New York: Academic Press.

Lehman, F. K. 1967. "Ethnic Categories in Burma and the Theory of Social Systems." In *Southeast Asian Tribes, Minorities and Nations,* edited by Peter Kunsstadter. Princeton: Princeton University Press.

Lewis, Helen M. 1970. "Fatalism or the Coal Industry?" *Mountain Life and Work* December: 6ff.

Lewis, Helen M., et al. 1978. *Colonialism in Modern America: The Appalachian Case.* Boone, NC: Appalachian Consortium.

Linz, Juan, and Amando de Miguel. 1966. "Within-Nation Differences and Comparisons: The Eight Spains." In *Comparing Nations, the Use of Quantitative Data in Cross-national Research,* edited by R. Merritt and S. Rokkan. New Haven: Yale University Press.

Lipietz, A. 1980. "International Regional Polarisation and Tertiarisation of Society." *Papers of the Regional Science Association:* 3–17

Lipset, Seymour Martin. 1985. "Canada and the United States: The Cultural Dimension." In *Canada and the United States: Enduring Friendship, Persistent Stress,* edited by Charles F. Doran and John H. Sigler. New York: Prentice-Hall.

Little, Arthur D., Inc. 1982. *Regional Economic Development in Appalachia.* Washington: Appalachian Regional Commission.

Llewelyn, E. 1986. "What is *Adfer?*" In *The Welsh and Their Country,* edited by I. Hume and W. T. R. Pryce. Llandysul, Wales: Gomer Press.

Lloyd, John. 1985. *Understanding the Miners' Strike.* London: Fabian Society.

Loevinger, Jane, and Ruth Wessler. 1976. *Measuring Ego Development* Vol. 1. San Francisco: Jossey Bass.

Long, Norman. 1975. "Structural Dependency, Modes of Production, and Economic Brokerage in Rural Peru." In *Beyond the Sociology of Development,* edited by I. Oxall, T. Barrett, and D. Booth. London: Routledge.

———. 1984. "Creating Space for Change: A Perspective on the Sociology of Development." *Sociologia Ruralis* 24:168–173.

Long, Norman, and P. Richardson. 1978. "Informal Sector, Petty Commodity Production, and the Social Relations of Small-scale Enterprise." in *The New Economic Anthropology,* edited by John Clammer. London: Macmillan.

Long, Norman, and Bryan Roberts. 1984. *Miners, Peasants, and Entrepreneurs. Regional Development in the Central Highlands of Peru.* Cambridge: Cambridge University Press.

Long, Norman, and Jan D. van der Ploug. 1988. "New Challenges in the Sociology of Rural Development." *Sociologia Ruralis* 28:30–41.

Lopreato, Joseph. 1967. *Peasants No More.* San Francisco: Chandler.

Lovering, J. 1978. "The Theory of the Internal Colony and Political Economy of Wales." *Review of Radical Political Economics* 10:55–67.

Lovingood, Paul, and R. Reiman. 1986. *Emerging Patterns in the Southern Highlands: A Reference Atlas* Vol. II, Agriculture. Boone, NC: Appalachian Consortium.

———. 1988. *Emerging Patterns in the Southern Highlands: A Reference Atlas* Vol. IV, Business. Boone, NC: Appalachian Consortium.

Macmillan, A. M. 1957. "The Health Opinion Survey: Technique for Estimating Prevalence of Psychoneurotic and Related Types of Disorder in Communities." *Psychological Reports* 3: 325–339.

McRobbie, Angela. 1978. "Working-class Girls and the Culture of Feminity." In *Women Take Issue,* edited by the Women's Study Group. London: Hutchinson.

Maggard, Sally. 1986. "Class and Gender: New Theoretical Priorities in Appalachian Studies." In *The Impact of Institutions in Appalachia: Proceedings of the 8th Annual Appalachian Studies Conference*, edited by Jim Lloyd and Anne Campbell. Boone, NC: Appalachia Consortium Press.

Marchione, Thomas, and Betsy Tabax. 1982. "Economic Crises in Eight States of Our Industrial Heartland: A Background Paper Prepared for the Regional Strategy Meeting of Ecumenical Agencies." Ohio Council of Churches, mimeo.

Markusen, A. R. 1980. "Regions and Regionalism." In *A Marxist View*. Working Paper 326. University of California, Berkeley.

Marshall, Ray. 1983. *Work and Women in the 1980s: A Perspective on Basic Trends Affecting Women's Jobs and Job Opportunities.* Washington: Women's Research and Education Institute.

Massey, Doreen. 1979. "In What Sense a Regional Problem?" *Regional Studies* 13:233–243.

Massey, Doreen, and Hilary Wainwright. 1985. "Beyond the Coalfields: The Work of the Miners' Support Groups." In *Digging Deeper: Issues in the Miners' Strike*, edited by Huw Benyon. London: Verso.

Mattera, Philip. 1985. *Off the Books: The Rise of the Underground Economy.* New York: St. Martin's Press.

Matthews, Ralph. 1983. *The Creation of Regional Dependency.* Toronto: University of Toronto Press.

Meilink-Roelofsz, M. A. P. 1962. *Asian Trade and European Influence in the Indonesian Archipelago.* The Hague: M. Nijhoff.

Merrifield, Juliet. 1980. *We're Tired of Being Guinea Pigs! A Handbook for Citizens on Environmental Health in Appalachia.* New Market, TN: Highlander Research and Education Center.

Miernyk, William H. 1980. "Coal." In *Collective Bargaining: Contemporary American Experience.* Madison, WI: Industrial Relations Research Association.

Miliband, Ralph. 1978. "A State of De-subordination." *British Journal of Sociology* 29 (4):399–409.

———. 1984. *Capitalist Democracy in Britain.* London: Oxford University Press.

Miller, Tommie R. 1976. Urban Appalachians: Cultural Pluralism and Ethnic Identity in the City. M.A. Thesis, University of Cincinnati.

Mitchell, Sharon, and Susan Abbott. 1987. "Gender and Symptoms of Depression and Anxiety among Kikuyu Secondary School Students in Kenya." *Social Science and Medicine* 24:303–316.

Moerman, Michael. 1965. "Who Are the Lue: Ethnic Identification in a Complex Civilization." *American Anthropologist* 67:1215–1230.

Moore, B. 1966. *Social Origins of Dictatorship and Democracy.* Boston: Beacon Press.

"More Gloom for U.S. Textiles." 1979. *Business Week* (April 9), 68–69.

Morris, Brian. 1977. "Tappers, Trappers, and the Hill Pandaram." *Anthropos* 72:225–41.

———. 1982. *Forest Traders: A Socio-Economic Study of the Hill Pandaram*, London School of Economics Monographs of Social Anthropology 55. London: Athlone.

Mouzelis, Nicos. 1988. "Sociology of Development: Reflections on the Present Crisis." *Sociology* 22:23–44.

Murphy, H. B. M. 1982. *Comparative Psychiatry.* Berlin: Springer-Verlag.

Murphy, Jane. 1986. "Trends in Depression and Anxiety: Men and Women." *Acta Psychiatrica Scandinavica* 73:113–127.

National Farmers Unions. 1979. *Ten Years of Underdevelopment/Ten Years of Struggle: Farming in Canada and the NFU.* Saskatoon, Saskatchewan: National Farmers Unions.

National Coal Board (NCB). Various years. *Report and Accounts, 1947, 1970, and 1984–1985.* London: HMSO.

Navarro, Peter. 1983. "Union Bargaining Power in the Coal Industry, 1945–81." *Industrial and Labor Relations Review* 36 (2):214–29.

Newby, Howard. 1980. "Urbanization and the Rural Class Structure: Reflections on a Case Study." In *The Rural Sociology of the Advanced Societies: Critical Perspectives*, edited by Frederick H. Buttel and Howard Newby. Montclair: Allanheld and Osmun.

———. 1987. *Country Life: A Social History of Rural England.* Totowa, NJ: Barnes and Noble.

Newfoundland and Labrador: Building on Our Strengths. 1986. Report of the Royal Commission on Employment and Unemployment. Ottawa.

Newman, Monroe. 1983. "The Job Future in Appalachia." In *Job Skills for the Future*, ARC Proceedings. Washington: GPO.

O'Conner, James. 1973. *The Fiscal Crises of the State.* New York: St. Martin's Press.

Organization for Economic Cooperation and Development. 1986. *Economic Survey: Spain.* Paris: OECD.

Osmond, J. 1985. "The Future of the Wales Congress." *Planet* 51:119–124.

Paynter, William. 1970. *British Trade Unions and the Problems of Change.* London: George Allen and Unwin.

———. 1972. *My Generation.* London: George Allen and Unwin, Ltd.

———. 1976, September 13. "Evaluation of the Wages Structure in the Mining Industry." Lecture, Oral History Project, South Wales Miners Library, University College, Swansea.

Peabody III, N. S. 1970. "Toward an Understanding of Backwardness and Change: A Critique of the Banfield Hypothesis." *Journal of Developing Areas* 4:375–386.

Peralta, Miguel. 1986. *Salir del Paro.* Diario de Terassa (Teradda, Spain), Fin de Demana 7 (June):5–7.

Perry, Harry. 1979. "Coal Conversion to Synthetic Fuels." In *Appalachia into the 80s*, ARC Proceedings. Washington: GPO.

Peterson, Jean Treloggen. 1978. *The Ecology of Social Boundaries. Agta Foragers of the Philippines*, Illinois Studies in Anthropology 11. Urbana: University of Illinois Press.

Philliber, William W. 1983. "Correlates of Appalachian Identification among Appalachian Migrants." In *The Appalachian Experience: Proceedings of the Sixth Annual Appalachian Studies Conference*, edited by Barry M. Buxton. Boone, NC: Appalachian Consortium.

Phillips, Paul. 1982. *Regional Disparities.* Toronto: Lorimer.

Photiadis, John D., and Harry K. Schwarzweller, eds. 1970. *Change in Rural Appalachia: Implications for Action Programs.* Philadelphia: University of Pennsylvania Press.

Plaut, Tom. 1979. "Appalachia and Social Change: A Cultural Systems Approach." *Appalachian Journal* 6 (Summer):250–61.

Portelli, Alessandro. 1984. "Two 'Peripheries' Look at Each Other: Italy and Appalachian America." *Appalachian Journal* 12:31–37.

Reed, John Shelton. 1983. *Southerners: The Social Psychology of Sectionalism.* Chapel Hill: University of North Carolina Press.

Rees, G. 1983. "The Political Economy of Rural Areas: Observations Based on Welsh Experience." *Papers in Planning Research* 62, University of Wales Institute of Science and Technology, Cardiff.

———. 1985. "Regional Restructuring, Class Change, and Political Action," mimeo.

Reich, Robert B. 1982. "Take the Money and Run." *The New Republic* (November 15), 28–32.

———. 1986. "The Hollow Corporation." *Business Week* (March 3).

Robens, The Rt. Hon. Lord. 1972. *Ten Year Stint.* London: Caswell.

Rodgers, Allan. 1970. "Migration and Industrial Development: The Southern Italian Experience." *Economic Geography* 46:111–135.

Rothblatt, Donald N. 1971. *Regional Planning: The Appalachian Experience.* Lexington, MA: D. C. Heath.

Rousseau, J. 1975. "Ethnic Identity and Social Relations in Central Borneo." In *Pluralism in Malaya: Myth or Reality*, edited by Judith Nagata. Leiden: Brill.

Routledge, D. S., amd K. S. Routledge. 1910. *With a Prehistoric People: The Agikuyu of British East Africa.* London: Edward Arnold.

Sacouman, R. James. 1977. "Underdevelopment and the Structural Origins of Antigonish Movement Co-operatives in Eastern Nova Scotia." *Acadiensis* 7:66–85.

——. 1979. "The Differing Origins, Organization, and Impact of Maritime and Prairie Co-operatives in Eastern Nova Scotia." *Canadian Journal of Sociology* 4:199–221.

——. 1980. "Semi-proletarianization and Rural Underdevelopment in the Maritimes." *Canadian Review of Sociology and Anthropology* 17:232–245.

Sager, Eric W. 1987. "Dependency, Underdevelopment, and the Economic History of the Atlantic Provinces." *Acadiensis* 17:117–137.

Saks, Daniel H. 1983. *Distressed Workers in the Eighties*. Washington: National Planning Association.

Sanday, Peggy Reeves. 1981. *Female Power and Male Dominance: On the Origins of Sexual Inequality*. Cambridge: Cambridge University Press.

Saunders, Robert J. 1972. *The Spatial Concentration of Industry in Appalachia: An Analysis of the Potential for Import Substitution*. Washington: Appalachian Regional Commission.

Saunders, S. A. 1984 (1939). *The Economic History of the Maritime Provinces*. Edited by T. W. Acheson. Fredericton, NB: Acadiensis Press.

Schacter, Gustav. 1967. "Regional Development in the Italian Dual Economy." *Economic Development and Cultural Change* 15:398–407.

Schneider, Peter, Jane Schneider, and Edward Hansen. 1972. "Modernization and Development: The Role of Regional Elites and Noncorporate Groups in the European Mediterranean." *Comparative Studies in Society and History* 14:328–350.

Schnelle, John F. 1979. "The Impact on Collective Bargaining of Oil Company Ownership of Bituminous Coal Properties." *Labor Studies Journal* 3 (3).

Schwarzweller, H. K., James Brown, and J. J. Mangalam. 1971. *Mountain Families in Transition: A Case Study of Appalachian Migration*. University Park: Pennsylvania State University Press.

Seltzer, Curtis. 1979. "Occupational and Environmental Health Issues of Coal Production, Combustion and Synthetic Fuels." In *Appalachia into the 80s*, ARC Proceedings. Washington: GPO.

——. 1985. *Fire in the Hole: Miners and Managers in the American Coal Industry*. Lexington: University Press of Kentucky.

Sewel, John. 1975. *Colliery Closure and Social Change: A Study of a South Wales Mining Valley*. Cardiff: University of Wales Press.

Shapiro, Henry D. 1978. *Appalachia on Our Mind: the Southern Mountains in the American Consciousness 1810–1920*. Chapel Hill:

University of North Carolina Press.

Simkin, C. G. F. 1968. *The Traditional Trade of Asia*. London: Oxford University Press.

Simon, R. 1984. "Regions and Social Relations: A Research Note." *Appalachian Journal* 11:1–2.

Sinclair, Peter R. 1985. *From Traps to Draggers: Domestic Commodity Production in Northwest Newfoundland*. St. John's, NS: Institute of Social and Economic Research.

Smith, Adam. 1937 (1776). *An Inquiry into the Nature and Causes of the Wealth of Nations*. New York: The Modern Library.

Smith, Barbara. 1986. *Women and the Rural South*. Lexington: Southeast Women's Employment Coalition.

Smith, D. 1984. *Wales! Wales?* London: Allen & Unwin; New York: Routledge, Chapman, and Hall.

Statistics Canada. 1987. *Education in Canada 1986*. Cat. 81–229.

———. 1988a. *National Income and Expenditure Accounts*. Cat. 13–531 Occ. and Cat. 13–201.

———. 1988b. *Provincial Economic Accounts: Historical Issue 1961–1986*. Cat. 13–213S.

———. 1989. Cat. 93–110.

Staub, M. 1982. "There's No Quittin': The Struggle to Save Yellow Creek, as Told by the People Who Live There," mimeo.

Stephenson, John B. 1968. *Shiloh: A Mountain Community*. Lexington: University of Kentucky Press.

Stephenson, John B. 1983. "Escape to the Periphery: The Commodifying of Appalachia." Paper presented to British Sociological Association, April 7, Cardiff, Wales.

Stephenson, John B. 1984. *Ford: A Village in the West Highlands of Scotland*. Lexington: University of Kentucky Press.

Tickmyer, Ann R., and Cecil Tickmyer. 1987. *Poverty in Appalachia*, Appalachian Data Bank Report No. 5. Lexington: University of Kentucky Appalachian Center.

Town, Stephen N. 1978. *After the Mines: Changing Employment Opportunities in a South Wales Valley*. Cardiff: University of Wales Press.

Toyne, Brian, et al. 1984. *The Global Textile Industry*. London: Allen Unwin.

Ty Toronto Socio-economic Research Group. 1977. *A Socio-economic Strategy for the Valleys of South Wales*. Aberfan, Wales.

U.K. Ministry of Power. 1972. *Energy Statistics*. London: HMSO.

———. Various, a. *Guide to the Coal Fields, 1970, 1973, and 1985*. London: HMSO.

———. Various, b. *Statistical Digest, 1961 and 1962*. London: HMSO.

Urry, J. 1981. "Localities, Regions and Social Class." *International Journal of Urban and Regional Research* 4:455–474.

U.S. Bureau of Labor Statistics. 1980. *Technology, Productivity, and Labor in the Bituminous Coal Industry, 1950–79*, Bulletin No. 2072. Washington: GPO.

U.S. Congress, Office of Technology Assessment. 1986. *Technology and Structural Unemployment: Reemploying Displaced Adults*, OTA–ITE 250. Washington: GPO.

Valli, Linda. 1986. *Becoming Clerical Workers*. Boston: Routledge and Kegan Paul.

Vandergeest, Peter. 1988. "Commercialization and Commoditization: A Dialogue between Perspectives." *Sociologia Ruralis* 28:7–29.

Veltmeyer, Henry. 1979. "The Capitalist Underdevelopment of Atlantic Canada." In *Underdevelopment and Social Movements in Atlantic Canada*, edited by R. J. Brym and R. J. Sacouman. Toronto: New Hogtown Press.

———. 1980. "A Central Issue in Dependency Theory." *Canadian Review of Sociology and Anthropology* 17:198–213.

Wadel, Cato. 1969. *Marginal Adaptations and Modernization in Newfoundland*. St. John's, NS: Institute of Social and Economic Research.

Walls, David. 1977. "On the Naming of Appalachia." In *Appalachian Symposium*, edited by J. W. Williamson. Boone, NC: Appalachian State University Press.

———. 1978. "Internal Colony or Internal Periphery? A Critique of Current Models." In *Colonialism in Modern America: The Appalachian Case*, edited by Helen Lewis, Linda Johnson, and Don Askins. Boone, NC: Appalachian Consortium.

Warde, A. 1985. "Comparable Localities: Problems of Method." In *Localities, Class and Gender*, edited by L. Murgatroyd, et al. London: Pion.

Warren, Bill. 1973. "Imperialism and Capitalist Industrialization." *New Left Review* 81:3–45.

———. 1980. *Imperialism: Pioneer of Capitalism*. London: New Left Books.

WCCPL (Welsh Campaign for Civil and Political Liberties). 1985. *Striking Back*. Cardiff.

Wein, Fred. 1988. "Canada's Regions." In *Understanding Canadian Society*, edited by James Curtis and Lorne Tepperman. Toronto: McGraw-Hill Ryerson.

Weis, Lois. 1990. *Working Class without Work: High School Students in a De-industrialized Economy*. New York: Routledge.

Weisner, Thomas S., and Susan Abbott. 1977. "Women, Modernity, and Stress: Three Contrasting Contexts for Change in East Africa." *Journal of Anthropological Research* 33:421–451.

Weller, Jack. 1965. *Yesterday's People: Life in Contemporary Appalachia*.

Lexington: University of Kentucky Press.

Welsh Office. 1967. *Wales: The Way Ahead*. Cardiff: HMSO.

———. 1976. *Welsh House Condition Survey*. Cardiff: HMSO.

Wenger, C. 1982. "The Problem of Perspective in Development Policy." *Sociologia Ruralis* 22:6–16.

Whisnant, David E. 1973. "Ethnicity and the Recovery of Identity in Appalachia." *Soundings* 6:124–138.

———. 1980a. "Developments in the Appalachian Identity Movement: All Is Process." *Appalachian Journal* 8 (1):41–47.

———. 1980b. *Modernizing the Mountaineer: People, Power, and Planning in Appalachia*. Boone, NC: Appalachian Consortium Press.

———. 1983. *All That Is Native and Fine: The Politics of Culture in an American Region*. Chapel Hill: University of North Carolina Press.

Whiting, Beatrice B. 1977. "Changing Life Styles in Kenya." *Daedalus* 106:211–226.

Whiting, Beatrice B. and John W. M. Whiting. 1975. *Children of Six Cultures: A Psychocultural Analysis*. Cambridge: Harvard University Press.

Whiting, John W. M., and Beatrice B. Whiting. 1975. "Aloofness and Intimacy of Husbands and Wives: A Cross-Cultural Study. *Ethos* 3 (2):183–207.

Williams, C. H. 1977. "Non-Violence and the Development of the Welsh Language Society." *Welsh History Review* 8 (45):426–55.

Williams, Cratis D. 1961. The Southern Mountaineer in Fact and Fiction. Ph.D. dissertation, New York University. University Microfilms, 1973.

Williams, G. A. 1979. "When Was Wales?" BBC Radio Lecture. Cardiff: British Broadcasting Company.

Williams, G. A. 1980. "Industrialization, Inequality and Deprivation in Rural Wales." In *Poverty and Social Inequality in Wales*, edited by Gareth Rees and Teresa L. Rees. London: Croom Helm.

———. 1982. *The Welsh in Their History*. London: Croom Helm.

———. 1985. *When Was Wales: A History of the Welsh*. Harmondsworth, Middlesex: Penguin Books.

Wolf, Eric R. 1982. *Europe and the People without History*. Berkeley: University of California Press.

Wolfe, Margaret Ripley. 1975. "Aliens in Appalachia: The Construction of the Clinchfield Railroad and the Italian Experience." In *Appalachia: Family Traditions in Transition*, edited by Emmett M. Essen. Johnson City, TN: Eastern Tennessee State University Research Advisory Council.

Wood, Phillip J. 1989. "Marxism and the Maritimes: On the Determinants of Regional Capitalist Development." *Studies in Political Economy* 29:123–153.

Zelinsky, Wilbur. 1973. The Cultural Geography of the United States. Englewood Cliffs, NJ: Prentice Hall.

Index

About the Contributors

Susan Abbott is an associate professor of anthropology at the University of Kentucky.

Richard A. Couto is a professor in the Jepson School of Leadership at the University of Richmond.

Graham Day is a senior lecturer in sociology at the University College of North Wales.

John Gaventa is an associate professor of sociology at the University of Tennessee-Knoxville.

Benita J. Howell is an associate professor of anthropology at the University of Tennessee-Knoxville.

Glenn A. Mitchell is a program evaluator in the Florida Office of Program Policy Analysis and Government Accountability and coordinator of the North Florida Network of Practicing Anthropologists.

Phillip J. Obermiller is an associate of the Appalachian Center at the University of Kentucky.

Nelda K. Pearson is a professor of sociology at Radford University.

William W. Philliber is a professor of sociology at the State University of New York at New Paltz.

Peter R. Sinclair is a university research professor of sociology at Memorial University of Newfoundland.

John B. Stephenson is the former president of Berea College.

ISBN 0-275-94835-8

HARDCOVER BAR CODE